FIRST INTO ACTION AGAIN

*To my mother Pauline.
I dearly wish I had known you beyond the one year,
my first year, that we were together.*

FIRST INTO ACTION AGAIN

DUNCAN FALCONER

MIRROR BOOKS

MIRROR BOOKS

All of the events in this story are true, but some names and details have been changed to protect the identities of some individuals where appropriate.

© Duncan Falconer

The rights of Duncan Falconer to be identified as the author of this book have been asserted, in accordance with the Copyright, Designs and Patents Act 1988.

All rights reserved. No part of this publication may be reproduced, stored in a retrieval system, or transmitted, in any form or by any means without the prior written permission of the publisher, nor be otherwise circulated in any form of binding or cover other than that in which it is published and without a similar condition being imposed on the subsequent purchaser.

1

Published in Great Britain and Ireland in 2024 by Mirror Books, a Reach PLC business.

www.mirrorbooks.co.uk
@TheMirrorBooks

Print ISBN 9781915306708
eBook ISBN 9781915306715

Editing and Production: Ian Levy, Christine Costello
Cover Design: Chris Collins

Photographic acknowledgements:
Duncan Falconer personal collection

Every effort has been made to trace copyright, Any oversights will be rectified in future editions.

Printed and bound in Great Britain by
CPI Group (UK) Ltd, Croydon, CR0 4YY

CONTENTS

Author's Note	7
Prologue	9
England	29
Spain	45
The Atlantic	71
USA	90
Palestine	106
Afghanistan	122
Liberia	148
Iraq	191
The Congo	224
Russia	235
Iraq, Saudi Arabia, Yemen	250
Israel & Palestine, Sri Lanka, Afghanistan	267
Kurdistan	288
Epilogue	301
Acknowledgements	304

AUTHOR'S NOTE

I HAVE SURVIVED FIVE EXPLOSIONS, two only just, a mock execution, been shot at on numerous occasions, chased by machete-wielders, hunted by man and beast, survived a near-drowning, a faulty parachute opening, an air-crash and several vehicle crashes, blacked out with anaphylactic shock, walked through a minefield (unwittingly), barely escaped capture by fanatical terrorists when others were caught and executed, and experienced close calls so many times I have forgotten most of them. Grabbing life with both hands is a given, but pursuing a lifetime of dangerous adventures perhaps suggests a flaw in my rationale. My life has not been a model to follow. The truth is, if I were to go back to my teens, knowing what I do now, which forks in the roads I picked that led to where they did, I would probably have chosen to be an accountant. I accept that my survival on most occasions has been more luck than judgement. But having done what I have and survived it all, I feel I have lived a life to its full, although I could always probably fit in just one more adventure.

So why is it that, after surviving such perils, I kept going back for more, without hesitation, knowing the dangers? I was always aware that my risk appetite was greater than my ability to mitigate. Failure was ever within reach. Perhaps supreme confidence, or simply blind foolishness, kept me going. I learned so much about the world while still learning about myself. When I was young I was certain I wasn't brave. Perhaps I was always trying to prove I was, but always doubting it.

My greatest success was not letting anyone know that fear was my closest companion.

DUNCAN FALCONER

PROLOGUE

I WAS SITTING AT A desk in a small studio apartment on the second floor of a wing of the Al Hamra Hotel in Karada, Baghdad, working on a new book. It was called *The Bomb Surgeon* – the irony of that title will become clear shortly. My publishers later asked me to change the title because of the London bombings earlier in the year. I renamed it *The Operative*. The hotel was in an area of the city designated the Red Zone. The Green Zone was the relatively safe area of Baghdad that contained government buildings and embassies and was protected by Iraqi and US soldiers. My wing of the hotel was practically empty. It was usually packed with Western news crews, but most had left the city for the weekend. That was fortunate, as many would have died that morning.

Beyond my bed was my balcony. It overlooked the street, the far side of which was lined by 3m-high concrete blast walls that formed a perimeter around the hotel complex. My balcony doors were closed to keep out the dust. Everything was quiet that Friday morning, the holiest day of the Muslim week.

At 08:12 a small truck, laden with an estimated 250lb of explosives, made its way along a residential street outside the perimeter. A few hundred metres behind it was an even bigger truck carrying some 3,000lb of explosives.

The smaller truck eased between houses and blocks of flats, one of them 10 floors tall overlooking my building, colourful washing hanging on the narrow balconies. It slowed to a stop against the perimeter wall to the right of my balcony some 30m away. The hotel's baker-boy, a young Iraqi lad who lived nearby, walked past the truck, heading for the hotel entrance, as he did every morning.

The truck driver had been parked for only a few seconds when he detonated his load. The explosion disintegrated the truck, instantly killed the baker-boy, and blew down several sections of the perimeter wall.

The pressure wave, closely followed by shrapnel, struck my building, blew my balcony windows inwards and flung me out of my chair. I was hurled across the room, smashing into the kitchen cabinets close to the ceiling. I fell to the floor along with a shower of debris, and lay there, dazed but conscious.

As I lay stunned, a warning fought its way to the front of my mind: one explosion was often followed by another, or by an armed assault. I had to get to my feet. But I had no idea if I actually had feet left to stand on. I wasn't in any great pain – had I lost my limbs, I might not have realised it immediately. I could see, although everything was blurred. The room was filled with dust. My ears were ringing and of no use.

I pulled my arms and legs beneath me – thankfully I still had them – and pushed myself up into a standing position. I stood unsteadily, barefoot, in my shorts and T-shirt. Nothing felt broken. I gave no thought to how badly I might be wounded.

PROLOGUE

I'd soon find out. I had to move quickly – if there was going to be an assault, it would come immediately.

My thoughts snapped to my weapons. Daylight streamed in through the gaping hole where the balcony doors and curtains used to be. The air was filled with dust, the floor covered in twisted debris, my bed, sideboard and wardrobe all trashed. My assault rifle and pistol had been by my bed but I couldn't see them.

Meanwhile, outside, the second truck came to a stop just behind where the first had been. I expect the driver's objective was the main tower of the hotel 100 yards further inside the perimeter wall. An explosion there would have probably brought down the entire 16-storey structure, a feat many terrorists have tried to emulate since the Oklahoma City bombing some 10 years earlier.

The attack was following a popular model. The initial vehicle bomb was intended to blow through the perimeter so that the following vehicle, carrying a much greater load of explosives, could continue into the compound and attack the primary objective. The tactic failed more often than it succeeded. There was no science involved, no Munro Effect calculations that mathematically improved the impact and accuracy of explosive charges. The major flaw was that the first bomb invariably failed to clear a way through the perimeter, either due to insufficient explosives or because the blast was too powerful and left a huge crater beneath the vehicle. At the Al Hamra, the blast walls had been shattered but the large pedestal bases remained in position, blocking the way.

The second truck could go no further. The driver wasn't going to get any closer to his objective.

FIRST INTO ACTION AGAIN

I started to make my way towards where I thought my weapons might be near the balcony. I considered going outside to see if an assault was in progress. Had I done so, I would've been vaporised by the second explosion.

If my actions so far seem like they took a long time, that's because it felt that way. I was surprised to later learn that there had been less than half a minute between the two explosions. The first was caught on the Al Hamra Hotel's CCTV cameras – they were destroyed by the bomb but the hard drives survived. The baker-boy can clearly be seen moving around the small truck as it exploded. The second blast was recorded by various cameras around the city.

I took a step forward, resting a hand on a huge supporting pillar which I always considered an inconvenience because it took up so much space in my room. A voice in my head told me to stop and take shelter behind the pillar. I have no other way of explaining what I did next. I put my hands to my head and rested my forehead against the pillar. I was still in a daze. The pillar was between me and the balcony.

I've been close to a few bombs going off. I had also been an explosives instructor in the Special Boat Service. But I'd never been so close to such a massive blast. A human body within 100m of a 1,000lb bomb was generally considered to be at risk of serious damage, even if behind cover. I would have stood no chance being 30m from a 3,000lb bomb. The sheer power that tore through my room, more than 10 times that of the first blast, should've sucked me along with it. It was a long building, six apartments in a line and six floors high. Huge support pillars, like the one I was standing behind, were spaced along the length of the building's interior. Without them, it would've

PROLOGUE

surely collapsed. Every door and window was blown in or out. Every false ceiling was brought down. Walls cracked open. My bathroom floor was covered in wall tiles, the sink and toilet shattered. The building's structure was severely damaged but it somehow remained upright.

The science of explosions is fascinating. Although indiscriminately destructive, there can be small areas left completely untouched. I remember a picture of a soldier in a First World War trench after a bomb had fallen on him and several comrades. He was virtually unscathed, yet his fellows had all been reduced to unrecognisable piles of minced meat spread around their boots. Perhaps something like that had happened to me and I had been in one of those untouched spaces. The blast wave went through my room and into the building. Everything was in shambles. When the shockwave had spent its fury, I was left behind my pillar, unscathed but for a tiny piece of shrapnel that had burnt my groin.

I don't know how long I stayed behind the pillar. Probably less than a minute. The threat of assault was still on my mind. I hadn't entirely escaped the blasts – I would not be myself for weeks. A concussion perhaps. Regardless, I had to concentrate, pull myself together and get going.

I stepped out from behind the pillar and picked my way over the rubble, pieces of wall and ceiling mixed in with the mashed furniture. I quickly dug through it and managed to locate my AK47. It appeared to be okay. And also my pistol and holster. I also found my trousers, which I quickly pulled on, and my boots, but no socks. In my trouser pocket was $600 and an invoice for the plastic membrane I had employed a local company to fit over all the glass doors to my balcony. I'd only been in that particular room a few days. The membrane was designed to prevent shards of glass from flying through the room in the event of an explosion. I'd been in the Al Hamra on two other occasions when nearby massive bombs had blown in most of the windows. It was a common occurrence in Baghdad. Some opted to remove the windows entirely and replace them with plastic sheeting that popped out when a bomb went off and could then be put back. The membrane on my windows had done its job.

I paused as my hearing slowly returned. Sounds filtered in from outside but no shooting. I ventured on to the balcony and peered over the parapet. What I saw left me stunned. The last time I had stood there and looked out on the residential area beyond the perimeter, it had been a normal Baghdad scene – homes, vehicles trundling by, kids playing, people going about their daily lives. Now it looked like the aftermath of an atomic bomb. Fires burned. Smoke filled the air. I could hear screams. The block of flats opposite was badly damaged. A corner of balconies had simply disappeared all the way to the roof. Not a single window was unbroken and many of the exterior walls had collapsed on various floors, exposing the rooms like a doll's house. Rubble was everywhere. Cars were crushed by bricks and slabs of concrete. The fronts of several three-storey buildings to my right had collapsed, spilling piles of bricks onto the street, leaving the interior rooms exposed. Palm trees were stripped of fronds. Bodies lay amid the rubble and on the street where they'd fallen from the apartment building. The perimeter blast walls in front of me resembled a row of broken teeth, several toppled over. All the cars along the interior street were wrecked, windows smashed, covered in dust and rubble.

PROLOGUE

As I stared at the devastation, people began to appear, dazed survivors wandering out of the shattered buildings, stunned like me by what they were seeing.

My thoughts suddenly went to the possibility of casualties inside my own building. I went back into the room and found my large medical bag. As I made my way to the door that was lying in pieces in the corridor, I heard the crunching sound of someone approaching. A figure stepped into my doorway, startling me, until I realised it was John, a former SAS lad who worked for NBC. His bureau occupied the top floors of the main hotel tower. When the lads had recovered from the initial shock and looked out from their trashed balconies they could see the epicentre was in front of my building. There were half a dozen security lads with NBC at any one time, most of them former SAS: Brits, Kiwis and Aussies. I was a frequent visitor, at mealtimes mostly. I worked and lived alone in the hotel, advising a couple of dozen clients, and they felt sorry for me, food-wise, as I only had the hotel restaurant where the meals were not particularly good. NBC had its own cook and imported its employees' victuals from Israel. While much of Baghdad had to make do with basic staples, NBC staff enjoyed lavish meals washed down with an enviable wine selection.

'Fuck, me!' John muttered as he took in the sight of me, caked in a thick layer of dust, standing amid the rubble of my room. 'We thought you were dead, mate.'

He couldn't believe I'd been in the room when the bombs went off. He must've said 'fuck me' half a dozen times as he looked around the room and back at me to confirm I was still in one piece.

He got on his phone and called the lads up in the tower. 'He's fuckin' alive,' he told them.

I greatly appreciated him coming to look for me. I could've been badly wounded. But I had to get going and check on my clients and anyone else who might be in the building. John left to help his own people while I headed out to navigate the rubble and begin a door-to-door search.

Hardly any of the corridor floor was visible. Every inch was covered with fragments of doors, windows, false ceilings and plaster. Wires and strip lights hung from the ceilings like morbid decorations and water flowed from broken pipes. Walking was a slow and treacherous procedure. All the rooms on my floor appeared to be empty. There were bloody hand streaks on the stairwell wall as I climbed to the next floor. I never found out who they belonged to. I called out as I went. Every room I checked was empty until I reached the *Chicago Tribune*'s bureau on the top floor. Liz Sly, the bureau chief, was there along with several of her staff, all shaken but uninjured. Their office was at the back of the building and had been spared the brunt of the explosions. By the time I got back downstairs and out onto the street, the US military had arrived in force and was taking care of the wounded.

A line of knee-high bushes stood near the entrance to my wing of the hotel. Lying neatly on top of one was the entire skin of a face, as if it had been surgically removed, like a mask. I assumed it was one of the suicide bombers, or the baker-boy. On the ground was a foot and, a little further away, a penis. Such macabre detritus would turn up in all kinds of places for weeks to come.

Over a dozen civilians had died, with many more injured.

PROLOGUE

Such assaults were not uncommon, mostly claimed by Al Qaeda. But there was reason to believe this might not have been the work of insurgents. I suspected something even more disturbing had taken place – and I wasn't the only one.

I might well have dismissed it as just one more insidious layer to the dirty games of war and politics had not the BBC turned up to add, what appeared to me, a bizarre twist.

Several hours had passed since the explosions. The Iraqi authorities were doing what they could to help while the US military assisted and provided security. I was taking a break, sitting outside my battered hotel annex with several fellow hotel residents, all media people, Liz Sly among them, when the BBC team arrived. They set up the camera and the reporter got to work. We listened to them describe how the Al Qaeda attack was believed to have been aimed at a police compound a few streets away and that, due to the police security and defences, the bombers changed their plans at the last minute and targeted the hotel instead.

I was baffled by the report, which didn't make sense on several levels. Surely the reporter knew what we all did with regards to the motives for an attack on the hotel. They didn't even hint at something we all suspected.

As the BBC team made ready to leave, Liz Sly, a feisty lady, approached to say something in a manner that I took to convey criticism of the report. I couldn't hear exactly what Liz was saying but she appeared to be exasperated. The reporter didn't appear interested in defending their report and departed.

I couldn't understand why the BBC team had been so quick to suggest that, not only was the hotel a secondary target, but that the perpetrator was without any doubt, Al Qaeda. Al

FIRST INTO ACTION AGAIN

Qaeda would certainly be the prime suspect under normal circumstances. But they were not the only contenders on this occasion. The BBC theory of the bombers being diverted from the police compound to the hotel was, to me, deeply flawed and hastily arrived at. Inaccurate reporting was usually the result of lack of time, poor intelligence, peer pressure, the need to race to be the first to report, laziness, desire for fame, political bias, or coercion (internal or external).

The BBC's theory that the suicide bombers initially targeted the nearby police compound and suddenly and inexplicably changed their minds struck me as implausible. Well-laid plans certainly select secondary or alternative targets in case circumstances change. The RAF during World War Two for instance had alternative targets, but that would have required only a minor alteration to the flight path of the bombers. This kind of targeting was very specific. If the police compound was the target, the planners would have conducted a reconnaissance, identified routes and all possible obstacles and taken steps to mitigate them. Imagine bank robbers taking weeks to plan a heist on a specific bank and, come the day of the robbery, they see a police car parked outside and then immediately select another bank nearby without as much detailed knowledge of how to rob it. To change an attack in mid-flow requires a very good reason and then a great deal of expertise to pull off. The two drivers would not have made the decision on their own. They had to receive orders from a controller able to observe the target and make critical and timely decisions. Suicide bombers, due to the limitations of their employment, are not experienced professionals and doubtless have little else on their minds but their route, their final objectives and pushing the button to end

PROLOGUE

their lives. I once sat with one in his prison cell in Sulaymaniyah while he was being interviewed by a CNN journalist. He had intended to blow himself up *inside* a bank and had been caught when a suspicious security guard wouldn't allow him entry. He had walked away in a daze, not knowing what to do, no doubt fearful of whatever punishment his superiors had threatened if he were to fail in his mission. He was so intensely brainwashed that he didn't even detonate his explosives when the bank guard stopped him – because his very specific instructions were to blow himself up inside the building. There was no room in his incredibly stressed mind for detailed instructions on a secondary target. To expect a pair of suicide bombers to calmly re-coordinate their own deaths in seconds by radio was utter fantasy.

Al Qaeda usually claimed responsibility on their website soon after an attack, but on this occasion no-one did. It took several months before an Al Qaeda online comment suggested they were responsible. Al Qaeda was known to claim responsibility for attacks they had not initiated.

So, if not Al Qaeda then who – and why?

There was another organisation on the suspect list of many in the media and it had the capability and motive for carrying out such an attack.

One of my clients was *Voice of America*, a news programme funded by the United States Congress. They were a small team based in a room at the Al Hamra Hotel and usually consisted of an American journalist and a local driver, fixer or translator. It would be no surprise to learn that, because of who funded VOA, it received intelligence from various US military sources that ordinary media organisations might not have access to.

Another way to look at it was that VOA was a convenient mouthpiece the US military or intelligence organisations might use to feed information to the general public. VOA's special relationship with the US government was no secret either. The news organisation had been the focus of hostility – and not only from insurgents. It was heavily criticised by the Iraqi government for exposing dodgy goings-on inside various Iraqi ministries. Living and working in the Red Zone, VOA was a vulnerable piece of the US government communications apparatus. One of VOA's Iraqi personnel was killed a year earlier and the case remains unsolved. The team needed full-time protection but its budget could only afford my occasional advice and training. I had several clients like them in Baghdad. All I could do was teach them the many dos and don'ts, ensure they had the right equipment and how to use it, and provide operational procedures in the hope that they would use them. Whenever they left the hotel in search of stories, which they frequently did, they were on their own.

A few months before the Al Hamra attack, VOA had exposed the existence of interrogation centres operated by Iraqi government security forces. This probably originated from US intelligence sources. The Iraqi police were doing terrible things inside these places to suspected terrorists, insurgents and anti-government agitators, on a level that Saddam Hussein would've been proud of. One of those interrogation centres was inside the police compound near the Al Hamra Hotel, the same one the BBC suggested was the original focus of the attack.

NBC took up the story of the interrogation centres – perhaps no coincidence, since the two bureaus were in the same hotel. Together, VOA and NBC brought the news to the world's

PROLOGUE

attention. This was an embarrassment for the Iraqi authorities. Middle Eastern governments historically exercised a high level of control over their news outlets, but there was little hope of the Iraqis dictating to the dozens of foreign news organisations operating in the country. That didn't stop them from trying though. The threat against the lives of VOA personnel became so serious that the bureau eventually had to quit Baghdad altogether. I personally supervised the closing down of the VOA bureau after the team suddenly left the country and I shipped their equipment back to the USA. I had spent many hours hanging out with VOA and was privy to some conversations. That was an advantage to having so many media clients. I heard many stories that never reached the public ear, usually because there was no official comment.

One snippet connected the Iranians to the Al Hamra Hotel plot. The Iranian consulate was located not far from the hotel. Both suicide vehicles needed to pass by the consulate in order to reach the section of hotel perimeter the planners had decided was ideal for the attack. The Iranians had a checkpoint on that road, but it was apparently stood down the night of the attack. A coincidence perhaps. Al Qaeda had no influence over the Iranians. But the Iraqi government did. This information supposedly came from communications monitoring, which would have been carried out by US intelligence services and passed on to VOA.

The rumour was that the attack on the Al Hamra was intended to punish Western news providers, notably NBC and VOA, for exposing the interrogation centres.

If the Iraqi government had anything to do with the attack then any media reports that blamed Al Qaeda would be welcomed. The Iraqi government wouldn't have blown up one of its own police stations/interrogation centres.

There was a piece of my puzzle missing. If I did believe the BBC was trying to curry favour with the Iraqi government, there had to be a theory attached to it.

In the earliest days of reporting in Iraq, many news personnel died in the pursuit of their work, either through ignorance of the dangers or murdered because they were news people or simply Westerners. It became obvious they needed to employ professional armed protection. CNN was one of the first, employing AKE, the company I worked for, which I will describe in more detail in a later chapter. Before long, every major news organisation that could afford it employed armed security in Iraq and Afghanistan. The good security providers, like AKE, not only employed quality soldiers, many of them former Special Forces, they provided intelligence services and training for the news crews. They also ensured that every security operator was properly vetted, equipped with quality weapons, body armour, communications and navigation equipment, and was qualified in the various skills necessary for the task. These included medical first-aid to a high degree, navigation, risk assessment and analysis, journey planning, communications skills, knowledge of explosives including booby-traps and mines, environmental survival and vehicle management. The top security companies also provided a 24/7 operations room to manage the numerous teams in different locations at the same time and, most importantly, provide an effective emergency response to serious incidents such as medical evacuations and kidnappings. We also provided journalists with trackers which were monitored by our ops room in Hereford. That lost its popular-

PROLOGUE

ity when more than one journalist was noted hanging out in places they shouldn't have been. On one occasion I was flown to New York to provide evidence that a journalist, who wrote a story about meeting rebel fighters in an isolated house in Syria that came under attack, never actually left Lebanon. That put AKE in a difficult position for a time because our clients began to suspect we might be there to monitor as well as protect. But I digress. Only a handful of private security companies could provide such services at the highest level. The best companies were not cheap and only the wealthier news organisations could afford them.

I was on the street one day with a Fox News team a year or so before the Al Hamra attack. A vehicle bomb had destroyed a prominent Iraqi restaurant frequented by westerners and several had died. Baghdad was not a town to eat out in, no matter how romantic or exotic the city might once have been. But westerners, it seemed, news people included, needed to be blown up a few times before the penny dropped.

The BBC rocked up beside us and I gave a hello to their lone security guard whom I didn't recognise. Making polite conversation, I asked what security provider he worked for. I'd heard the BBC had ditched its contractor. To my surprise, he didn't work for a security company and was self-employed and hired by the BBC on a monthly contract. I noted he had a pistol and AK47, which was significant for reasons that will become clear. The fact that the BBC no longer employed a registered security provider and had switched to hiring individuals struck me as highly irresponsible for several reasons.

Engaging a professional security provider in Iraq was considered an essential Duty of Care. The alternative was to employ security guards on an ad hoc basis. To anyone unaware of the complexities of operating in Iraq, this might seem like a reasonable way of saving money. The cost of security guards had reduced as the conflict continued and more companies entered the business, increasing competition – but the good ones that provided the kind of comprehensive service described above were still expensive. When the BBC decided to ditch its professional provider, it initially offered to pay its guards more than the going rate in the hope of attracting quality operators. They were still saving money. Some lads went for it, but the wiser ones appreciated there was a significant disadvantage for themselves as well as for the client when operating in Iraq. The self-employed guards had to provide much of their own specialist equipment. This was a significant financial outlay. Giving up a professional security provider also meant the news teams would be without access to essential services such as real-time local intelligence fed directly to operators on the ground, a speedy back-up and replacement system for personnel and equipment, and a dedicated operations room run by professional soldiers to coordinate tasks, as well as provide emergency responses to crisis situations that required specialised knowledge, experience and the security industry contacts. All of this was far beyond the everyday capabilities of a news organisation, even the BBC. Another important loss was the vetting of self-employed security personnel. A news organisation would never have the same access to a soldier's true background that a professional security company would have. Duty of Care would be severely watered down. The BBC could get away with it as long as nothing serious ever happened. It was rolling the dice.

But there was one more glaring red flag that waved above all

PROLOGUE

others. The BBC was breaking an Iraqi law every time its news teams went out on the ground with armed security. This could have led to serious consequences.

Soon after the new Iraqi government was formed it fought to take control of the vast number of armed foreign civilians operating in its country. Anyone could get a gun – in the early days I could pick up an AK47 for around $25. And at that time there was no security licence that required vetting and qualifications. Anyone could get a job as an armed security guard. Former postal workers, bartenders and hairdressers who'd never held a rifle in their lives before suddenly found themselves on deadly security patrols across the country. Hundreds of them died over the years. One US engineering company won an Iraqi contract and needed armed security. The CEO walked into a biker bar somewhere in the American midwest and offered $500 a day to anyone who wanted to go to Iraq. He hired some 50 biker dudes that night. Within four months, after several locals had been shot and several bikers were killed in ambushes, the engineers they were hired to protect refused to go on site or on the road with them.

To combat this problem, the Iraqi government established its own weapons licensing system. Only bona fide, registered security companies operating in Iraq could apply for a rifle and pistol licence. And there was a significant caveat. Every foreign security company that wanted a licence had to invest in an Iraqi partner who would have a level of ownership of the Iraqi-based operation and took responsibility for the awarding of and execution of the weapons licence and its terms. AKE was one of the first to be licensed in Iraq (the first round of applications were in alphabetical order). Those who continued to operate and carry firearms without a licence risked having their weapons confiscated and the offenders incarcerated until they sat before a judge. Iraqi army and police checkpoints were instructed to demand proof of weapons licences. The impact on teams operating illegally could be disastrous. Iraq was an incredibly dangerous place for any westerner to travel in. If a team's weapons were confiscated miles from home, they were vulnerable to death or capture for the rest of the journey. There were not only insurgents to deal with but also a burgeoning criminal class. More than one of my clients reported being pursued by bandits at night. *The Times* was a client of mine when Stephen Farrell's team contacted me one night, having narrowly escaped capture by bandits after an irresponsible late night stay in the city. They had headed home after the curfew when the streets were empty, except for bandits looking for prey. Shots had been fired at their vehicles. I had to retrain the team over the next week and hammer home the operational procedures for Iraq. Farrell should have known better, having already experienced a kidnapping. He went on to be kidnapped again in Afghanistan, which cost the life of his fixer and one of his British SAS rescuers, and several years after that I was involved in a mission to retrieve him in Libya after a team he'd joined was kidnapped. For some journalists, getting the story trumps safety and security. It's unforgivable when they expose those they employ to the same risks.

As far as I could see, the BBC was breaking the new licensing law by continuing to employ unlicensed, unvetted, unsupported armed security guards. The BBC couldn't apply for the licence without taking on Iraqi partners. But then it wasn't a security company so it wouldn't qualify anyway. The corporation saved

PROLOGUE

money, but at a risk to the lives of their staff and local employees. It also risked its operating licence. Breaking Iraqi law made the BBC vulnerable.

The Iraqi government was never officially accused of the Al Hamra Hotel bombing. I'm not suggesting the BBC concocted the ridiculous report about the Al Hamra bombing to appease the Iraqi government in order to keep its operating licence because it had been caught carrying unlicensed weapons. That would be ludicrous. But it was the height of irresponsibility to put itself in such a position.

My AKE clients during my stay in Baghdad included:

The Daily Telegraph
The Times
The Financial Times
CNN
Fox News
USA Today
The Los Angeles Times
The Wall Street Journal
The Washington Post
The Chicago Tribune
Time Magazine
Newsweek
ABC
Getty Images
Voice Of America
Al Jazeera
NHK
The Guardian

FIRST INTO ACTION AGAIN

Being a security risk manager was high-risk with small financial reward. It wasn't the money that kept me in it – I was doing okay as an author. I was an adventure freak. I loved nothing more than turning up in war zones, usually in places I'd never been to before, and existing amid the turmoil while trying to figure out how I was going to keep my team alive so that they could achieve their objectives. If an organisation needed to operate in a hostile and challenging environment and wanted to greatly improve its chances of achieving its aims, I was one of the people it employed. Plus it gave me material to write about from a first-hand perspective.

I thought my days of wild excitement had come to an end when I left the SBS. I had no idea the best, and worst, was yet to come.

1

ENGLAND

THE DAY I DROVE OUT of the Special Boat Service headquarters in Poole, Dorset, saying goodbye to my life in special forces and the Royal Marines for good, I assumed it would also mean the end of my military adventures. I had served over 11 years, half of what was considered a full career. Despite climbing the ladder of promotion and looking forward to greater responsibilities, I felt compelled to resign and move on. There's a sixth sense inside all of us that influences our decisions. You come to a fork in the road. Do you take the right or the left? What is that decision based on? Chance? Instinct? Perhaps it's something spiritual. I knew from experience how crucial such decisions were and that they were not to be taken lightly. When I was 17, my first major fork in the road was either an office job or the military. I was wise enough to know that whichever road one takes, one must be positive and embrace the consequences.

I resigned from the SBS not just because I felt it was time to explore other avenues of life. Change was in the air in UK SF (Special Forces). There was a move towards more conventional warfare and larger combat teams. It would be fantastic stuff, I had no doubt. But I preferred working alone or in small teams and those days looked to be numbered.

Since leaving school I'd known no other life than the Royal Marines and the SBS and, despite having no doubts about leaving, I was somewhat bewildered. I had no plan. That was odd for someone who, professionally, never did anything without a plan – objectives, contingencies, equipment, procedures, finance. I hadn't considered any of those to any serious degree. I had to make money of course. No more monthly cheques come rain or shine. An obvious choice was commercial diving in the oil sector. That would provide good money, especially if I opted for the more hazardous saturation diving. But my internal decision-maker didn't budge at the thought. Life would be too predictable and I couldn't see much adventure in it, not the type that would light me up. Private security was another obvious choice, but I knew little about the sector. It sounded like mostly bodyguard (BG) work, which I didn't fancy. A friend from the 14th Intelligence Detachment had just got fired from a BG task in London. He'd been looking after a Saudi family. He was told to take the children shopping to Harrods one afternoon. How depressing. He hated it. When he got back to the house the mother was waiting at the front door to greet her kids and asked where the other one was.

'There was only three,' he said. He wasn't the sharpest tool in the box.

'I've got four,' she said.

They rushed back to Harrods and found the kid in the manager's office.

I left the SBS on a Friday. The following Sunday afternoon

ENGLAND

the phone rang in my bungalow in the sleepy village of Lytchett Matravers, a few miles outside Poole. I lived alone and wasn't expecting any calls. My initial surprise was the identity of the caller. It was my first commanding officer in the SBS who'd retired some years earlier. I'd no idea what had happened to him. We didn't exactly mix in the same circles, him being an officer and 20 or so years my senior. He talked to me in a personable manner, addressing me by my first name, which sounded odd coming from him. I called him sir. He was known as RAM and I had enormous respect for him. He was one of those iconic military figures, a hero from the Borneo Confrontation who as Commanding Officer of the SBS had pioneered a new path for the unit and was credited with putting it back on the road to competing with the SAS. He was chief architect of modern maritime procedures for capturing ships and oil platforms. RAM overflowed with determination, mentally and physically, and led by example. In his spare time he did things like tackling the longest and most gruelling canoe race in the world, 124 miles from Devizes to Westminster, entering it more than a dozen times and often without much training due to his busy schedule. He was in his sixties the last time he took part in the race.

Everyone in the SBS knew that RAM considered it their duty to be fit and ready at a moment's notice to take part in any operation that they were trained to do, day or night, weekends and holidays. RAM liked to put the squadron to the test without notice, much to the annoyance of those who were not always in the best of shape.

I'd been in the SBS only a few months when, one Monday morning parade where, unusually, the entire squadron was mustered, RAM turned up and ordered everyone to be back in five minutes dressed in running kit. Our much-vaunted Sergeant Major, Derek, was on hand with a checklist to ensure no-one slipped away. Several trucks were waiting and we climbed aboard.

The SBS wasn't very large and could squeeze into a handful of four-tonners. The trucks drove into the countryside, somewhere on the Purbecks, and each of us was given a photocopy of a sketch map showing our route via a couple of manned checkpoints to a pick-up-point 30 miles away. A marathon plus.

We weren't given any water, that was for us to sort out for ourselves on the way. I regarded myself as one of the fitter members of the unit in those days. I didn't smoke and could nurse half a pint all evening. I agreed with the boss' philosophy that every man who wore the cap badge should be physically fit enough to do the job for which he took the Queen's shilling. Considering the growing demands, the level of fitness required was not small.

The least fit members of the SBS at that time could be found among the 'old and bold'. My generation was a new breed of SBS coming through, all part of RAM's facelift. He wanted the SBS to conduct maritime tasks that no other special forces in the world could achieve, such as climbing the world's largest oil platforms in the worst of weathers without being detected, using enough men armed and equipped to recapture the towering structures from a terrorist force. RAM wanted to achieve the same against all manner of ships while underway, from beneath the sea, on the surface or from the air. Such feats required operators with high levels of strength, stamina and determination. A bit of madness was also essential. Teams couldn't afford

ENGLAND

a weak link in the human chain. Every individual had to be on form or the operation could fail. It was a very serious business.

I was amused by the groans and dour expressions of those unfit members on seeing the distance they'd been ordered to cover. Thirty miles at short notice wasn't a doddle. It wasn't a race – we were given a reasonable time to complete it. The only expectation was to keep going and to be in enough of a fit state, mentally and physically, to conduct a task at the end of it. Quite a few failed to complete the run, and several who did were in no condition at the end of it to achieve anything other than crumple to the ground exhausted. A few careers were ended that day. Men had been marked. The boss was cleaning house and clearing a way for the new generation.

RAM's telephone call to me that evening began with congratulations on my years in the service and a welcome to civvy street. To my surprise, he had my departure date circled in his calendar. I was flattered. He asked me what plans I had for my future and I told him I was considering my options. He asked if security work was on my list and when I said it was, he suggested we meet at his home in Poole for a chat the following day.

I put the phone down, elated. A call from RAM for the purpose of possibly recruiting me was indeed a compliment. I didn't know what kind of security work he did but I suspected it wasn't anything ordinary. I'd been a pretty decent operator with no major black marks against my name. But we never really knew just how good we were or what our peers really thought of us. If a man was fit, reliable, punctual, tenacious, intelligent, capable, informed, knew the job, had good skills and was good company during long, boring waiting games, then he was an average member of the SBS. I felt I was at least average. I was looking forward to the meeting, with a sneaking feeling that it might be interesting. I would not be disappointed.

I drove into Poole the following morning and found RAM's house near Sandbanks. When the door opened I was pleasantly surprised to be greeted by a familiar face, RAM's old secretary from the SBS HQ who'd joined him on his civilian venture. She welcomed me in with her usual broad smile and I waited in the hallway. There were photos on the wall of RAM and his two amazing daughters. One was a world-ranked free-faller, the other a triathlete. No great surprise there. RAM did his first triathlon with his daughter when she was 15 years old.

RAM arrived and after some pleasantries we remained in the hallway while he explained about his company. Much of the work required the skills one learned with the SBS and military intelligence. His operators generally worked alone or in small teams, although there might be the occasional large team job. He went on to underline one important reality, emphasising that I needed to grasp its implications before agreeing to join his organisation. The significant difference between working for him and for the Ministry of Defence was that his operators could expect little or no support if things went wrong. If anyone ran up against foreign authorities while on a mission, for whatever reason, they were very possibly on their own. It was up to the individual to deal with such problems and extricate themselves. Any injuries or deaths that occurred as a result of a given task would not be the responsibility of the company. And, unfortunately, due to the nature and confidentiality of the tasks, operators were unable to get any kind of insurance.

'If those conditions don't suit you, then we should take this no further,' he said.

ENGLAND

I shrugged. The Royal Navy had an injury compensation scheme but I'd never given it any thought. There were many serious things that could go wrong resulting in death or injury – those were the risks one accepted. As for support on operations when things went wrong, there would occasionally be something in place where possible, an emergency response or quick reaction force. But for most of the high-octane tasks I'd taken part in, a response force wouldn't have been of much help because they were usually too far away. We could be compared to high-wire trapeze artists swinging from rung to rung far above the ground without a safety net. If that had worried me, I wouldn't have been in SF.

'That all seems perfectly fine to me,' I said. The job, as he described it, was music to my ears. Especially the part about small teams and mostly individual work.

He invited me to join him in the operations room. It felt a little awkward being so familiar with him in such personal surroundings. I had only ever seen glimpses of him when he was the squadron boss, coming in and out of the lines, listening to him talk from a podium or seeing him observe our training. I think he spent more time in London than he did in Poole. One never spoke to him. He was the God Frog, as the CO was affectionately called in the SBS. And now, here we were, chatting like mates. There was a bit of the eccentric professor about RAM and I was the inveterate protégé eager to please.

There were several maps on the walls of the ops room. One that caught my attention was of Iran with various pins along the coastline and notes attached. Iran had been in the news a lot. The Shah of Persia had been deposed by an Islamic revolution led by Ayatollah Khomeini, the US embassy in Tehran had been stormed and its personnel taken hostage, and Iraq, led by Saddam Hussein, had invaded the country in the hope of reversing the revolution. That war was still ongoing when I met RAM that day.

RAM's map showed pencil lines across the Persian Gulf connecting the Iranian coastline with Bahrain and Qatar. He explained how he'd recently conducted an operation to rescue an Iranian doctor from the country. RAM had taken on the biggest risks of that operation, flying into Tehran under the guise of setting up a tour company and then secretly meeting with the doctor, who was on the run from the Revolutionary Guard. The doctor had no passport and could not legally cross any borders. RAM returned to the UK and put together a team of former SBS operators, setting up a base in Bahrain from where they drove a speedboat under cover of darkness to the Iranian coast. RAM made his way a mile inland to a prearranged rendezvous. The doctor failed to turn up and RAM returned to Bahrain. A week later he set up a new operation out of Qatar from where he took the speedboat to a different piece of coastline to attempt another extraction. While RAM was heading for this new rendezvous the doctor was captured by agents of the Revolutionary Guard. RAM missed them by minutes. Had he been caught, he would've shared the same fate as the doctor, who was tortured and executed. The story served as an appropriate introduction to RAM's unusual security business.

At that time, RAM was running the largest private bodyguard operation in UK history, providing close protection for the media tycoon, Rupert Murdoch, in London during the so-called 'siege of Wapping'. Murdoch had just bought *The Sun*, *The Times* and

ENGLAND

News of the World newspapers. He planned to modernise the industry with technology that required just 10% of the current workforce. The unions didn't approve. Murdoch went ahead and switched production from the Fleet Street printing presses to new ones in Wapping, shedding 6,000 workers in the process. The union bosses went ballistic. Murdoch and his family received death threats. There was even a bungled attempt to kill him and his wife. Murdoch wanted former Special Forces to protect his family and executives and RAM was called in to do the job. I wasn't particularly interested in bodyguard work but it was something to do while waiting for a more stimulating task.

My first day on the job provided a pleasant surprise when I walked into our Kensington Hotel. The team consisted of around a dozen guys at any one time. I was to revive an old partnership from my days in the 14th Intelligence Detachment. Mac was there to greet me (aka Max in *First Into Action*).

It was almost like old times, without the guns and IRA threats, of course. The job was mostly as boring as expected, with many hours spent hanging around in vehicles, expensive restaurants or the Wapping print factory. One of my responsibilities was running the back-up car, which meant ensuring no other vehicle got between me and the client. The London black taxi cabs were notorious for pushing in. When I was a kid, cycling through Sloane Square, a black cab deliberately tried to push me into oncoming traffic as I overtook it and I've harboured a grudge against them ever since. I thought nothing of nudging them out of the way when they persisted. It was a form of entertainment, I suppose. On one occasion, after bumping an aggressive black cab out of the way prior to dropping Murdoch off at the Savoy, I was pursued by a whole team of them, using their radios to try to corral me in the back streets. I needed to stay in the area and wait for Murdoch to leave, so I had to lose them. The cabs were no match for my Ford Granada, tearing through the narrow streets around Charing Cross, and I soon shook them off.

When Mac and I weren't looking after Murdoch we were usually with his number two, a big Aussie called Bruce Matthews. He was a classic hard-arse from down under, tough, liked his drink, and a good bloke once you got to know him. He didn't like any of us poms at first and tried to get us replaced. When he heard he was getting former Brit Special Forces as bodyguards he was impressed, but was disappointed when we turned out to be less physically imposing than he'd imagined. I suppose his idea of a bodyguard was some hulking brute who could knock down a wall with his forehead.

When Matthews was told he was stuck with us, he treated us rudely and was generally dismissive, regularly ignoring our recommendations. That all changed one evening when, against our advice, he decided to visit one of his old hangouts, a Fleet Street pub popular with newspaper types. As soon as Murdoch's main man stepped inside to down highballs with his chums, word got out and several union thugs turned up. Three of RAM's lads were with Matthews that night. He had told them to wait in the car, as usual, as he didn't want to be embarrassed by his petite guards in front of his mates. The lads ignored the orders and stealthily entered the crowded bar to keep an eye on him. Matthews mingled raucously with his colleagues, having a great time loudly swilling drinks in the smoke-filled room. Being loud and over 6ft tall, he was easy enough to spot.

In walked the three union heavies with dark purpose in their eyes, making their way through the crowd towards their target.

ENGLAND

What they didn't know was they'd been seen by those whose job it was to look out for such characters. The thugs converged on Matthews, shoving his colleagues aside. Matthews was a hard bugger – he showed no fear and squared up to them with a sneer. Tough as he was, at 60 or so years old he would've been challenged to handle these heavies. Before they could make their move, hands shot from behind them and seized their throats and testicles in an iron grip. The leader's eyelid was grabbed, pulled and twisted between thumb and forefinger.

'You steer a horse by its mouth and a man by his eyelids,' I remember an instructor once saying. The discomforted thugs stiffened in pain. They were turned about, briskly marched back to the door and unceremoniously ejected onto the street. The operation was deft, calmly efficient, without fuss or noise, and so swiftly executed that few punters were even aware what had occurred. Matthews was impressed. From that day on he could be heard bragging about 'his lads' whenever the subject of bodyguards was brought up. Small but effective. Before that day he wouldn't allow us to enter a restaurant with him, making us sit outside in our cars until he was ready to leave. Finding time to get a decent meal as a bodyguard was always a challenge. That all changed. Now we were always invited to join him – at a separate table, but never far from him.

The only other noteworthy thing about that job was Mac being inadvertently responsible for the biggest headline *The Sun* ever ran during peacetime. Mac and I were driving through the city with Matthews and a female freelance journalist in the back who was Matthews' bit of stuff on the side. Mac had taken the weekend off and I asked him what he'd been up to. Mac said he'd been to a party where Freddie Starr had turned up.

At the time Freddie was the country's most famous comedian and a world-class celebrity. Mac described how Freddie, who was having a great time at the party, mentioned he was hungry. As a joke, he was presented with the hostess' pet hamster – whereupon the comedian rolled it up in a slice of bread and bit its head off. I couldn't believe it but Mac insisted it was true. The woman journalist behind us had clearly been listening. She leaned forward, insisting Mac repeat the story, which he did. We thought little of it.

A couple of days later I was leaning over a rail in Wapping looking out over the printing presses when I spotted *The Sun*'s headline as the papers were stacking up: FREDDIE STARR ATE MY HAMSTER!

I called Mac out of the tearoom to show him. 'Loose lips,' I said, wryly. We laughed heartily. Mac never did get a slice of the profits.

I stuck with the Wapping job because it paid well and was mildly entertaining but I still hoped something more interesting would turn up. Many jobs probably did come into the office while I was in Wapping but, as in the SBS, only those who were involved ever knew anything about them.

When I was eventually invited back to Poole it was to sit in on a warning order with a bunch of other lads for what, still today, remains one of the most extraordinary tasks I'd ever heard of. It was the stuff of Hollywood movies. A Chinese man had arrived in London with a small entourage seeking assistance, and not the kind that was normally advertised anywhere. RAM was called in to hear his proposal for an operation that most private security agencies would have run from. RAM took the task seriously and presented us with his outline plan. There were no

ENGLAND

maps or details at this stage but enough to inform everyone of the risks. And as per usual, those who preferred not to take part could leave before more details were given.

The Chinese man was the leader of a local clan in a remote village on the east coast of the Yellow Sea. The villagers made a living in husbandry, fishing, various cottage industries and trading with neighbours. This particular village also ran a mining operation, although it wasn't mentioned what the mine produced. The remoteness of the communities, combined with a distrust of central government and its economic apparatus, meant that the villagers didn't use banks or any other government services. The village's wealth, which had been accumulated over hundreds of years, was hoarded in the form of gold, precious stones, valuable artefacts and some currencies. There were advantages to isolation, such as freedom from taxes and official rules and regulations. The main drawback was a lack of protection from others who also preferred to live out of reach of the law, such as marauding bandits. The situation sounded more like something from the 16th century than the 20th, but that's how it was in far-flung parts of China in those days.

The villagers couldn't support a militia large enough to drive off the bandits and so paid a levy to be left alone. The reason the Chinese man had come to London was that a new band of marauders had arrived in the region and, instead of a mere levy, they wanted all the village's wealth. When the elders refused, the bandits attacked, destroying property and killing several villagers.

The wealth was well hidden and the few who knew its location were among those who'd escaped. It was hoped the bandits would eventually grow tired of searching and move on.

But after several months it was evident they would stay until they either found the treasure or consumed all of the supplies and destroyed the village. The elders therefore went in search of help and eventually found their way to England.

RAM didn't plan to take on the bandits in a fight. That would have required a large force with substantial weaponry. He wanted a low-risk operation. A SF solution. If everything went to plan there would be no need for direct conflict with the bandits. A dozen men would sail a workboat from the Philippines and land on the Chinese coast near the village. Weapons would be required for self-defence and in case things went wrong, and the Philippines were an ideal place to source them. The force would work in two groups, one to create a diversion and draw the bandits away from the focus of the second group, whose job it was to retrieve the treasure. The ground operation was expected to take no more than 12 hours. It reminded me of the old Japanese movie *Seven Samurai*, remade years later by Hollywood as *The Magnificent Seven*. I was grinning from ear to ear as I listened. It was absolute madness and I couldn't wait to take part. Invading China would look good on my resume.

The risks weren't as great as they might appear. The boat would have no problem sailing into those waters. The Chinese navy and coastguard were practically nonexistent in those days. There were no soldiers or police within hundreds of miles. The village was two miles from the coast across easy terrain. And the elders would provide guides. The devil was in the detail of course, but that was RAM's stock in trade. I can't remember exactly what the pay was but it was around £50,000 for a regular operator with the team leaders on a little more. What with the boat procurement and all the other

ENGLAND

logistics, it was an expensive task. Everything needed to be paid up front, including salaries.

I returned to London and carried on with the Murdoch job while waiting for the Chinese operation to get the green light. A month later I was called back to Poole to attend a briefing. I arrived at RAM's house late in the evening to find the place very quiet as I entered the ops room. Other than RAM, I was the only one there. I asked about the China job and RAM explained the elders were still trying to raise the money to finance the operation. Despite their claims to have more than enough wealth to cover the costs, no investor was willing to take the risk of staking them. I never heard another word on the subject. Another in a long list of operations that never got beyond the planning board. But there were many that did.

RAM brought me in on a completely new task that was most interesting. It had come from London, having bounced through various corridors of power to end up in front of RAM. The task would take several months and I was to conduct my part of it on my own. It involved a foreign government, terrorists and anti-terrorists and could not be performed by any official UK security service. The powers that be in London, however, had allowed it to be carried out by a private UK specialist. A kind of deniable operation, if you like, to use the Hollywood expression. There were to be no direct ties to the UK government. I'd need a few changes of civvies, ablutions, and my military field equipment, of which I had plenty. Weapons would be provided on arrival and I'd be away for three months.

After packing my gear, I shut down my house, a process I was used to, and took a taxi to Hurn Airport near Bournemouth where I caught a late flight to Bilbao. Once there, I'd make clandestine contact with someone who would take me to a secret location in the hills above Vitoria, where I would commence my task.

This felt more like what I was designed to do.

2

SPAIN

MY FLIGHT FROM BOURNEMOUTH LANDED at a cool and drizzly Bilbao Airport around 11pm. I climbed down the steps with the rest of the passengers to collect our baggage that had been lined up on the wet tarmac. It was a quiet airport. We appeared to be the only plane operating. In the shadows, beyond the lights, I could make out a handful of silhouettes. Glistening helmets and ponchos. Rifles. Some dogs. Soldiers quietly standing about, watching. Spain was having its own battles with militant separatists and my task was directly related to the situation.

The short version is the Basques wanted independence, Spain was reluctant to grant it, and the Basques were divided on how to achieve that goal. The Basque Nationalist Party (PNV) was a political organisation focused on accomplishing its objectives through peaceful means, while ETA (Euskadi Ta Askatasuna – Basque Homeland and Liberty) was a militant/terrorist outfit. The PNV had won a form of autonomy from the Spanish, a heavily watered-down version of self-government, which only served to antagonise ETA who accused the PNV of making a defeatist compromise with the enemy.

At that time the IRA was the most destructive terror organisation in Europe. When all the deaths and kidnappings were added up, Spain's ETA ranked second. One of the conditions of Basque autonomy was that it had to join the Spanish Government's fight against ETA. However, the only armed force the Spanish permitted the Basques to operate was their president's armed protection unit, a relatively small number of bodyguards. The PNV argued that, since ETA was a substantial terrorist force, any PNV counter-terrorist unit would have to be equal to the task. This put the Spanish government in an awkward position. They were reluctant to let the Basques have a significant military force, and certainly not a specialised one. But they had to concede the PNV couldn't take on ETA without possessing the tools for the job. Grudgingly, the Spanish agreed to an increase in the size of the Basque president's protection force and to a broadening of its mandate.

The PNV took full advantage of the concession and was keen to build its own special forces unit. It wanted an SAS-style outfit capable of handling operations comparable to the Iranian Embassy siege in London. Not only that, it wanted the skills to storm a hijacked commercial aircraft parked on a runway, and even the ability to recapture Basque oil platforms in the Bay of Biscay should they ever be seized by terrorists. Lofty ambitions indeed.

Initially, someone in the PNV thought the Israelis might be a good fit and they did get involved at one stage, but the Basques eventually turned to the British. The UK was an old ally and one of the few countries capable of delivering such a complex

SPAIN

package of skills. The Israelis didn't have the knowhow to tackle an oil platform in the Bay of Biscay, for instance. The request was passed onto a certain London company in the private sector that in turn brought in RAM, who of course relished the challenge.

The proposed Basque unit was given the official name Berrocci Berezi Taldea (Berrocci Special Group). It was going to need a headquarters, training grounds, living and working facilities, instructors, training programmes, operational procedures, manpower vetting and selection processes, an internal organisational structure, equipment procurement systems, vehicles and communications, all held together by an effective administrative infrastructure. And Berrocci had to be as clandestine as possible. The latter consideration was driven by one particularly dark and dangerous factor.

Although the Spanish government had given its blessing to the unit, that didn't mean it wouldn't take opportunities to hamper its progress. The Basques had a serious enemy, a right-wing militant group called GAL (Grupos Anti-terroristas de Liberación). GAL was essentially a death squad and only avoided being classed as a terrorist group because it was created and run by officials within the Spanish government itself. General Francisco Franco, who'd ruled Spain since the beginning of World War II, had spent much of his tenure doing his best to crush the Basques and had died only 11 years before my arrival in Spain. His friends and followers were still thick in the Spanish government. GAL was primarily focused on destroying ETA, but it would target any and all who assisted the Basques' pursuit of independence. My task was to spend three months on my own with the Berrocci men at their secret location, training them in many of the foundation skills the unit required. If Spanish intelligence knew my purpose, that information could find its way to GAL and I could have a problem.

As I walked down the steps to the tarmac I began to experience a familiar feeling, the same I felt every time I arrived in Northern Ireland as an undercover intelligence operator. Stepping off a commercial flight, on my own, in civvies, pretending to be someone other than who I really was. I was back in that groove in many ways. There was one significant difference, though, as RAM had stressed to me on joining his team – I was on my own if things went wrong. When I asked RAM how the Spanish might react if they knew why I was there, he couldn't be sure they'd be happy about it. Theoretically, I should've been fine. The Spanish had technically given it the okay. But then there was the GAL factor.

I picked up my bag and joined the line of passengers heading for the terminal building and the subsequent immigration and customs checks. I doubted the Spanish knew what I was doing there. They wouldn't have found out from the UK side. Any leaks would have originated from the Basques and that depended on how well Berrocci had been infiltrated, which was, apparently, a factor I needed to take seriously. There was little doubt ETA had eyes and ears within Berrocci and it was safe to assume the Spanish did too. But since I was still at an administrative level, my engagement and transit details were known by very few. I would soon find out.

I entered the arrivals hall and joined one of the lines that led to an immigration kiosk. When my turn came, I handed over my British passport and smiled politely at the officer who

SPAIN

inspected it. He glanced at me with that classic immigration officer expression of serene, unblinking blankness and handed it back. There was no indication that he had any interest in me.

I moved on to the customs hall. It was the last hurdle to the exit. If I was going to get pulled, this was where it would happen. There were several customs officers standing about eyeing up the passengers. In the background was a handful of armed soldiers. As I walked towards them, one of the officers looked me in the eye. I moved my gaze straight ahead. Someone in front of me was pulled over to turn out their suitcase. I wasn't stopped. I made my way through the arrivals hall, out the other side, onto the street and into the night air once again. So far so good. Onto the next hurdle before I could consider myself safe, at least relatively speaking.

My instructions were to turn right, make my way to the end of the terminal building and wait. The area was poorly lit and when I reached the corner I stepped into the shadows from where I could see all of the approaches to my location. I watched as passengers climbed into cars and taxis and within a few minutes I was the only person there. It was very quiet. Everything was wet from the light rain, the black tarmac road surface glistening under the random security lights. I had been in such situations many times. Standing silently alone in a strange place, waiting for someone, usually a stranger, to meet me. The usual things went through my mind. How long should I give it? Where should I go if no one turned up? The contingencies had been loosely covered. If the authorities were to question me, I would claim to be a tourist. If no-one from Berrocci came to meet me, I was to make my way into town, find a hotel, contact RAM and take it from there. It was past midnight and all the taxis had left. I began to contemplate the long walk into town.

It turned out my contacts were there all the time, concealed by the darkness while they watched me. The people of Berrocci were a paranoid bunch and justifiably so. I'd been there some 20 minutes when I saw two figures heading across a nearby empty car park towards the terminal entrance and then along the pavement in the same direction I'd come.

They stopped in front of me in my shadowy corner and one of them uttered the agent contact phrase. I can't remember exactly what it was now but it was something like, 'Have you come to visit the Bilbao Museum?' His English was very good. I replied something like, 'I'd rather go to the cinema.' Agent contacts were obviously a two-way confirmation code allowing each party to confirm the other's legitimacy. It was old-school WWII SOE procedure typical of RAM.

'I'm David,' said the one who'd made the contact. He was something of a Clark Gable lookalike. David gave me a welcoming smile and offered his hand. I shook it and gave him my name. The other was Umberto, a squat individual who looked like he could lift the engine end of a car on his own. I don't remember him ever smiling. I would later find out that David was the senior officer of the Berrocci team I was to train.

Umberto picked up my bag and David looked around with an assertive air before leading the way at a brisk pace. They looked in all directions as we moved without talking. When we arrived at the car, I caught a glimpse of Umberto's pistol in a holster on his hip as he opened the trunk and placed my bag inside. They climbed into the front and I sat in the back. Umberto started the car and drove out of the car park. They remained watchful

SPAIN

as we left the airport behind us, mostly looking to our rear in case we were being followed.

We drove in silence all the way to Berrocci, the secret camp that shared the unit's name. I'd never been to that part of Spain before and sat back watching the countryside fly by. There were few lights. We passed through several small towns and villages. There was hardly any traffic. After driving through the outskirts of Vitoria we continued south-east along a long, broad, gently curving road that climbed steeply up into the hills. After 15 or so kilometres from Vitoria, after a good gain in altitude, we turned onto a gravel track. A pair of headlights appeared behind us and kept pace. David and Umberto paid no attention to the accompanying vehicle.

Five or so kilometres further on we arrived at a collection of buildings, some of them old. The new-builds were large and resembled hangars. We came to a stop alongside some other vehicles. Apart from two armed men in fatigues watching us from across the car park, there was no-one about. I wasn't important enough to warrant a greeting from any official.

David took my bag and led the way to an isolated log cabin in a field a few hundred metres from the main cluster of buildings. It was a large, single-storey hunting lodge made of hewn logs on a foundation of granite boulders. Not a shoddy affair either. The surrounding countryside was open grassland stretching to distant trees on two sides, with a grassy slope rising several hundred metres to meet the night sky. The lodge interior was grand. The spacious main room had a substantial stone fireplace with a stag's head above it, as one might expect. A couple of leather armchairs stood either side of it. A chunky wooden table that could comfortably seat a dozen people dominated the central floor space. There was a small kitchen beside a doorway that led to several bedrooms. It was all very clean and tidy. David left me to explore the place for myself. I was tired and, after taking a shower, I was soon in bed listening to the sounds of the unfamiliar countryside outside my small window.

As usual in a new location, potential threats dominated my thoughts. There was always the chance of an ETA attack and I wished I had been left with a pistol, if only to help me relax. I didn't get much sleep that first night: there were too many creaks and bumps keeping my ears busy.

I got up soon after the early light came in through the window above my bed. After finding the makings of a cup of coffee and boiling a pan of water on the gas stove, I decided to take a look around the camp.

It was pretty obvious the place was originally a farm complex. RAM had discovered it, part of his original brief being to set up a training establishment. He recommended it after jogging the perimeter, which was a few dozen kilometres. A long-abandoned church was a part of the property. RAM had turned it into what we termed a killing house, hopefully not too sacrilegious a decision. A killing house, in this context, wasn't an abattoir but an interior shooting range. Steel plates 8ft tall and 4ft wide covered the inside walls of the nave with long rubber sheets suspended a few inches in front of them to catch ricochets. Wooden framed partitions simulating walls, doors and windows could be moved around to create rooms and corridors. It was quite excellent, all things considered, and saved Berrocci the cost of having to create a purpose-built facility. It missed some useful accessories such as an overlook control room, mood light

SPAIN

controls, speakers and so forth, but it was a great starter that could be improved over time.

David found me and took me to the cookhouse for breakfast. The men, recruits for David's new team, all shapes and sizes, trickled into the dining hall. Thirty or so altogether. David took the opportunity to brief me on the camp and the various procedures. The men eyed me curiously as they ate, no doubt wondering what kind of instructor I was going to be. They had already gone through two months of training with another of RAM's team and David sounded confident they were close to operational readiness. That I doubted. It would take more than a few months to turn a bunch of civvies into an effective SWAT-style team. I'd want six intensive months to get the same number of Royal Marines Commandos to that level.

I'd been a special forces instructor for many years but I'd never faced quite this kind of challenge before. Three months on my own to get this bunch operational was, frankly, ridiculous. To add to the difficulties, I spoke neither Spanish nor Basque and I doubted many of them spoke English. David couldn't be expected to interpret for me all of the time because he was also a student. I would need to split them up into smaller groups at times, working on different subjects. I was going to need a dedicated interpreter.

To kick things off, I asked David to set up three demonstrations. The first was a simple pistol shoot of 20 shots into a figure 11 at 10 metres. The second was a conventional troop-level advance-to-contact in open country, with blank rounds of course – I wouldn't risk a live-fire exercise until I knew them. Finally, I wanted to see a single-team room assault with a live hostage extraction, again using blank ammo. I wanted to see their best, most polished performances and gave them three days to rehearse – a day for each display. But before they got started, I wanted to see the lads at 6am the following morning for a little jog. A sort of greeting. That gave me the rest of the day to scout the area, get to know the place and go through the equipment I had available.

There was a knock on the door of my log cabin that evening. It was the cook bringing my supper. I had been wondering about the evening meal. He asked me something in Basque and when I shrugged ignorance he went into the kitchen and dragged a huge wicker-covered glass bottle out from under a table. It was too large for him to lift on his own. It looked like a giant Christmas tree bauble. He pulled a cork the size of a tennis ball from the neck and tilted it to fill a jug with red wine. An unexpected treat. I had the fire going, so I lit a couple of candles, of which there was an abundance, sat at the table and ate my dinner, which was delicious. Afterwards, I retired to the log fire with a book and a glass of wine and settled in for the evening. One had to take advantage of such moments. I still missed a pistol by my side and decided to ask David about getting me one, when the timing was right.

The following morning I met the lads outside their accommodation. They were certainly a mixed bunch: fat, thin, tall, short, beards, moustaches, bushy-haired, a couple of baldies, but all with dark, olive skin. Their attire was also mixed, ranging from shorts and T-shirts to trousers, boots and trainers. Some looked fit and muscular and keen to get going, while others clearly weren't used to such an early start to the day.

The air was fresh and I was looking forward to stretching my legs. RAM had been training for a triathlon when he found

SPAIN

the location and had mapped out several routes of different lengths. I decided five miles would be a reasonable start. The area was hilly and offered some challenging climbs.

I gave a smile and a 'hi' which was returned dryly, verging on suspiciously by some. Without further ado, we got going. The group set off with enthusiasm, mostly due to David's robust encouragement. There was no doubt he wanted the men to impress. But within a mile, only about half of them were still with me. I'd been running at a slow, easy pace, but the hills had taken their toll. There was a strong core of tough individuals who stayed with me, David among them, but the rest formed a long line of stragglers. A handful had taken to walking. I paused and got those with me to do push-ups and sit-ups, while the rest caught up. We repeated that procedure throughout the remainder of the run so that we could all finish together. I left them with the understanding that some kind of early morning workout would be a daily routine and retired to my cabin for a shower while they set about preparing for their demonstrations.

Apart from the workouts, I spent the next three days with little to do but explore the countryside. The landscape was stunning – a series of hills dotted with woodland and fields on what appeared to be a huge plateau. This would be my only down time on the task and so I made the most of it.

On the day of the first discipline, David came to my cabin early to inform me the men were ready. I had cancelled the workout that morning. We went to the range to find the teams kitted out with pistols, hip holsters and ready to go. Each man had his own target with his name on it. It was a simple exercise. Nothing fancy. I was looking for basic technique and accuracy.

The first row of men lined up. With David's help, I asked

them to face their targets and hold their weapons in both hands in the easy position, pointing at the ground. Each time I shouted 'fuego!' ('fire!') – it should really have been 'disparar!' ('shoot!') – they were to raise their pistols, fire a single shot, and lower them again. The only degree of difficulty was that they were to fire as soon as possible once the weapon was level with the target. I was looking for instinctive shooting rather than aimed shots. That meant keeping both eyes open. I noticed most were trying to aim with an eye closed, an impractical habit for the business they were in. At 10 metres, at a quick pace, I would expect a trained, instinctive shooter to get all of the rounds into a circle the size of a football. Inspecting the targets after the first group had fired, I could see their aim was poor, with many rounds failing to even find the boards. I made no comments and asked for the next group to take their shots. There was little difference in skill level between them all. At the end I thanked David and looked forward to the next discipline.

An hour later David led me to the top of a ridge overlooking a valley that ran across our front. The unit could field two rural teams but I only needed to see one. The dozen men, all in camouflage fatigues, appeared on the left side of the opposite slope about a quarter of the way up, spread out in an arrowhead formation and walking slightly uphill. I was in the perfect position to see things unfold. They moved slowly and deliberately and looked professional. The machine-gunner was near the centre of the group and I quickly identified the commander because he kept signalling the men to maintain formation.

They were halfway across the valley when I heard the pop of enemy gunfire. They dropped to the ground. More shots gave away the ambushers' position hidden in foliage to my right,

SPAIN

three-quarters up the slope about 200 metres from the patrol. I could hear shouting, no doubt the troop commander. The machine-gunner was joined by his partner and, as the others put down covering fire from their prone positions, the gun team ran uphill to the left flank. I expected them to push on to the top where they'd have a commanding position but they didn't. I had seen boxes of smoke grenades in the ammo store but the patrol didn't use any. This was the ideal time to hide one's movements from the enemy.

The machine-gun opened up with short bursts and half the troop got to their feet and charged forward a few metres before dropping down. Then the other half got up and advanced in the same manner. The ambushers remained dug into their position throughout. The machine-gun crew carried on firing in bursts but the charging troops were gradually edging uphill until the left flank eventually came between the machine-gun and the ambushers. The gun team realised their error and stopped firing in order to move to higher ground, which brought everything to a brief halt. When the gun team recommenced firing, so did the charge forward. But as they progressed, the two groups started to get out of sync. At times they were moving as a single unit with long periods of no shooting while empty magazines were changed. It reminded me of my first troop attack on my commando course. It had been an absolute shambles, far worse than what I was watching, and went from bad to worse when I was suddenly put in charge and fumbled to take control. Those days seemed an eternity ago.

By the time the Barrocci patrol finally reached the enemy position they had converged into a tight group and everything came to a grinding halt. There was no sweep through to beyond the enemy position. The gun group was called in to join the others and the assault officially ended.

After lunch I met the men at the church where David had assembled his best team for the room entry. I threw them a small surprise by announcing I would be the hostage. I'd miss seeing the approach, pre-entry and outer entry, but it was the final entry that I most wanted to see, and where better than from inside?

I sat in a plastic chair in the centre of the small room surrounded by furnishings that simulated a living room and three dummies as terrorists. The air was dusty from the gravel floor. I was wearing goggles because they would be using flash-crash grenades. I certainly wouldn't have chosen to be the hostage had they been using live rounds, an unnerving position I'd taken on more than one occasion during live firing exercises with the SBS.

I didn't have to wait long before I could hear the team stealthily approaching outside. The door was kicked open and I braced myself for the grenade, fragments of which struck me. There were four operators, all wearing gas masks. A hail of blank rounds was fired. I was roughly manhandled from the chair and out of the room, along the corridor and out the front door of the church into the fresh air. It was over in seconds. There are a number of fundamental techniques to conducting a room entry. Clearing the doorway for those behind to enter and engage. Avoiding tripping over obstacles when shooting in a confined space in poor visibility. What to do if an operator went down, or a weapon jammed. Entries were more complicated than simply bursting in with guns blazing.

I said nothing more except to ask David to muster the teams

SPAIN

in the briefing room the following morning and left them to de-service. I think David was miffed that I had offered no comments, compliments or criticisms about any of the disciplines.

I was called to meet the big boss of Berrocci for the first time. He had just arrived, a successful Basque businessman named Ramon who had been appointed by the PNV. He was a capable and natural leader whom RAM held in high regard. I went through my general plans for the training schedule and brought up the subject of an interpreter. Ramon was aware of the issue and explained how it had been a challenge because few people in the organisation could speak English well enough. An interpreter was an important position of trust and trying to fill it from outside Berrocci risked unwittingly employing a spy. Ramon was contemplating one possible solution but appeared to harbour some doubts about it and didn't elaborate. I needed to recommence training the next day and an interpreter was essential. He assured me he'd take care of the matter.

The following morning the men were assembled in the briefing room. I went to see Ramon to ask about the interpreter and was surprised to find a beautiful young woman sitting alone in his office, wearing a smart trouser suit. She glanced at me without a smile or any kind of acknowledgement. This was the first woman I'd seen at the camp.

I was about to politely withdraw when Ramon entered from an adjoining room and introduced her as his daughter Louisa. She was to be my interpreter. Louisa looked uncomfortable, as if she didn't want to be there. She'd just completed university and was available to work with me for the duration of my visit. Ramon would have preferred someone with military experience, but there was no-one else he could trust to take the position. I asked if she understood we'd be going into the field on occasion. My question was directed at Ramon but Louisa answered curtly in perfect English. Her father had explained the job requirements.

She was under a strict curfew for her personal safety and would have to be home in Bilbao every evening. My first thought was that meant I'd be without an interpreter for night exercises, but I kept it to myself. Without further ado I asked her if she'd join me in the briefing room where the men were waiting. She got to her feet and waited for me to lead the way without looking at me. She was petite and a head shorter than me. I couldn't tell if she was nervous or just being objectionable. A bit of both, probably.

The men were talking loudly when I entered the room and didn't quieten down until Louisa appeared behind me. I later learned David was the only person who knew she was Ramon's daughter. She looked uncomfortable standing at the front of the room beside me but her chin was proudly up.

I introduced her as my interpreter, which she then of course had to interpret. She spoke clearly and confidently. I got straight on with it. After saying how pleased I was to be at Berrocci and how much I was looking forward to the training, I turned to the subject of the demonstrations. Louisa seemed to have no problem and translated fluidly. I had no idea what she was saying, of course, but David gave me a reassuring nod when I glanced at him.

I pulled no punches, explaining I wasn't impressed with what I'd seen and that the teams had fallen short of my expectations. Louisa was silent. She seemed to be contemplating what to say.

SPAIN

The men waited expectantly for her translation. She leaned close to me and whispered that I couldn't say that.

'Say what?' I asked.

I couldn't criticise the men in that way.

Seeing my confusion, she explained they were proud Basques and my words would be taken as an insult.

I was annoyed at being edited in this way. Perhaps I could've been more diplomatic. But then we weren't some snowflake institution that needed its delicate sensitivities pandered to. Soldiers had to be blunt and to the point. I didn't want to alienate my students if I could avoid it, but honesty struck me as more important right now. I was irritated by her stubborn refusal to interpret what I'd said and wasn't sure what to do. The men were waiting.

I considered asking David to interpret for now, but decided against it. If Louisa was to be my interpreter, this had to be sorted out. I walked out of the briefing room and went to find Ramon.

He looked up in surprise from his desk as I entered. He was even more surprised when his daughter followed, looking flushed. I explained what had happened. He spoke to her in Basque. She replied loudly and heatedly. Ramon inquired if I could find a more diplomatic way of criticising the men. In my earliest days as an SBS instructor I had been lambasted for my occasional lack of tact and was aware of my shortcomings in that department. But over the years I thought I'd improved. Ramon was right, of course. I agreed to try a softer approach, but at the same time I wanted assurances my comments wouldn't be watered down. Roman looked at his daughter, who appeared to agree, if somewhat reluctantly. She was as strong a character as he was.

We returned to the briefing room. The men were talking loudly but went quiet as we entered. They looked expectantly at us once again, but seemed to sense something was wrong. Perhaps they had enough English between them to work out what I'd said. I babbled on about how disappointed I was with the demonstrations. Louisa looked displeased but went ahead and interpreted me. It must have been an accurate translation, judging by the response. There was a brief silence while the men digested the comment. Then came a loud burst of angry voices. I couldn't understand what was being said but it was clear from their tone and body language that they were not happy. They retaliated with a barrage of questions. Louisa was overwhelmed as she tried to select comments to translate for me. The men were upset and demanding explanations. I tried to placate them by stressing there were many positives and that we would work together to fix the negatives. Louisa tried to make herself heard above the cacophony but the men were in no mood to listen. This was not a very good start at all.

I asked David to join me outside. He wasn't pleased with what he'd heard either. But I wasn't about to back down. They either accepted it or kicked me out. I think David appreciated that a lot of time and effort had gone into getting me to Berrocci. I was clearly not their choice of instructor but to replace me now would be a major inconvenience.

He sucked it up and asked me what I wanted to do first. My plan was to begin with pistol shooting, a fundamental discipline for the unit and its ambitions. I told him to muster the men the following morning in light fatigues, carrying only pistols. He asked how much ammunition he should bring.

'None,' I said.

SPAIN

He was perplexed and asked for confirmation.

'No bullets,' I said and left him. I needed to spend the rest of the day researching the facilities and to come up with a plan.

Being disliked as an instructor wasn't new to me. When I was part of the SBS Land Air Training team we usually had four instructors. The boss, a sergeant, was always helpful though tough, while the other lads were generally humourless and businesslike. The fourth member, myself, was nicknamed Mr Nasty because, on top of his training responsibilities, it was his job to make the recruits' lives hell. When they were woken at 2am, having gone to bed at midnight after a typically gruelling day, and taken for a mud run or freezing swim and workout till dawn, it would be me in charge. My mission was, essentially, to help trim the fat so that we were left with the core players who would eventually join the SBS. The mere sight of me turning up at any time of the day was enough to fill them with dread.

I decided to forgo PT the following morning and requested the men to be at the hangar that doubled as a gym and training facility wearing fatigue trousers, T-shirts and trainers. The men ambled in after breakfast with a general air of indifference. There was little energy about them. When Louisa arrived she was equally apathetic. I smiled as if all was normal and got down to it.

As bodyguards and SWAT-style operators, their engagement with an enemy was mostly, but not exclusively, going to be within 10 metres. Their primary weapon was the pistol – their SMGs (submachine guns) pushed too much to the right when set to single shots. To get these guys firing pistols accurately, I needed to go back to fundamentals.

Like boxing, good pistol shooting begins with the feet then

works its way up the legs, through the hips, back, shoulders, down through the arms and finally to the hand grip and trigger finger. Once the body has acquired the right techniques and muscle memory, a person can shoot from any position with a far greater likelihood of hitting the target. Getting the right muscle memory was the key. Body strength improved the entire system. Hand-eye coordination was a given. A most important component was the position of the pistol in the hand or hands. The hold had to be strong and constant, especially with instinctive shooting. Each time the pistol was drawn it needed to be in the same configuration in a vice-like grip. A simple test was to stand and aim at the football-sized circle on the figure 11 target at 10 metres and shoot into it, holster the weapon, then close your eyes, draw the pistol and fire again at the target. If your rounds were inside the football 10 out of 10 times, consider yourself a professional. If you could do the same while kneeling, sitting and lying then consider yourself an expert. All that one-handed and you were a god.

I wasn't expecting the men to reach professional level during my tenure but I hoped to get close. The first step was for them to become completely familiar with their weapons and so I began the day with them stripping and assembling their pistols, racing against each other then doing it blindfolded. Louisa remained cool towards me but as the tempo of the training picked up, so did she. I constantly interrupted sessions with bouts of push-ups, pull-ups, sit-ups etc, aimed at strengthening their bodies while playing games. They leaped over gym horses, climbed ropes and ladders, always holding their pistols in one or two hands. As the days went by, I increased the degrees of difficulty. Loading and unloading with blank rounds. Swiftly

SPAIN

changing magazines. Drawing against each other, Wild West style. They were very competitive, which accelerated improvement. A fiery and passionate bunch. There was lots of shouting and screaming during races, as encouragement or to try to put each other off. Louisa would join in enthusiastically. And every so often I'd pause for them to carry out the blind eye test – eyes closed, draw, aim, then look to see if they were on target. They became aware of the importance of the pistol position in the hands.

At the end of the first week David asked when they were going to use live ammunition.

'Not yet,' I said. The men were having fun but I wasn't sure they grasped the full value of what I was doing at this stage. My relationship with Louisa had not really improved despite her increased enthusiasm. She didn't greet me in the mornings and left at the end of each day without saying goodbye.

On week two I introduced them to wax bullets. I found a box of 38 special revolvers in the store. The bullets and gunpowder were removed and the casings filled with wax. The percussion cap was powerful enough to fire the wax as a soft, slow bullet, though it stung painfully when it struck flesh. It was the precursor to paintballing, which wasn't around in those days.

I built an assault course around the walls of the gym using ropes, ladders, swings, rings, nets, horses and tunnels with Figure 11 targets spread about. Each man had to scramble over the assault course in turn, as fast as he could. Whenever I blew my whistle, no matter what position he was in, he had to draw his pistol from its holster and shoot a wax bullet at a target. Points were given for hits. It was difficult but a lot of fun. Each man eagerly awaited his turn. There were shouts of encouragement when someone was doing well, hoots of derision when a target was missed or a gun dropped, and laughter if someone fell or got hopelessly entangled. The value of the exercise was debatable but it was an enjoyable break from the more serious routines.

By the end of the week they were doing everything while wearing gas-masks and then at night in complete darkness, in pairs or in teams, using flashlights to move around the gym in search of each other, the hand-held lights a disadvantage as well as an advantage.

The last day of week two, I surprised them by taking them to the range where live 9mm ammunition was waiting for them. I conducted the same exercise as I had two weeks earlier – single shots on command into a target at 10 metres. The improvement was huge and a pleasure to see. Without having fired a live shot for two weeks, every round was on target, with most of them inside the football-sized circle. I had saved the targets with their names on from the first demonstration so that they could compare them.

I gave them the following day off, which was a Sunday, and went to my log cabin. I needed to start planning week three. As darkness fell there was the customary knock on the door and I opened it like Pavlov's dog expecting to see the chef standing there with my supper. Instead it was David and Umberto. David asked if I'd like to join them for dinner. I grabbed my coat. I assumed we were going to the mess hall but they led me to a car. I sat in the back and David handed me a pistol and a couple of spare mags before we drove off. He grinned as he explained that we weren't going off to do a hit. It was purely precautionary and for my own safety. We were going to a restaurant in Bilbao.

SPAIN

There were only a handful of bars and restaurants the men could safely frequent. A few days before I arrived, a couple of off-duty Basque police officers had been gunned down by ETA while leaving a bar in Vitoria.

Our restaurant was owned by the brother of one of the Berrocci bodyguards. David led the way inside. It was quiet but then it was early in the evening for Spaniards. I followed him through the room expecting to sit at one of the empty tables at the back. Instead we climbed a flight of stairs to a door at the very top. He opened it and indicated I should enter. I stepped inside and to my surprise saw all of my students standing behind lines of tables formed into a square. The men faced the centre in silence.

David led me to the head table where I was guest of honour. I felt awkward at first but they were taking it seriously and so I adopted the appropriate gravitas. Before anyone sat down David announced in Basque and English that, from this moment on, no-one would question my training methods. He handed me a glass of wine, held up his own, the men did likewise, and we made a toast. They presented me with a gift which I was encouraged to unwrap there and then. It was a large, serrated Rambo knife, a picture of Rambo on the packaging, with a hollow haft filled with various survival implements such as flint, fish hooks, snares and a compass in the screw cap. I wondered if the Rambo bit was some kind of dig. But these men clearly intended it as a serious gesture – the 'Rambo' allusion was merely commercial advertising. The Spanish are renowned for their knives and this one was extremely well crafted. It became my field knife of choice and I have taken it all over the world.

FIRST INTO ACTION AGAIN

The next day Louisa came to me with a genuine smile and apologised for not attending the dinner because of her curfew.

The next couple of months were spent switching between conventional soldiering and SWAT-style training. The Spanish authorities did their best to make things difficult whenever the opportunity arose. A supply of Spanish high-explosive grenades arrived and Ramon asked me to train the lads in their use. The first grenade detonated successfully but it was one of the few that did. I spent most of the day destroying the duds with plastic explosives.

The weeks went by quickly and the boys worked hard. Their enthusiasm was a delight. The last day of my training programme was a demonstration laid on for senior members of the PNV to show how Berrocci was progressing. The Spanish military sent several officers to observe. The teams were to carry out a complex assault on the old church in order to rescue hostages held inside by terrorists. It was to be a two-pronged entry, with one team using explosives to breach the ground-level entrance while another abseiled from the tower and gained access through an upstairs window. To add a degree of difficulty, the teams were to use CS gas, which meant conducting the entire assault wearing gas-masks. It was impressed upon the dignitaries that the teams would also be using live ammunition and real explosives.

Ramon had hoped I would use live hostages but I was against it. The guys had greatly improved but that was a risk I wasn't prepared to take. I doubt I could have found anyone stupid enough to volunteer anyway. I would be happy if we completed the exercise without any of the men shooting each other. I was to be disappointed.

SPAIN

The officials were ushered into a roped-off area outside the church where they'd be safe against ricochets. The military observers would no doubt be most curious to see what the Basques had achieved. Back in my SBS days we conducted a number of entry demonstrations for top brass and politicians. We usually invited them to stand inside the actual killing room behind a white line wearing ear defenders and goggles to get the full experience. We would often place a vase on a stand within a few feet of them which was deliberately shot to add dramatic effect.

The lads were up for the assault. They didn't lack enthusiasm and their skills were good. I was concerned about the usual unforeseen mishaps ruining the demonstration, such as a tangled rope on the abseil or a detonator failing during the explosive entry.

The entry went off without a hitch. I remained until the dummy hostages were dragged out and the exercise was brought to an end. White smoke issued from the old building as the men came outside. David said it had gone perfectly. Normally I would have lined up the guys at that point and officially cleared their weapons, but it was time to start treating them as professionals and they returned to the barracks to de-service in their own time. I slipped away to avoid being noticed as anything other than one more observer. Everyone knew about the foreign trainer but having him on view wasn't considered appropriate.

As I headed towards the barracks I heard a shot ring out from inside, immediately followed by a prolonged scream. I ran into the block and along a corridor to where several of the men were crowded in the doorway to one of the rooms. I pushed my way through. Lying on the floor was one of the men. I could tell right away that he wasn't in any immediate danger of dying. He'd been shot through his bicep. I inspected the wound – a pinhole where the bullet had entered and a hole the size of a cherry where it had exited, with hardly any blood. The bullet had missed the artery but shattered the bone. Very painful. Fortunately, none of the dignitaries were aware of the incident.

I left Berrocci a couple of days later, never to return. Most of the lads were attending a function somewhere and I was happy to slip away without fanfare. I was just a hired hand anyway. There's usually a certain kind of bond between instructor and students, especially in such circumstances, and that was evident in this case. But I always hated those kinds of goodbyes. To my surprise, a couple of days before, Louisa asked if she could join me for dinner in the cabin, just her and me. Her father had allowed her to stay late. It was a memorable evening.

I didn't keep in touch with anyone from Berrocci but I kept an eye out for them. A few years later I heard they were involved in a gun battle with an ETA terror cell in a Bilbao park. They killed a couple but at the cost of one of the lads. I never knew who, and I didn't try to find out. Of my many adventures, even though it was uneventful as far as personally seeing action was concerned, I've always thought most fondly of my time with Berrocci. Many years later I wrote a book influenced by the experience, a highly fictionalised account set in Central America called *Mercenary*. I also wrote a screenplay. Fingers crossed!

One day I plan to return to Berrocci and conduct a drive-past posing as a silly old lost tourist.

3

THE ATLANTIC

NOT LONG AFTER RETURNING HOME from the Basque country, I received an urgent call from RAM asking if I was available for an immediate high-priority task. It was my favourite kind of start to an operation. Within an hour I was stepping into RAM's briefing room where he was busy scribbling notes. I waited with my usual impatience to find out what it was.

'There's a terrorist threat against a British cruise liner,' he said without drama. He went on to explain that the intelligence services didn't know which particular vessel was under threat but it was being taken seriously.

There were many British cruise ships dotted about the globe at any one time and the intelligence services were working hard to cover all of them. They wanted at least one man on board each where possible and he would have to be thoroughly versed in all aspects of ship-boarding techniques, from air and sea. That narrowed it down to SBS since the SAS didn't do maritime. Several Hereford lads had joined SBS teams on ship-boarding exercises, but there was a big difference between having done it once or twice and having lived it. However, due to operational commitments there was a shortage of SBS operators on hand at such short notice, which was not unusual.

London gave RAM a call. Knowing he employed former SBS, they asked if he had anyone on the books qualified to cover one of the high-priority vessels that would soon be departing UK waters. The SIS (Secret Intelligence Service – MI6) would permit the task to be managed by a private UK civilian security provider as long as the operator selected was a recent member of the SBS with maritime anti-terrorism experience.

Due to time constraints and the practicalities involved, there would be no attempt to evacuate the cruise ships already at sea. Nor would they cancel those vessels about to depart. That would cause widespread panic, especially if the media got hold of it. Everything had to appear normal. Any leak of the threat would create pandemonium aboard the cruise ships at sea. The best solution was to place a specialist on board each vessel they could readily get to, and manage any threats using response methods for those they could not.

The QE2 was departing Southampton the following afternoon for New York, stopping in port for six hours before returning to Southampton. I was to be on it for both the outbound and return legs.

The QE2 had been the target for terrorists a few years earlier while on its way to New York from Southampton and the SBS parachuted a team into the Atlantic to climb on board to find a bomb. Just two years back the cruise ship Achille Lauro was hijacked in the Mediterranean by the Palestine Liberation Organisation. A passenger was executed on that occasion. While I was a serving member in the SBS we were put on

THE ATLANTIC

standby twice to fly to a cruise ship in response to a threatened terrorist attack. Both times the situation had been resolved before we could get into the air. The risk to cruise ships was real enough.

My brief was to pose as a regular passenger, secretly equipped for my response duties. If the terrorists were to appear, either by somehow gaining access to the ship while it was in transit or disguising themselves as passengers or crew, I was to secure an exterior space for UK or US special forces to retake it by helicopter or assault boat, depending on where the ship was in the Atlantic at the time.

I'd never been on a cruise ship before. I'd been aboard many types of commercial vessels but never a floating luxury hotel.

'Do you have a tuxedo?' RAM asked.

'No.'

'A suit?'

'Not really.' I had some horrible, cheap thing I'd bought years before for some function or other. I wrote down my clothing measurements and was told that suitable garments would be on board by the time the ship sailed.

The SBS was arranging the specialist equipment I'd need which would also be on board for me. That would include weapons of course. It was technically illegal for a UK civilian to possess lethal weapons. A special dispensation had been provided for me for the task. The ship was departing around 1600 the following day. I needed to be on board no later than 1400.

I immediately began thinking about potential scenarios and what I needed to pack. I confess to having visions of me running around the ship like some action movie hero. It was an irresistible thought. I would be lying if I said I wasn't looking forward to it for all kinds of reasons. But all silliness aside, it was within my capabilities. How could anyone not wish for a chance to do for real what they'd spent years training for?

We spent the next few hours going over the planning, what I'd need, what might happen, what my responses would be, communications, operational procedures, et cetera, et cetera. It was all familiar territory for me.

By late afternoon we were satisfied that we'd covered everything. There were always loose ends and the unknown, but a comprehensive list of contingencies had been compiled in that respect. Basically, if the terrorists appeared, I would be on my own until the lads arrived, making decisions as the situation developed. That was why a maritime anti-terrorist specialist was required and not just any old SF type. RAM reported to his London contact that I would be on task and all was in order at our end. I was set to go.

RAM suggested I go home, sort out what personal kit I needed and get a good night's sleep. A car would collect me and my wife around noon and take us to Southampton.

I paused, having been thrown off balance. I didn't have a wife.

The news gave RAM pause too. For some reason he thought I was married. He said a girlfriend would do, assuming she was up for it. I didn't have one of those either. I was so often away for long periods, it was tough to maintain a relationship in my line of work.

Not having a wife or girlfriend was a major stumbling block. RAM was concerned it could jeopardise the task. A young man on his own would attract attention and arouse suspicion. Terrorist elements might already be on board and on the lookout for a sea marshal. RAM's immediate response was to replace me. He asked if I knew anyone else qualified for the task, who was married. I didn't. But I didn't want anyone else to do it. In my head, I was already on my way to the boat. RAM had several former SBS members on the books, but none had my level of current maritime knowledge and experience. Most had left the SBS several years before, while I had been a civvy for barely six months.

There was no time to find someone else. It had to be me. I blurted out that I had an ex-girlfriend who I thought might do it. It was true. She'd be perfect, in fact. She was easygoing, cool, calm. I hadn't spoken to her in months. Our parting had been amicable, we were still friends and I was sure she'd be up for it.

RAM asked me to call her and confirm right away. There weren't cell phones in those days and I didn't carry an address book. I had her number at home. RAM wanted her passport details as soon as possible.

I left the office feeling anxious. I'm sure RAM was too. I couldn't let him down. I couldn't carry out the task without a partner and I couldn't not go either. Lives might be at stake. Reputations too, since RAM had already told the SIS I was good to go.

It was early evening by the time I got home and I went straight to my contacts book and the phone. As I listened to it ring at the other end, I realised I didn't know quite what to say. I couldn't tell her about the threat, not at first. If she agreed to the trip then I'd find a way of telling her. I'd drive round to her place and discuss it face-to-face.

She picked up the phone. I was relieved and immediately started chatting. She was surprised to hear from me and sounded pleased. Without wasting any more time, I explained I had two tickets for a trip to New York on the QE2. Would she like to go? She immediately got excited and was totally up for it, adding that her boyfriend would love it too.

Boyfriend?! I was stymied. I told her I meant her and me. Now she was equally off-balance. She thought I knew she was in a serious relationship. I apologised. She laughed it off, telling me she was flattered, but declined the offer and wished me luck finding a partner.

I put down the phone in panic mode. What was I to do? RAM was correct about the importance of having the appropriate cover. A single young man on a QE2 cruise would attract attention from passengers and crew. I could always claim that my wife had gone down with a sudden illness. But I'd look stupid telling that to anyone and everyone I met on the ship. I'd still stand out. RAM wouldn't be happy and neither would the SIS.

There was nothing for it. I had to find a girl, and I had until the next morning to do it. I thought about calling some mates and asking if they knew of anyone. But that wasn't really on. There would be too much explaining to do and I couldn't tell anyone about the operation. It would get complicated.

I wasn't going to achieve anything by sitting at home. Perhaps if I went out I might bump into someone I knew. Some old girlfriend I'd forgotten about, whose number I no longer had. A pub. It was a long shot but it was all I could think of. The thought of letting RAM down was becoming incredibly stressful.

As I changed into something a bit smarter, I went through the various pubs I knew, trying to decide which ones might be best. And then it struck me. A wine bar. Bournemouth. Sour Grapes. I'd been there a few times. Wine bars were more upmarket.

THE ATLANTIC

Sour Grapes was well-known for attracting a more classy girl. When it came to a cruise on the QE2, a wine-sipping young lady was trumps over one who drank pints. I knew not every girl who went to pubs drank pints but the wine bar angle was appealing. It was the best place to start.

I arrived at Sour Grapes around 8pm. It was already getting busy and music filled the air. I ordered a glass of Liebfraumilch, the de rigueur beverage at the time, and looked around, with more hope than confidence. It would have been perfect if I found someone I knew. All she had to do was enjoy a trip to New York on the finest cruise liner in the world. No strings. Just act like a partner. She didn't have to be amazing. Ordinary was fine. Less than ordinary would work too. We just had to look the part together.

I strolled around the room looking at the girls, feeling like a stalker. I got to the end of the room without seeing anyone I knew and retraced my steps. Disappointment loomed. I tried to think of other wine bars I might try. And then I saw her.

I didn't know her at all. I'd never spoken to her before. But I recognised her. She was as tall as me, thin and leggy with a pretty face and long, brown curly hair that dropped off her shoulders. Very pleasing to the eye. I'd seen her on a couple of occasions in the same bar, the month before I left for Spain, but all I'd ever done was look.

I wasn't the chat-up type. I found it difficult to go up to a strange girl and just start talking to her. It felt predatory. What I remembered most about this particular girl was that the last time I saw her she'd actually returned my gaze and there'd been the hint of a linger. On those rare occasions when a girl did show any sign of interest in me, I was still reluctant to go over and chat to her. I was hopeless at it. It was better that they thought pleasant things about me from afar than label me a beast of prey once I moved in and opened my mouth.

She was currently deep in conversation with another girl. She probably wouldn't remember me. Not that it mattered anyway. She was a complete stranger and I needed to find someone I was already acquainted with. I wasn't just trying to sell a girl a boat trip to New York in the same cabin as me, but a trip that might be hijacked by terrorists. I groaned inwardly at the ridiculously impossible task.

I glanced at a couple more girls entering the wine bar. I didn't know them. My eyes returned to the tall pretty girl to find she was looking at me. I stared back, frozen. This time there was definitely more than the hint of a linger. She looked away. I continued to stare at her. Then she looked at me again, and this time she smiled ever so slightly, before turning back to her friend. She must have said something about me because her friend glanced at me and after a brief exchange they both chuckled. She looked at me again, this time raising her eyebrows as if to say 'are you just going to stand there and look?'

The pair giggled again. There comes a point when a mysterious man who just stares at girls from across a crowded room and nothing else starts to appear dodgy. This was ridiculous. I still couldn't move. I was pathetic. But then it was as if someone else took over my body and I found myself walking over to her. I knew it was crazy. I needed someone I knew. Starting from scratch with a complete stranger was wasting valuable time. But I couldn't stop myself. It was a combination of desperation and a lovely girl who had given me an invitation to engage with her.

I can't remember what drivel I started off with but it can't have been that bad because we struck up a conversation. Her friend slipped away. The girl was well-spoken, on the posh side, confident, and my first impression was that she was very nice indeed. She was a local girl attending a nearby college. I can't remember which one or what she was studying. Actually I hardly remember anything she said, except that she did a bit of modelling on the side and hoped to make a career of it. She asked what I did for a living and I told her I was a marine engineer. I'd been working on a cover story for the trip while at RAM's. I needed a profession I could talk about with some degree of confidence. I initially thought of being a deep-sea diver. But as a marine engineer I would have an excuse to walk about the ship in places a passenger might not normally go. I would have to conduct a recce once on board. I knew a great deal about ships from all the surveys I'd taken part in while in the SBS. Collecting data on various vessels was part of our familiarisation programme. I knew enough to flannel my way through as a marine engineer – as long as I didn't get into a conversation with a real one.

The girl was chatty and easy to talk to. But I soon started to get a nagging feeling that I was miles from my objective and wasting precious time. I absently checked my watch to estimate how long I had left to try out another location. She saw me and, probably thinking I was bored, said she had to be going home. I apologised and made the excuse I was conscious of the time because I had to travel to New York the following day. She beamed, suddenly excited. She'd never been to New York and was looking forward to going one day. The Statue of Liberty was something she particularly wanted to visit. I said the statue would be one of the first things I would see since I was arriving by boat. She was even more impressed when I told her it was the QE2. She asked how expensive it was. I told her I had no idea because it was work-related.

'A stoker's cabin next to the engine room, then,' she chuckled.

'Actually, no,' I replied, looking down my nose in mock self-importance. 'Top floor with a balcony.'

She was green with envy. 'Who are you taking?' she asked. 'You can't go alone.'

I told her I would certainly have invited my girlfriend along – if I had one.

'Okay, I'll go,' she said with a giggle.

She was joking of course, but it was no joke to me. I was desperate. 'Okay,' I said. 'I'll pick you up in the morning.'

'Okay,' she said, continuing the line.

'I hope you have an evening gown. I recommend two or three if you don't want to wear the same ones twice. Captain's table and all that.'

She said she did indeed, having collected quite a few dresses as a model in lieu of payment.

There was a pause as we both grinned.

'Well, that's sorted then,' I said, knowing it was far from.

Another long pause. She suddenly looked unsure. 'I was only joking,' she said.

'I know. I was just fantasising... Actually, being a large state room means it can have separate beds. So I could take a friend. But I'd rather not take a bloke. All those cocktail parties... dinners in tuxedos... I'd take my mum if she was still with me.'

She became thoughtful.

So did I. I can't remember what I was thinking by that stage. It was late. Probably too late to go anywhere else. I would give it until closing time. Maybe there was a nightclub. I never went to discos if I could help it. I'd really be scraping the bottom of the barrel if I ended up in one of those places. I could hear myself shouting above some god-awful racket. 'Fancy a cruise on the QE2 then?'

'Which way are you going?' she asked.

I snapped out of my thoughts. 'I can give you a lift home,' I said. 'If that's okay with you,' I quickly added.

She thanked me. We finished our drinks and headed outside. My car wasn't far away and we climbed in. She lived in Parkstone, towards Poole.

'How long is the trip?' she asked as I drove.

'Four days there, four days back.' There was something about the way she'd asked the question that tickled my hopes.

'And you'd be working?' she asked.

'Yes.'

'Doing your marine survey?'

'Well, it's not as if I'd be in a boiler suit,' I said. 'Mostly casual chats with the engineers.'

'And you work for a proper company?' she asked.

'Of course.'

'In Poole?'

'Yep.'

She thought about it some more and glanced at me. 'I could probably take a week or so off,' she said.

'Are you serious?' I asked, giving her a double take.

'Single beds, right?'

'Absolutely!' I was getting excited. 'No strings. I'm a complete gentleman,' I added with total conviction, selling myself, or rather giving myself away.

'Someone from your company, your boss, would have to talk with my parents. To prove it was all genuine.'

'Absolutely.' I couldn't believe it.

'I get the feeling you're genuine.'

'I am,' I assured her. 'You can certainly trust me. I couldn't afford for you to be less than happy the entire trip or I could lose my job,' I said, desperate to find anything that would give her confidence in me.

I asked if she really meant it – that if my boss physically met her parents, she'd consider joining me. She said she would. I was stunned. Not only would I have fulfilled my obligations to RAM, I'd get to spend time with this rather lovely girl. I told her she'd have to be ready to go by midday at the very latest. She chuckled and confessed she'd already been thinking about her wardrobe. I suggested I meet her parents when I dropped her off and if that went okay I'd get my boss to pay a visit in the morning. I had no idea if RAM would agree to it. She said that would be fine.

And so that was it. I had a brief meeting with her parents, who seemed to like me. I asked for her passport and gave her my home number in case she changed her mind.

Now, to be honest, I can't remember exactly how our conversation went line by line that evening. It was a long time ago. She was certainly how I described her. There were never any innuendos, no sordid suggestions, it was all very sweet and purely platonic. I was overjoyed at my good fortune. But I still had a few rather awkward hurdles to clear. The looming obstacle ahead was called 'the absolute truth'.

I drove directly to RAM's to give him the girl's passport and explain the situation – well, kind of. RAM was old-school, the type who married his childhood sweetheart. If I'd told him I'd solved the problem by picking up a strange girl in a bar, he'd probably have had palpitations. So I told him I contacted a girl I knew – not a lie – and that he could see for himself in the morning because I'd told her parents he was coming to meet them. He wasn't too pleased about that part, but I made it clear that if he didn't meet them, she wasn't going. It put him on the spot. When I mentioned that I'd not yet told her about the terrorist threat he became uneasy. I reassured him that I would do so in my own time and that I believed she wasn't the type to be put off. RAM didn't have a great deal of choice since he'd already told London he had the job covered. He had to put his trust in my judgement.

At 9am RAM turned up at the girl's house to introduce himself. He called me when he got back to his office to say it all went well, the parents had given the trip their blessing and the girl was eager to go. All he had said about the task was that it was related to marine risk – he'd leave it to me to tell her the bit about a potential terrorist attack.

A car and driver were laid on to pick me up and we made our way to the girl's house. There was an awkward goodbye with her parents who, despite all the assurances, must have thought the whole situation was bizarre. She confessed she had gone to bed wondering if she was doing the right thing, but woke up feeling positive about the trip.

I still wasn't sure when or how I was going to tell her about my real purpose. There was a risk she would change her mind when she learned the truth. If I waited until we set sail, she might get hysterical and demand to get off the boat. That would be a nightmare. It was reason enough not to tell her at all.

FIRST INTO ACTION AGAIN

That wasn't as ridiculous as it sounded. She didn't have to know anything about it. My SF gear was with the only person on board who knew my real identity. As long as the terrorists didn't strike, she'd be none the wiser. And if they did, well, it wouldn't matter anyway. The more I thought it through, the better I felt about keeping her in the dark. It was going to work.

All the way to Southampton she rambled on about New York, how excited she was about visiting the city for the first time by ship, like so many hundreds of thousands of immigrants back in the day, and how her first sight of the town that never sleeps would be the Statue of Liberty. She was a delight to be with, apart from that small black cloud called the truth.

We arrived at Southampton, our paperwork was processed and our baggage taken on board. As far as the cabin was concerned, I really had no idea what to expect. RAM had explained there were several reasons why I needed to be as high up as possible. I would have a satellite phone so I needed to be above the waterline, as close as possible to the bridge and the captain's quarters. Plus, I needed to be near the uppermost deck so I could more easily secure it for the potential arrival of response forces such as the SBS or Navy SEALs, who would rope down onto it.

We got the VIP treatment as soon as we arrived at check-in. We were escorted onto the ship and upstairs to the uppermost cabin deck. The room was luxurious indeed, with a separate sitting room and a balcony. A bottle of champagne and a bowl of fresh strawberries were waiting for us.

After inspecting the view from the balcony with glee, she sat on the couch, savouring her opulent surroundings. There were two single beds as promised, a nice bathroom and plenty of cupboard space. I cracked the champagne and we toasted the adventure. And for a brief moment I felt rather very good.

There was a knock at the door.

'That'll be the baggage,' she said.

I opened it to find a ship's officer standing in the corridor, a small, slender man in a white uniform, with a rather large suitcase beside him which belonged to neither of us. A twinge of concern rippled through me.

'Hello there,' he said as he struggled into the room, dragging the suitcase with him. It looked heavier than he did. He went back to close the door, then took a moment to catch his breath.

'I didn't enjoy dragging that thing all the way up here, I can tell you,' he said.

I, of course, instantly knew what the suitcase contained. 'My suits are in there,' I said, a little panicked.

'Yes, of course,' he said.

'Can't you keep it until I need it?' I asked hopefully.

He looked at me strangely. 'What good is it with me?' he said, half-smiling, as if he thought I was joking.

'Well, that's great,' I said, knowing he couldn't take it back. 'Thanks very much.' I headed for the door to see him out. My companion didn't need to see inside it. I could still get away with some bull about it containing engineering gear.

'Hold up,' he said, not moving from the suitcase. 'There's a bit of paperwork to do before I leave.'

'Oh,' I said, flustered.

'You have to check off and sign for each item,' he said, reaching for the suitcase lock. 'You know how it is. Especially all that gear.'

The security officer unlocked the case, threw the lid open

and started pulling items out, spreading them around the couch and floor. It was a Special Forces' Aladdin's cave. He had a list of items which he read out loud, ticking them off as he went through them. Body armour. Sat phone. Smoke grenades. Cyalumes, colours various. Climbing harness. Ropes. Flares. Goggles. Gloves. P226 9mm semi-automatic pistol with six spare magazines. Thigh holster. Magazine holders. Heckler & Koch MP5K submachine gun with suppressor. A chest rig and eight spare magazines. Several hundred boxes of ammunition. And finally, a tuxedo and an Armani suit.

I couldn't look at the girl. She hadn't screamed. There hadn't been a thud as she fainted and hit the floor. She hadn't uttered a sound.

'Right then,' the security officer said cheerfully when the check was complete. 'I think that's that. If you need any more clothing, like evening shirts, there's a decent shop on board. Just sign for what you take... Oh, one more thing,' he added, reaching into his pocket and taking out a key. 'A master key. It'll get you into every room on board, including the captain's. He knows you're on board somewhere but he doesn't know who you are.'

I took the key.

'Good luck,' he said, shaking my hand. 'Let's hope we have an uneventful voyage... Nice to have met you,' he said to the girl with a wink and a smile. He opened the door, looked up and down the corridor with the air of a master spy, and closed it behind him.

I finally turned to face her. She was staring at the MP5K submachine gun on the bed. She looked at me. I did my best to force a smile. 'I was going to explain,' I began.

'Who are you?' she asked calmly.

'Well... I'm not exactly who I said I was. I didn't fib, I just didn't tell you everything. Which I was about to. Kind of. Well, as much as I could. But I was secretly hoping I might not need to. Sort of.'

'What's going on?'

She wasn't panicky or flustered. She was quite cool actually. I sat down and explained the operation to her, telling her about the terrorist threat and what I was supposed to do in the event of an attack. I emphasised that if the powers that be really believed an attack was likely they wouldn't allow the ship to sail at all. It was probably all a hoax.

She listened with interest. I finally asked her how she felt, adding that she had time to get off the boat if she wanted to, but obviously praying she wouldn't.

I wasn't prepared for her response.

'Which gun is mine?' she asked.

I realised at that moment that I might have a completely different problem on my hands.

That evening we joined the other passengers for dinner in the huge, sumptuous dining room. I wore my tuxedo, my P226 semi-automatic tucked into my trusty shoulder holster under my left arm, through which she had linked her own arm. We clinked our champagne glasses , looking good and enjoying the experience immensely.

The trip turned out to be uneventful in the end. In fact, none of the cruise ships were attacked. I was never informed of what happened. If RAM knew, he never told me. Need to know basis. It was either false intelligence or the threat had been dealt with before it could develop. New York was fabulous. The whole thing was as close as I was ever going to get to playing James Bond. In that department, I failed on one significant level. I never seduced the girl. She was absolutely lovely but we were quite incompatible in the end. She was looking for a real boyfriend and realised I wasn't the type who would be home regularly, among other things I'm sure. No short fling for her, no matter how romantic it might be.

We had a lot of fun and played the young couple perfectly, even getting invited to the renowned Captain Lawrence Portet's table for dinner more than once. Back in Southampton we said farewell and I never saw her again. I did call her some years later, when I came to London to bury my father. As I was clearing out his flat, I came across an old notebook. Inside it was her parents' number in Bournemouth. I gave it a try. I don't know why. They were still at the house and gave me her London number. She sounded just the same and was as delightful as I remembered. She had pursued her modelling career and moved on to other things. I told her I was doing the same old kind of stuff. And that was that.

RAM managed to get a long-term contract out of Cunard after that task and provided security on the QE2 and other ships for some years. I did one more for him during the first Gulf War. I took an old girlfriend on that occasion. She was from Poole and had moved to Florida and was more than happy to take a luxury cruise around the Med with me. I didn't know she'd become a professional pole dancer in Fort Lauderdale. My hopes of keeping a low profile were dashed the first day on deck by the pool when she came to join me on a couple of loungers I was hogging. She removed her dressing gown to reveal a bikini that consisted of little more than a few lengths of string holding a couple of small triangular pieces of cloth to her front and rear. I think an old man fainted somewhere nearby and another got a sound slap from his wife for salivating. They were nearly all elderly people on board. We were invited to the captain's table on that occasion too, but I don't think it had anything to do with me.

I should have appreciated those kinds of jobs more than I did. They would be the last of my cushy operations. But I was looking for far more exciting adventures. And they were waiting for me – but not immediately. First there was a visit to Hollywood, which has to be mentioned because… well, it became a significant part of my life and was a much longer stay than I anticipated.

4

USA

I'D DEVELOPED A TASTE FOR the American way of life while I was in the SBS, during visits to the USA to play with the Navy SEALs. The urge to take a good, long look at the country had never left me. RAM had suggested I might look at Mexico and Colombia, where there was a thriving kidnap for ransom industry. Former members of the SAS were pioneering the commercial side of the business led by a UK company called Control Risks. I might well have caught a flight south to check it out had it not been for a former Metropolitan Police officer I'd worked with on the Murdoch Wapping job. He asked if I would be interested in joining an investigation task he was running in Los Angeles that required a surveillance specialist. I didn't need much of a push to try out the USA, so I caught a flight to California.

I took an immediate shine to life in LA. The surveillance job turned out to be boring and I wasn't disappointed when it came to an end after a couple of months. Security sounded like a good business model for me, so I set up a one-man office in

USA

Santa Monica. I hoped RAM and my other security contacts might use me as a footprint in the USA. I printed a stack of brochures detailing the company's capabilities, bought a car (a black Camaro Z28) and car-phone, and started peddling my business around town.

I soon discovered that Americans had little interest in hiring some former foreign special forces operator as a security consultant. They had their own home-grown specialists – former CIA, FBI and police – providing similar services. No-one had heard of the SBS.

The opportunity to get involved in K&R (kidnap and ransom) in South America was still available, but by the time I accepted my business was a failure I was flat broke and couldn't afford a plane ticket anywhere. I was the type to push such things to destruction.

In order to keep a roof over my head, I applied for three jobs I picked out of the newspaper and was offered all of them. Since I was skint I decided to accept all three to build up some cash. In the mornings I taught novice security guards in the San Fernando Valley, a class of around 60 guys. In the afternoons I worked as a graphic artist designing video covers for the South American department of a company called Media Home Entertainment (I had a school qualification in technical drawing). And in the evenings I was a bartender in Westwood.

They were long days. I traded in my Camaro for a 1000cc Kawasaki, which was the only way I could make it to any of those jobs on time. The traffic in LA was usually pretty heavy. But there was no helmet law, the weather was nearly always perfect and the bike was a beast, which altogether made the journeys bearable.

FIRST INTO ACTION AGAIN

After three months I'd stockpiled enough cash to quit the teaching job. It was the furthest away and the worst-paid. It also left the mornings free to go to the gym and take long runs on the beach.

I moved into an apartment a stone's throw from Santa Monica pier, around the corner from a British pub called the King's Head on Santa Monica Boulevard. It was a great place to pop in for a swift pint and a bite. Santa Monica was home to a lot of Brits. The pub's English manager was an affable, chatty type. One evening he happened to mention he was looking for a bartender. So I quit the other bar job, which was several miles up town anyway, and joined the Kings Head. It was a fun pub to work in, always packed in the evenings. The staff, mostly Brits and Irish, were a laugh, especially when we locked the doors at the end of a busy night and congregated for a group meal.

Around that time I was contacted by two local company directors interested in my security services. They'd seen my brochure somewhere and wanted to discuss a job. We met at the Polo Lounge of the Beverly Hills Hotel on Sunset Boulevard, a popular place to be seen for anyone in the film industry. I think there was a script on every table and most of the punters were either producers, actors hoping to be noticed, or agents and writers pitching their clients and movie ideas.

I wondered why we were meeting in that particular bar. It turned out neither of the company directors actually wanted to employ me as a professional security man. They told me they were writing their first screenplay and asked if I'd like to be their military action adviser. The offer took me by surprise but I went along with it. I think it was mandatory for everyone in

USA

LA to be working on a script anyway and so I got stuck into a story outline. My partners turned out to be flakes, but since I'd already come up with a scenario, I bought a book called *How to Write a Screenplay* and wrote the entire movie in about a month. Needless to say, it was no great work of art but I enjoyed the experience.

I met a lot of people while working behind the bar and, unsurprisingly, many of them were actors. Throw a stone in Los Angeles and it'll bounce off an actor and hit a writer. Martin Landau from the *Mission Impossible* TV show was a regular. Lewis Collins of Bodie fame from *The Professionals*, who also starred in the *Who Dares Wins* SAS movie a few years before, popped in over a period. I never told Lewis my background and looked suitably impressed as he described training with the SAS. Another well-known actor at the time was Paul Coufos, a powerful, handsome, German/Greek New Yorker and Ivy League Cornell University graduate. He'd been a successful TV actor, famous for his role in *Days Of Our Lives*, and had come to Hollywood to try his luck in the movie business. He'd just finished shooting a movie called *Busted Up* about a hardened heavyweight boxer and he certainly looked the part.

Paul was a regular and as I served him his first chilled beer of the evening I mentioned I had a script. He rolled his eyes, told me to fuck off and walked away. Did I mention he was from New York? When he revisited the bar for another beer, which was not infrequent, I took a different tack and asked for his advice about getting the script to an agent. He clearly figured he had to either agree to look at the script or find another watering hole, and he was fond of the Kings Head.

I never thought he'd actually read it. The truth is Paul was

FIRST INTO ACTION AGAIN

a big-hearted fellow and a man of immense generosity. He liked the script enough to send it to his agent without mentioning it to me. I received a call from the agent a few weeks later explaining how he'd sent the screenplay to Joel Silver, a major figure at Warner Bros. who had produced *Die Hard*, *Lethal Weapon*, *Predator*, *Commando* and dozens more. Silver had offered $55,000 to option it against $350,000 if it got made. In those days $55,000 could buy a new apartment in Santa Monica four blocks from the beach on Pico Boulevard.

I drove my bike to the agency just off Sunset Boulevard to find a bottle of champagne and a cheque waiting for me as well as an offer to represent me. I was, to say the least, stunned.

That was the beginning of my writing career. I'd only ever written SF operational reports up until then. If not for Paul, I probably would've taken the other fork and headed south for that K&R job.

While I was waiting for my big Warner Bros. script to get made, Paul asked me to write one for him. And he got it made. My first movie was called *To Die To Sleep* and starred Ami Dolenz (daughter of Micky of The Monkees fame), Charlie Napier (200-plus movies including *Rambo: First Blood Part II* and *The Silence of the Lambs*), Larry Gatlin, the Country and Western singer who wrote several great soundtracks (*Deep In The Heart*, *Next of Kin*) and of course Paul as the lead. Making that movie was an unforgettable experience and not just because it was my first. It was the perfect introduction to that ridiculous and irresistible industry. We shot it in St Louis. Due to the changing weather (we were hit by a snowstorm for a couple of days) and changing locations (we couldn't afford some and got kicked off them before we could finish the scene), I wrote most of it on

USA

the set while we were filming, handing the finished pages to the actors to shoot that day. The financier withdrew his money halfway through the shoot, having lost confidence in the project, and everything ground to a halt. The camera crew kidnapped the rolls of film we'd shot so far and held them for ransom since they hadn't been paid. Ken Dalton, the producer, declared he was going downtown to get drunk (which was no big deal since he was drunk every day anyway). He met some wealthy good old boys in a bar and by 3am, all drunk as lords, they agreed to finance the movie to the tune of $250,000. We recommenced filming the following day and completed it. I don't think they got any of their money back. Utter madness, but great fun.

To say the entire experience was a departure from the life I had led until then was an understatement.

I wrote another movie a few years later for Paul and the same crazy, alcoholic, drug-fuelled, lovable producer, Ken. At Ken's request, the entire film crew, 40 or so people moved into a hotel in Palm Springs and then sat around waiting for him to let them know when they could start setting up for the first scene. Ken had made a deal with the hotel to feature it prominently in the movie if he didn't have to pay a deposit for the rooms.

Ken remained in his room near the phone, waiting for the money to drop into the production bank account. The actors turned up mid-morning. The most entertaining of them, Morton Downey Jr (*Predator 2*), shared top billing with Paul. We hung around for hours, ordered lunch, which turned into beers, then cocktails, then shots, more food, all charged to the rooms. By late afternoon, sitting around the pool in a party atmosphere, I think many of us had forgotten why we were there.

Paul grew concerned and we went to find Ken in his room.

FIRST INTO ACTION AGAIN

He was drunk and high on other substances and explained that the film's finances, which apparently originated from a scrap-metal dealer in Poland, had turned out to be part of a money-laundering scam and had disappeared shortly after being deposited in the US bank. There was no money.

Paul and I went back to the pool to tell the actors and crew the bad news. No-one wanted to fork out for a day spent lounging around in Palm Springs. They'd all had to pay to get there anyway. Minutes later, suitcases began dropping out of windows at the back of the hotel into the car park, followed by their owners, to avoid having to pass through the hotel lobby. Paul and I were among them. We scrambled into our cars and hit the road back to LA. Ken woke up the next morning to a huge bill and a very pissed-off hotel manager. I don't know how he got out of there without paying but somehow he did. Such was the film industry.

I worked on the Warner Bros. script with Joel Silver's people in Burbank Studios for months. There were countless story development meetings aimed at refining the plot and characters, polishing dialogue, adding this scene, removing that one, until it bore little resemblance to the original idea. And then it was dumped. Selling a script was a long way from getting it made.

Nevertheless, the fact that Silver had optioned a script by me was no small deal in Tinseltown and my agent made the most of it. Literary agents' mission was to get their writers known and they put them in front of as many producers as possible to pitch their ideas. I had plenty of those.

Hollywood agents were generally cut from the same cloth as snake-oil salesmen. Mine actually was a snake, an English snake

USA

by the way. I had told him a little about my background, that I was former UK special forces, and he ran with it.

To say he embellished my past was an understatement. I would never know how he'd introduced me until the meeting itself, which was often an uncomfortable experience. Among his many descriptions of me, most of them *sotto voce* over the phone, were that I was a former British secret agent, a spy, assassin, sniper, bomb-maker, code-breaker, interrogator, the man who taught James Bond everything he knew, and that I could kill someone in seven different ways with my bare hands without getting out of my chair. I asked him to refrain from exaggerating. He agreed, but then carried on with the same bullshit.

The meetings kept coming. I gradually became indifferent to the exaggerations. In truth, I ended up the snake-oil salesman's willing partner. I started to enjoy denying the exaggerations with a swashbuckling laugh that might suggest there was some truth to them. A total wanker, I know, but it was hard to resist. Producers would usually meet me with one or two development staff and we'd begin with polite chit-chat. Most were very bright and purely interested in talking stories. Some were on the strange side. On more than one occasion I was asked how many people I'd killed. I was once invited to describe in detail what it was like to strangle someone. Another wondered if I'd killed many children. One producer asked me if I would tell him who really shot JFK. Denying anything only made it look as if I was being modest and evasive.

There were also many female producers, development staff or assistants who made it their mission to try to seduce me either during the meetings or immediately afterwards, on my way to the car park or via a message to my agent. A special forces operator turned writer was a rare commodity in Hollywood. Being an Englishman added to the mystique – think Bond. If it helped my writing career, I really didn't mind. Life as a writer was difficult enough not to take advantage of such things.

One of the most bizarre meetings my agent arranged was in a suite at a Holiday Inn on the junction of the 405 Freeway and Sunset Boulevard. There was no producer present. The room was full of male actors, more than a dozen of them, mostly quaffing Cristal champagne. The head guy was a huge Texan. I was sure I'd seen him in a Bond movie. He wore gold bracelets and had a row of gold teeth. Only when the meeting was brought to order did I learn the purpose of it. They intended to rescue Terry Waite from his captors in Lebanon. Waite was an Englishman who worked for the Archbishop of Canterbury. A few months previously he had gone to Lebanon to secure the release of four hostages but was kidnapped himself in the process. I was introduced as the UK special forces specialist who the host hoped would help plan the operation.

A round of applause followed and I found myself centre stage, nodding and smiling. What the fuck? It was surreal. The meeting lasted an hour or so, with speeches from various people. Then, fortunately, it descended into a piss-up. I sneaked out a couple of hours later, a little drunk after talking endless shite with these strangers while swigging champagne.

Such rogue endeavours were not uncommon in the US. An American oil tycoon had recently threatened to fly a team into Vietnam to rescue American prisoners of war because the US government had failed to get them out. Fortunately, our rescue operation never got past the pre-planning piss-up stage. Terry Waite was held for another four years in Lebanon before being

USA

released. He never knew how close he came to being joined by a bunch of old, alcoholic Hollywood actors and an idiot former Brit SF operator.

I soon became part of the Brit Pack of Los Angeles film-makers and celebrities. It was headed up by Julia Verdin, a lovely lady who started off as an actress and went on to produce, write and direct. I met her through my agent. Another one of those producer meetings. She invited me to my first Hollywood party, at her house, which was an eye-opener. I had never seen so many beautiful girls in one place. Many of them were from other US states, visiting LA either in the hope of making a career or just to have a good time. One of the lovely ladies I met that evening was Liz Hurley, who was living with Julia at the time. I confess to having had high hopes as we seemed to get on well, chatting away. Then the famous male actors started arriving and I ended up joining the rest of the writers consigned to a corner of the kitchen. Writers generally had little cachet in Hollywood. A few months later Liz achieved fame with her first major movie hit, *Passenger 57* opposite Wesley Snipes. Hugh Grant also appeared on the scene and my fantasies about an evening with her well and truly evaporated.

I worked on several projects with Julia Verdin over a number of years. I rewrote *The Set Up* for her, a bank heist movie based on a book. The original adaptation Julia was working with was pretty bad and she hired me to improve it. My effort turned out to be good enough to get the movie financed and I was able to rehearse scenes with such Hollywood greats as James Coburn (*The Great Escape, The Magnificent Seven, Our Man Flint*), Billy Zane (*Titanic*) and James Russo (*Django Unchained, The Ninth Gate, My Own Private Idaho*). I didn't get a writing credit because of contractual restrictions but I never bothered about such things in those days. I was happy enough to get the work.

The meetings kept rolling in and I was interviewed by *Paris Match* as an up-and-coming new writer – I suspect the interviewer saw through me.

I developed a project with Dick Donner, a famous director of movies such as *Superman*, *Ladyhawke* and the *Lethal Weapon* series. He took me onto the set of *Lethal Weapon 2* and introduced me to Mel Gibson and Danny Glover, at one point suggesting to Mel that I looked enough like him to play his brother. I thought it might have been the beginning of my acting career until Mel rolled his eyes and walked away. Perhaps I had dented his fragile US/Aussie ego by describing the superiority of UK SF. I went on to develop projects with Dick's equally famous wife, producer Lauren Shuler Donner (*You've Got Mail*, *Maverick*, *Deadpool*). Another very lovely lady. I worked with the great Mace Neufeld who produced *The Hunt for Red October*, *Patriot Games*, *The Saint* and dozens of other hits. Our project was about a special forces assault on an oil platform. I was well into the script development when he called me in to tell me a film had just been completed called *Under Siege* with Steven Seagal which was too similar to our project for us to carry on.

Another interesting character I worked with on several projects was Peter Kent, Arnold Schwarzenegger's stunt double for a dozen years or so, who handled all the dangerous stunts in *The Terminator* movies, *Total Recall* etc.

As long as I'm shamelessly name-dropping, I might as well mention the time I walked past Julia Roberts as I was leaving a lunch meeting at the Warner Bros. studio lot restaurant. She did a double take as she passed and gave me that dazzling smile

USA

of hers. She'd filmed *Pretty Woman* not too long before. Very, very hot in real life too. I collided with the doorframe of the exit as I looked back at her while leaving. No-one believes me but I swear she was smiling at me.

Embrace of the Vampire was a movie I wrote for a company called The Ministry of Film. It starred Martin Kemp of Spandau Ballet and *EastEnders* fame, with Alyssa Milano playing the female lead. I'd met Martin years before in a pub in Poole when I was in the SBS. He was married to the sister of a Royal Marine. He didn't remember me, of course. I later created a TV series for the same production company called *Pacific Blue* that ran for 101 episodes over five years on the USA Network and ended up on TV sets all over the world. I got ripped off by around $2m by the producers and later discovered my slimeball agent was in on the deal.

An assistant at the agency called to meet me for lunch one day and explained he knew I had been screwed over and would provide evidence for $150,000. I decided against taking it to court. It would have been an expensive gamble, so I put it down to experience. As it was, I did well enough out of the project financially to move to Corral Canyon in Malibu, where I lived in the studio quarters of a lovely house that once belonged to Bing Crosby's daughter Mary. The house was now owned by the wonderful actress Alice Krige (*Chariots of Fire* and too many others to mention) and her director husband Paul Schoolman (*String Caesar, Persona*). It was a beautiful location overlooking the Pacific Ocean. Peaceful and remote. I enjoyed some five years there and wrote several screenplays, as well as my first book, *First Into Action*. I left shortly after a fire swept up the canyon, only narrowly avoiding our homes. Ten years later the buildings weren't so lucky when another canyon fire burned them to the ground.

I spent 13 years in Los Angeles all told and made a dozen movies. I wrote under several pseudonyms, some taken from distant family members, others just made up. But by the end of the millennium I began to feel I wasn't where I wanted to be. LA was a seductive town in many ways and most unsatisfying in others. As far as my career as a screenwriter was concerned, it felt like success was always just around the corner. To make the majors, I was going to need luck and more experience and talent. But the truth is, I was on the wrong road.

Writing on its own wasn't enough. I craved adventure. But I had little hope of finding any. I'd let all of my contacts from the old days go cold. I also felt out of date. I needed another fork in the road to present itself.

It arrived in two stages.

The first was a chance encounter back in England with a Glaswegian lad named Ian. He was a former British Paratrooper who later joined the famous Rhodesian Selous Scouts. When the unit was disbanded Ian opted to stay in Africa and carry on fighting – but this time on the side of wildlife. He became a poacher-hunter or, as he preferred to be known, a conservationist.

Ian was planning a ranger training task in Nigeria when I met him. He agreed I could come along as an unpaid assistant. The location was a couple of hundred miles north of Lagos, a place called Kiangi National Park near the town of New Bussa.

It was a fascinating couple of months. Our mission was to turn 90 locals into rangers in order to tackle the rampant poaching. The local governor had visions of creating a safari

USA

park for international visitors, but poachers had already wiped out all its elephants and rhinos and continued to kill any animal they came across.

The poachers were a brutal, murderous lot who had killed and maimed several rangers over the years. The local police were of no use and the desperate governor sought outside help. The Greek Consular to Nigeria, an avid birdwatcher, was horrified by what he'd seen during a visit to the park and agreed to finance a clean-up. Ian was given the job.

We lived in a run-down compound in the centre of the vast park and soon after arriving got stuck into an intense training programme: weapon handling, patrolling, obstacle crossing, ambush drills, arrest procedures and medical training. A two-seater powered hang-glider had been donated along with funding to train a pilot. The aircraft was used to search for signs of poachers, such as smoke from fires, and to resupply patrols in the field.

I volunteered to take the first test flight once the craft was assembled, filming the take-off from my seat above and behind the pilot. Unfortunately, the craft veered to one side as we left the ground and crashed into trees. The pilot and I were hanging upside down inside the framework covered in fuel when we were rescued. We were lucky not to have sustained serious injury.

A week later, after the craft had been repaired, I insisted on joining my trusty pilot for a second attempt, camera in hand. Once again we trundled down the runway, both nervous, but this time we took off successfully. I was to spend many hours airborne over the next few weeks. Those were some of my greatest flying experiences, soaring over the jungle and savannah, following rivers, often below the tall jungle canopy, skimming across the water.

After the training came the more serious business. Before we could leave the newly formed teams to conduct operations on their own, we needed to put them through their paces. It was during the last of these patrols that I found myself in the middle of the most ridiculous gun battle I've ever been in.

Around midnight I went with 10 rangers along a river to check out a distant light one of the boys thought he'd seen. We heard what sounded like a dozen poachers inside a dense patch of woodland the size of a football pitch. We moved in to flush them out.

We hoped they would surrender but it was not to be. I sent a couple of the boys around to the far side of the wood and placed the remaining men in two cut-off teams who would intercept the poachers as they fled the flushers. It was pitch-black and everyone waited silently in position.

The operation began with the flushers screaming and firing their guns in the air. Unfortunately, the cut-off team with me mistook the screams for cries of battle and charged into the wood, leaving me on my own. Then the poachers bolted from the wood. They must have ran past my cut-off team in the dark, dense woodland. Everyone seemed to be firing wildly at anything. The poachers were running straight at me. My weapon was an over and under shotgun. I had a pouch filled with solid and seven shot. I fired and reloaded as quickly as I could, unable to see anything in the darkness except muzzle flashes. The other cut-off team clearly felt they were missing out on the action. They left their position and ran to where they could engage the fleeing poachers. That put them directly

USA

opposite me. Bullets and lead pellets were whizzing around all over the place.

The battle lasted no more than 10 minutes. All but one of the poachers escaped. To my surprise, no-one on our side had been hit.

In the morning we found several blood trails heading into the bush. Some of the poachers had been hit pretty badly, judging by the amount of blood. We considered following the trail but it was decided I should leave the camp as soon as possible. If word got out – and it would – that a white foreigner had shot local poachers, even though I had been with the rangers, the police would come looking for me and there was no predicting what might happen.

That suited me anyway. Two months had been long enough. The following day I was on the road back to Lagos and the airport.

A couple of months later a terrible, world-altering event occurred that affected so many lives. Aeroplanes crashed into the Twin Towers in New York City. It created another major fork in the road for me, and this time I had no uncertainty as to which path I wanted to take.

5

PALESTINE

A COUPLE OF MONTHS AFTER the 9/11 attacks I got a message from Mike, an old SBS buddy. We'd joined the unit at a similar time and he'd stayed on to complete his full service, only recently becoming a civvy. He was a manager at a specialised risk management company in Hereford run by a former SAS sergeant. Mike was looking for someone with SF skill-sets for a range of tasks and asked if I was interested. I was certainly up for any kind of adventure but I had to come clean and admit that as far as my old SF skills were concerned, I was on the rusty side.

He explained the job was more about planning and conflict risk analysis than leaping through windows with a dagger in my teeth, although it would be in my interests to stay fit. He declined to elaborate. He did say that my years of experience operating on my own in hostile places would be a great advantage. Mike was famously tight-lipped.

I was intrigued. If I wanted to know more, I would have to go to the offices in Hereford and meet the boss. Mike stressed that sooner rather than later would be preferable as things were hotting up on a global scale.

That sounded all very enticing and I shot over to Hereford.

The company was AKE Limited (Andrew Kain Enterprises). I met with Andrew, an exceptionally intelligent, well-read, well-informed, mild-mannered Scotsman from Mull only a couple of years older than myself. The interview was brief. He'd learned enough about me from Mike and other sources to be confident that I was capable of the work. He wanted to see for himself if my personality and his company ethos were compatible.

He'd started the business a few years earlier, providing journalists and TV news-gathering teams with the basic skills to operate in hostile and challenging locations with reduced risk. It was the first school of its type. Andrew had created the concept after coming across a statistic showing the high number of news personnel who'd died in the course of their work. After examining the causes, he concluded that most of the fatalities could have been avoided. News people needed to be familiar with weaponry, how combatants operated, first-aid to a high degree, navigation, and transport over land, sea and air.

There were certain similarities between special forces and news teams heading to a conflict zone: small groups of self-sufficient individuals, travelling to places they'd probably never been to before, with little to no support, providing their own food and water and facing extreme dangers. The news teams needed to identify the risks, mitigate them, have the right equipment for the job and know how to respond when things went wrong – which, according to Murphy's law, they inevitably would.

AKE's main client at the time was CNN. It was said that every government leader, including the President of the United

States, watched CNN whenever there was breaking news at world crisis level.

CNN was the first news organisation to grasp that news teams would be more successful if they were better prepared for the risks. It bought into the logic of being taught by former special forces operators. Before long, news organisations from all over the world were signing up to AKE's risk awareness training courses.

The five-day courses were conducted in a hotel secreted in the Welsh hills and included personal, home and office security, self-sufficiency, journey management, ambushes, driving accidents, kidnapping and interrogations. AKE's medical course was based on a SF operative's training, focusing on dealing with serious injuries when days from the nearest medical facility.

CNN went a stage further after realising it would be even better to include a risk manager in the news-gathering team. But the requirements for such managers went beyond military experience. They needed to be able to control civilians, many of whom had no experience of conflict zones, panicked in the face of danger, were tardy, and argued against tactical decisions. They needed a level of self-control that prevented them from strangling the clients in frustration.

The partnership turned out to be a great success and AKE's operations room was soon bustling with activity as it managed a large number of news teams on the ground around the globe. Insurance companies reduced the risk insurance premiums of news personnel who completed AKE awareness training.

At the end of my meeting with Andrew he asked when I could start. I was ready to go right away. He shouted to a lady in another office to book me on a flight to Tel Aviv the following

PALESTINE

afternoon. That lady happened to be his darling wife, Bethan. I would be joining an operational team already on the ground.

By the time I got home to pack my stuff, I had received an email from AKE's sophisticated intelligence cell containing all the information I required for the task. AKE was run like an SAS operations room. All of the guys were former military, mostly SAS, SBS, Paras or Royal Marines. Andrew had intentionally set up his operations HQ in Hereford because there was plenty of local manpower. And with a former SBS operator as AKE's 2IC (second-in-command), he also had a direct line to the SBS in Poole.

On arrival at Tel Aviv airport I was met by a local CNN driver who drove me to the American Colony hotel in Jerusalem, where all CNN bureau personnel were accommodated apart from local Israeli and Palestinian staff. The big news was the Second Intifada, a Palestinian uprising against the Israeli occupation of the West Bank and Gaza. Despite the coalition invasion of Afghanistan kicking off, the Palestine situation was significant. The Middle East was a powder keg and had become the centre of the world's attention.

I quickly learned the broad political landscape, as far as we were concerned. The Israelis didn't like western media organisations in the country because they were perceived to be biased towards the Palestinians. The Palestinians appreciated the western media presence because it highlighted their plight.

Soon after I arrived I was sent into the city of Ramallah to relieve a former SAS lad who was looking after a CNN apartment. Ramallah was where the Palestinian government headquarters, the Mukataa, and its incumbent leader Yasser Arafat were located. The Mukataa was the centre of tension between the Israelis and Palestinians. The roof of the CNN apartment overlooked the headquarters, providing a dramatic backdrop for reporting regional news.

The CNN apartment was unoccupied due to a lull in activity. An AKE operator was keeping a watch on it and I was sent to relieve him. I set off alone from the Jerusalem bureau in one of our 4x4s. It was early afternoon. That should have given me ample time to get to the Ramallah apartment before the 10pm curfew since it was only 12 miles away. Distance wasn't the challenge. There were two checkpoints to navigate and they could be unpredictable.

First was the Kalandia border crossing between Jerusalem and the West Bank. A few miles on was the main checkpoint into Ramallah. Both were manned by the IDF of course. There were a couple of back routes into Ramallah, but as I was unfamiliar with the area I decided to stick to the main routes. There was a cross-country footpath used by Palestinians who needed to avoid the checkpoints, such as smugglers, but it was a dangerous option. Israeli settlers lived on the high ground overlooking the pass and, on occasion, found it sporting to shoot anyone using it since they were unlikely to be Israelis. A French news crew ignored the warnings against using the footpath a few weeks before my arrival and one of them caught a bullet. I never learned if he survived or not.

I arrived at the Kalandia checkpoint to find it crowded with vehicles and pedestrians on either side. One of the unpredictables was the IDF deciding to close the checkpoint without warning, often for hours at a time. There would be no Israelis using it because they were forbidden from entering the West Bank. Four hours later I was through.

PALESTINE

Less than a mile further on I arrived at the checkpoint into Ramallah where half a dozen vehicles were lined up ahead of me, mostly Palestinians returning from work. The IDF soldiers took their time inspecting documents and vehicles before allowing them through. Towers with machine-gun barrels poking out overlooked the checkpoint. Concrete chicanes impeded vehicle speed should anyone decide to break through. An escaping vehicle or a runner wouldn't get far. It was Berlin Wall rules.

I sat in my 4x4 as darkness fell, wondering if I should go back to Jerusalem. Holding up vehicles at the checkpoint until curfew was a particularly spiteful ploy. Ramallah was heavily patrolled by the IDF during curfew and it was dangerous for anyone caught on the streets. The Kalandia crossing back into Jerusalem would soon be closed for the night anyway so I had little choice other than to wait it out. My mission was to get to the CNN apartment that night and so that's what I'd do.

I called the number I had for the SAS lad I was relieving. He answered with a gruff hello. Bob was his name. I told him my situation. All he could offer, in his Scottish accent, was that they were a bunch of wankers and that I should give him a call when I was close to the apartment.

It was well past 10pm by the time it was my turn to drive up to the soldier running the checkpoint. He looked 15 years old with an attitude, doing his best to appear menacing, but it wasn't working on several levels. For starters, his uniform was a couple of sizes too big, including his helmet, which he kept having to push back so that he could see anything other than his own feet. He checked my passport and media licence and asked what I was planning to do in Ramallah. I told him I was going to the

FIRST INTO ACTION AGAIN

CNN bureau. He said I couldn't go through but didn't give a reason. The little prick was enjoying his moment of power. He didn't care what nationality I was.

I played my usual innocent act, asking simple questions, trying to pander to his sense of superiority without satisfying his attempts to rile me. I did wonder why he was giving me as much of a hard time as he might give a Palestinian. The only explanation I could think of was my news media credentials.

I asked if I could stay at the checkpoint for the night because it was too late to go back to Jerusalem. He said no. So I couldn't go back, couldn't go forward, and I couldn't stay there. I asked if I could speak to his officer. He asked me why. I politely told him he was the first Israeli soldier I'd ever spoken to and I wanted to see if the officers were as stupid as he was. He didn't seem to take offence and walked away. Ten minutes later an officer, with a holstered pistol and no headgear, approached my vehicle and asked politely where I was going. I told him it was the CNN house. He asked if I was aware there was a curfew. I told him there wasn't one when I arrived three hours earlier. He calmly said I could depart and walked away. The dark motive behind his decision was obvious.

As I drove out of the checkpoint and through the chicane that led to the main road into the city, I had an uncomfortable feeling about the next leg of my journey.

The main street into the town was broad with buildings spaced out either side. There were no street lights and no signs of life. I kept my speed down, searching everywhere for soldiers. It was unnerving.

What first struck me about Ramallah was how cracked and broken it looked. The stone pavements had been crushed at intervals by heavy tracked vehicles such as tanks and troop carriers. Parked cars had been run over. I passed a pile of five or six cars, one on top of the other, all flattened by tanks, a monument to the bullying.

I consulted my map as I drove into the town. I needed to leave the main road and take the side streets but every one of them, left and right, was blocked off to vehicles by concrete barriers. I finally came to a junction where all options were open and took a turn towards the apartment that was still half a mile away.

A hundred metres along the dark street, several figures stepped from the shadows onto the road up ahead. A couple of flashlights shone at me and I slowed to a crawl. There were about a dozen of them. Their silhouettes became more clear as I got closer. They were wearing helmets and carrying rifles. Israeli soldiers. I stopped the car and turned off my headlights. I knew what it was like to be a soldier facing an oncoming vehicle at night in a hostile environment. Flashes of Northern Ireland.

They moved towards me at an easy, confident pace and surrounded the vehicle. There was a tap on my window and I opened it. A soldier leaned in aggressively to look me over and said something in a language I didn't understand. I said I was English. The soldier switched to pretty good English and told me to turn off the engine. Then came the questions. He was antagonistic. I told him I worked for CNN and was going to our apartment. He wanted to know why I was out during the curfew and I gave him a brief explanation. Others behind him were saying things to him in their language. Someone chuckled. They were mostly youngsters. He told me I couldn't go to the apartment and that I was to drive back the way I had come. I asked him where I should go. He said he didn't care but if he saw me again I would be in trouble. I thanked him and started the engine.

I turned the vehicle around and headed to the main road, turned right and continued back the way I'd originally come. I couldn't make for the checkpoint – I risked getting shot approaching it at that time of night. I drove on for a few hundred metres and came to another turn towards the apartment that wasn't blocked. I went for it. As I eased along the dark residential street with closely packed two- and three-storey buildings on either side, I gave Bob a call. He answered right away. I told him I wasn't far away but I'd run into an IDF patrol. He warned me the soldiers were at their most dangerous during curfew.

I arrived at a junction but the road I needed was blocked. My only option was a turn that took me back to where I'd encountered the soldiers. I took it in the hope the next left would be clear. It wasn't. I stopped the vehicle and began to make a U-turn to find another way.

As I backed up, a brick struck the roof, startling me. Dark figures ran towards me. It had to be the same patrol. It would be suicide to try to escape, so I stopped. The soldiers were shouting and aiming their rifles as they closed in. They surrounded the vehicle, banging on it as they crowded around me. There was a heavy thud on my window and I opened it. It was the same soldier as before. In a foul temper, he ordered me out of the vehicle. I opened the door and was immediately grabbed roughly by several hands, one around my throat, and slammed up against the vehicle.

The commander was incensed that I'd disobeyed him. He pressed the barrel of his pistol painfully against the side of my head. One of the others said something, the commander agreed, and they hauled me to the side of the road and thrust me against a low wall with a steep incline on the other side. The pistol returned to my forehead. I believe they were just trying to scare me, have a bit of sport by threatening to shoot me and let my body fall down the hill. The one with the gun to my head kept shouting. I suspect my refusal to cower infuriated him. Looking death in the eye wasn't new to me. Nor was being bullied. I reacted as I always had done. Cold, defiant but otherwise unresponsive.

A car horn sounded down the street and headlights flickered. A 4x4 came to a stop and the driver climbed out. He stood beside it, calling to the soldiers. They turned their attention to the intruder. The commander removed his pistol from my head and confronted the newcomer. A conversation began between them. I was unable to understand at first but I heard the commander say the name Bob. He turned back to me and said that if he ever saw me out at night again he'd kill me. Hatred for him welled up in me. I wanted to smash his face in. He'd ignited a violent fury in me. But I picked up the stuff the soldiers had taken from my pockets and thrown to the ground, including my passport, moved past them, and climbed into my vehicle. I drove over to the man who'd arrived to save my bacon.

Bob was a powerfully built Scotsman, cool as they come. He got back in his own vehicle and I followed him to the apartment building a couple of blocks away.

Looking back, I doubted they intended to execute me. All Bob would say was that you never knew with that lot. Brutality came easy to them. Many Israeli soldiers in Ramallah at that time were sons of Russian immigrants. They were usually based on the Lebanese border where they were more suited to the brutality of the front line. He didn't think many, if any, were even Jewish. It was well-known that many Russians had claimed to be Jews to be allowed to leave the Soviet Union. Bob had been in Ramallah for a month. The soldiers had tried to intimidate him at first. They wanted CNN out of there. Bob might have looked like a thug, but he was intelligent, educated and eloquent. He'd befriended one of the local commanders, not a Russian but an immigrant from Brooklyn. According to Bob, he wasn't such a bad bloke once you found the civvy in him.

A month later I was in a small bar in Ramallah, one frequented by foreign news people even during the curfew. The Israelis left it alone for that reason. While I was seated at a table with friends I noticed a pair of surly-looking Palestinians watching us from across the smoky room. The place was dimly lit but I could see their expressions, their dark, cold eyes. One of them stared at me intently and drew his index finger across his throat. Palestinians left western media alone, but only because we were useful to them. I knew that under other circumstances, it would not be a mock execution where this guy was concerned.

Bob was a man of few words. He made a pot of tea and smiled as he handed me my cup, as if we were meeting in the waiting room of a quaint English country train station. I got the impression the evening's events had amused him. But I was wrong. He was just being Bob. A hardened SAS veteran of many campaigns spanning a couple of decades, he had the build of a nightclub bouncer, a chiselled jaw and unwavering eyes that warned he was not to be trifled with.

There was something familiar about him. I'd worked with many SAS operators in my time, but that was over a decade ago and I couldn't place him. Bob knew a few SBS lads and I asked

PALESTINE

after several SAS men I'd known back in the day. We were from the same era and chatted well into the night. He also knew my face from somewhere. And then we figured it out. It had been a brief encounter. We almost flew to Chile together in a helicopter during the Falklands conflict, an operation to spy on Argentinian airfields that was sadly cancelled at the last moment. His full name was Bob Shepherd and several years later he wrote a book called *The Circuit*, a first-rate account of his days in the private security world and well worth a read. I spent a pleasant week working with Bob and couldn't have had a better mentor for my purpose and responsibilities in Israel and Palestine.

Bob was replaced a week later by another former SAS lad, Smudge, just as things were beginning to heat up at the Mukataa. The Israelis surrounded the complex and brought in cranes and bulldozers, threatening to tear the entire place down if Arafat didn't surrender. I don't doubt the Israelis had considered storming it but that would've been a bloodbath, and not entirely one-sided.

Our resident CNN correspondent for that week was Ben Wedeman, a journalist of great acclaim. Wedeman was one of the great characters of CNN and a lot of fun, along with his camerawoman Mary. He had a wicked sense of humour and, as one of the few correspondents who could speak Arabic, was in great demand in the Middle East. As we stood on the rooftop overlooking the Mukataa and the build-up to the Israeli attack on it, Ben remarked (while grooming his coiffure in preparation for a stand-up) how it was a pity we couldn't actually broadcast a report from inside the building.

One of the advantages for news teams in having former military as security managers was that soldiers understood how other soldiers operated. The Israelis had surrounded the complex, but they lacked polish and discipline, too many conscripted kids. We soon noted weaknesses in their procedures, spotting significant gaps in their perimeter coverage. A small team could get through to the Mukataa without being challenged. There would be a risk while crossing an exposed floodlit car park between the perimeter and the main buildings. But everyone was up for it.

I can't remember the finer details so long ago after the event, but we didn't take high risks when it came to our clients so we must have been confident in reaching the Mukataa without being challenged. Five of us, a correspondent, producer, cameraman, myself and Smudge, made our way through back alleyways and across gardens, pausing in the shadows between the residential buildings that abutted the road that surrounded the Palestinian Authority HQ. The bulldozers and cranes had fallen silent. The entire complex was bathed in bright lights from an array of portable floodlights the Israelis had erected. The purr of generators was constant. It was around 2am. Groups of soldiers congregated at either end of the street from us, chatting, smoking, switched off as they had nothing to fear. They'd been there for weeks. Many were sleeping.

A couple of sentries ambled past down the street. It was our cue. The next patrol would be in half an hour or so. When they were out of sight we stepped from the shadows, me carrying the camera tripod, crossed the road and clambered over the rubble that was all that remained of the Mukataa's perimeter after the Israelis had torn it down. Anxieties increased as we crossed the floodlit car park, past Palestinian Authority cars that had been trashed by the bulldozers. We reached the main entrance of the

PALESTINE

building, which was in shadow. Not a single Israeli soldier was watching the car park, as we had hoped.

We knocked on the main door of the Mukataa and it was opened by a Palestinian in a smart suit. He was taken completely by surprise. We introduced ourselves as CNN. He was quick to react, aware of the dangers as well as the opportunity, and quickly ushered us inside.

CNN was a magic word I learned to use to great effect during my time as a media risk manager, even when I wasn't working for them. The rest of the world's media were crammed on the roofs of a couple of tall buildings a mile away watching the Mukataa through high-powered lenses. They'd be envious when, a couple of hours later, as daylight came and the Israelis resumed their mechanical pounding of the Palestinian Authority's headquarters, CNN broadcast a live interview with Yasser Arafat from inside the building itself. It was no wonder heads of states tuned into CNN.

The Israelis were livid, of course. I don't doubt heads rolled that day. This wasn't the first time a couple of former British SF had smuggled a CNN news team into the Mukataa right under their noses. On the previous occasion the Israelis threatened to shoot the entire news team on leaving the building. And so the AKE lad in charge tied a white sheet to a pole and, after alerting the rest of the world's media on top of the tall flats a mile away, they filmed him, broadcasting live to the world as he stepped out of the Mukataa wearing a vest with PRESS written on it. The Israelis could hardly shoot him while he held a white flag in front of millions of witnesses.

We didn't need to go to such lengths that day. The Israelis were furious, but they'd learned their lesson from that previous

FIRST INTO ACTION AGAIN

incident. They'd been outmanoeuvred. Again. And by CNN and the same security advisors.

We spent half a day at the Mukataa. I was wandering through the building, being my usual curious self, when I paused to let a dozen schoolchildren, who'd just arrived, walk past me up a flight of stairs. The Palestinians had taken advantage of the intense press coverage to bring in some local school pupils to meet Arafat. The Israelis could hardly stop them with the world watching. I followed them up the stairs to find them lining up to have their photo taken with the man himself. Not to miss an opportunity, and being naturally mischievous, I joined the line. When it was my turn I shook Arafat's hand as he smiled at the camera. I think he assumed I was another kid at first because his smile faded when he looked up at me. But then the smile returned, he nodded hello and continued on to the next kid. A month later a Lebanese lady fixer working for CNN came up to me in the Jerusalem bureau and handed me the photograph. She'd seen it pinned to a wall along with the photos of the children and thought I'd like it.

I spent about three months in Israel and Palestine, Christmas in Bethlehem, and made several trips to Gaza. It was a most illuminating introduction to the news business. I got to see its weaknesses, the battles between different news organisations, the variety of standards, the politics of story-editing, the untruths by omission, the bias, the peer pressure and competition to sell news. Witnessing world events live from the footlights was a unique experience.

During one of the many demonstrations we attended, we spent the day hunkering down with the Palestinians, watching them throw stones and Molotov cocktails at the Israeli soldiers who fired rubber bullets back in return. Days later we joined Israeli soldiers in a similar riot, hunkering down among them, watching the Palestinians attack us. Pressed together, under the barrage of stones and Molotov cocktails, a form of camaraderie grew, the soldiers sharing jokes, cigarettes and coffee as if we were united in the conflict. Who else but journalists had the privilege of experiencing such violently opposed positions so intimately?

I was to spend the next 15 years taking news teams into hostile environments. There was so much going on in the world. While I was in Palestine, coalition forces invaded Afghanistan while more prepared to go into Iraq. I headed home for a break but with one eye on the news, wondering where I would be sent next.

It wasn't long before the call came. I was on my way to Afghanistan. I couldn't wait.

6

AFGHANISTAN

BY THE TIME I ARRIVED in Kabul to manage the CNN bureau, the conventional war was coming to an end and the insurgency was beginning. My first visual impression of the city was a somewhat romantic one, but then only because it was covered in a thick blanket of snow. A storm had been raging in the region, which grounded all flights and left me stuck in Islamabad. I had to find a way into Kabul. I contacted the UN and talked my way onto a supply convoy heading through the Khyber Pass. I'd recently read a book about the British Army's retreat from Kabul along the Khyber Pass at the end of the First Afghan War which provided an interesting perspective on the trip. The UN convoys frequently came under Taliban attack.

As I headed out of my hotel with my bag to join the convoy, our local fixer called to say he'd managed to get me a seat on a Pakistan Airlines cargo flight into Kabul that was leaving in a few hours. Time was a priority and so I had to take the flight.

I'd have felt safer with the UN convoy. The plane was a

AFGHANISTAN

creaking wreck. There were just a handful of seats. The cavernous, grubby, peeling interior was largely devoted to cargo, mostly food, some of it live. I sat between an old Afghan man and a goat. The in-flight meal of rice and some kind of meat was okay. One couldn't afford to be a fussy eater in my line of work.

We didn't appear to climb high above the terrain, which made for a bumpy ride. At one point I could see nothing but snow-covered mountains towering above us on both sides as we crossed the Hindu Kush.

I was to spend three months in the Afghan capital. Within a week of my arrival the snow melted, revealing the city's true grime and squalor. The melting ice also released the stench of raw sewage. Everything was grey – the mountains that surrounded the city, the local stone, even the air itself, as wood fires were the main source of heating and cooking. The fine dust in the air meant most newcomers developed what was known as the Kabul cough within days. During their period of occupation, the Russians had built numerous apartment blocks and government buildings, dismal concrete cubes that contributed to the depressing atmosphere. The roads were heavily potholed and the pavements uneven and crumbling.

As usual when I arrived in a new location, I spent the first few days driving around, familiarising myself with the geography. What struck me was how colourless the place was. Black and grey were the dominant hues, which included the clothing.

The CNN house was in a densely populated suburb at the foot of a barren treeless hill, the long, narrow crest dominated by an eroding British fort from the days when the British Empire ruled Afghanistan. Coalition forces maintained a heavy presence in the city but internal security was lacking. The newly formed Afghan police force struggled and crime and thuggery were rampant. At night it felt like insurgents and bandits lurked in every shadow of the unlit streets.

It wasn't just the West's military that had arrived in force. Droves of non-governmental organisations (NGOs) had moved in: aid charities, de-miners, water providers, medics, food suppliers and, of course, the news media. The majority of these westerners were young men and women who seemed oblivious of the fermenting dangers. Come evening, they were in the mood for entertainment, but there were no clubs, pubs or discos. Booze and food were plentiful, flown in by entrepreneurial companies such as German Supreme Foods. I was to work for them years later, designing security solutions to truck in avgas (aviation fuel) from Pakistan – but that's another story.

My first night in Kabul, the AKE operator I was relieving, former SAS, introduced me to one of the ways bureau staff unwound after work – an NGO house party. Apparently I'd only just missed the CNN bureau's monthly bash.

That evening's venue was the DHL compound a short drive away. We arrived around 7pm to find the normally sleepy residential backstreet jammed with vehicles. The house was packed, music blaring, coloured lights flashing and a disco ball spinning in the living room. The conservative Muslim neighbours must have hated it. But they could do nothing against the might of the western occupiers. It was part of the price they had to pay for ridding the country of the Taliban.

I was taken aback by the DHL party. But it was the norm in Kabul. The Taliban hadn't attacked any of these western play gatherings yet, but it was only a matter of time.

AFGHANISTAN

We'd been at the rave for an hour when four young Afghan men entered the living room. They were dressed like westerners and stood looking around as if searching for someone. There were several Afghan NGO workers at the party, so the newcomers didn't look out of place.

Their leader saw I was watching him. He came over and examined me with a sneer.

'I'm going to kill you,' he said in a guttural voice, eyes fixed on mine, wagging his index finger towards the ceiling beside his face in a manner that suggested he was in collaboration with a higher authority.

He was so nonchalant I assumed it was a joke of some kind. He looked like the driver who'd picked me up from the airport that morning. Wondering if this was some kind of initiation gag, I smiled as I looked around for my SAS partner.

'Why you smile?' the Afghan growled, his frown deepening. 'I'm going to fucking kill you.'

His English was clear with a thick accent. My smile faded. I began to suspect he had nothing to do with CNN or any NGO. One of his buddies muttered something in his ear and pointed to the kitchen. He repeated his threat to me, sounding like a bad actor in a low-budget movie. Then he headed for the kitchen with his mates.

Why me, I wondered?

I found my SAS partner and told him what had happened, suggesting it might be wise to get our people out of there and back to the bureau. At that moment the Afghan who had threatened me suddenly flew backwards out of the kitchen. He landed heavily on the floor, hands up to his face, blood seeping through his fingers. I saw one of his colleagues in the kitchen fall to his knees in pain, clutching his gut. The leader got unsteadily to his feet, then he and the rest of his gang fled like scolded children, shouting threats as they ran out of the house, through the garden and onto the street.

My SAS partner went into the kitchen. I saw him talking with several large, rugged white men who had delivered the beatings. I later learned they were SAS – to be precise, three were 21 SAS (reserves) while their boss, a dark-skinned islander, was a sergeant from 22 SAS. The Afghans had made a similar threat to kill one of them. The SAS men were the British Embassy VIP protection team. They had been in Kabul for several months, were clearly experienced in the ways of Afghans and had little patience for such antics.

We rounded up the crew and headed back to the CNN house. The next morning we learned that not long after we'd left the DHL house, the indignant Afghans returned with AK47s and fired bursts of automatic fire at the building from the street. Fortunately, we were not the only ones to decide it was time to call it a night and only a handful of people were still at the party. Amazingly, no-one was killed or injured. It was an interesting introduction to the city.

Before my SAS partner flew home he handed me a semi-automatic pistol, a poor Iraqi copy of a Browning 9mm. It was on the loose side and had a dodgy return spring, but was better than nothing. The gun was a secret among the AKE security personnel. Neither CNN nor the AKE bosses back in Hereford knew about it. It wasn't an official policy to carry weapons at that time, but our intel from various sources, including the embassy VIP protection lads, suggested it would be wise to have a weapon. The insurgency made no distinction between western

AFGHANISTAN

media personnel, charities or military. We were all legitimate targets. It was illegal for civilians to carry weapons and there would be repercussions if we were caught. But the pros outweighed the cons. I'd brought my trusty shoulder holster with me and carried the pistol everywhere I went.

There were a couple of reporters in residence the first month I was there and at least one of them went out every day accompanied by me. I preferred to drive myself. I didn't trust our Afghan staff. An American and Brit pair who ran a private security company were murdered one night by their Afghan employees while out on a task. The Afghans had been working for the company for a couple of weeks and apparently intended to kill them all along. The problem was every western company needed security guards, the only manpower source was local, and reliable vetting was impossible. Guards could turn on their western employers at any time.

I soon got to know the city. It bustled in the daytime. Chicken Street was the most popular for shopping, among us tourists at least. I bought the usual stuff – rugs, cushions, and a British Army cavalry sword and infantry rifle from the previous occupation.

There was one significant problem at the bureau. I was informed of it the day after I arrived and officially took up my post. The staff hadn't been paid in two months. We had a cash flow problem. The bureau employed eight armed guards, three cooks, a cleaner, two fixers, three drivers and an odd-job man. They had bills to pay and mouths to feed and wouldn't remain appeased for long. I hoped they knew CNN could be relied on to come through with their pay but the Afghans were a suspicious lot. US dollars were on their way with the new bureau chief, but he'd been delayed. I could've done without the added concern.

My task was plagued by mission creep. I began as security risk manager, intelligence-gatherer, military liaison, logistics manager, victuals and vehicle manager, staff manager and medic. By the end of my three months I could add producer, cameraman, treasurer and bureau psychiatrist. I acquired the latter designation early on in the tour.

I answered a knock on my room door one evening to find a guy standing in the corridor looking at me strangely. I'd shared only a couple of words with him since my arrival. He was highly intelligent and the only comments he ever made at our communal dinner table suggested he might be a conspiracy theorist. One of those 'flat Earth' types. He was weird. So, a typical engineer really. It was apparently something to do with all the radiation they absorbed from the satellite dishes.

He wanted to discuss something in private. His accent was midwestern USA. I invited him in and we sat facing each other in a pair of tatty armchairs. I waited patiently while he considered how to begin.

He finally told me in a calm, grave tone that he was contemplating suicide. I did a good job of keeping my expression blank, nodding thoughtfully while wondering how the hell I was supposed to deal with this. I had gained much experience in my life but I felt far from qualified to manage mental health issues at this level. I recalled scenes from movies where therapists discussed such matters with patients. I understood that the basic approach was to let the patient do all the talking while maintaining an expression of suitable gravitas. I got him to describe his home life back in Kentucky with his dog and

AFGHANISTAN

mother. I wondered if his desire to end it all might be linked to the recent death of his beloved dog. We must have talked for an hour. It was the most awkward conversation I'd ever had. Every moment I sat there, every earnest nod and utterance, I felt like a fraud. I wanted to ask why he'd come to me but I refrained. I would have to do my best.

He would drift into moments of contemplative silence. I believed him when he said he felt suicidal. When he eventually left I knew I'd failed to relieve his anxieties. All I could think of was how he might top himself and how I would get his body home. I also wondered how we were going to manage without an engineer. I considered calling his line managers, but then I remembered the rules of patient confidentiality, something else I'd learned from the movies. He only had a couple of weeks left with us and swapping him out would take that long anyway. I felt pretty helpless on all counts. He agreed to another 'therapy session' and I hoped to string them out until his departure.

A week later one of the staff banged on my door. The engineer had locked himself inside his room and wouldn't answer. I sprinted along the corridor and broke down the flimsy door to find him lying unconscious on his bed. My first thought was that he'd gone and topped himself. The room stank of kerosene, which wasn't unusual because every room had a kerosene heater. The winter nights were cold. Those heaters were dangerous pieces of kit – I only used mine to warm the room when it was really bitter, and made sure I wasn't around while it was on. My preferred solution was to wear more clothes.

His pulse was weak. I dragged him into the corridor where the air was fresher and made one of our staff give him mouth-to-mouth. I'd been conducting medical training for everyone and this was a perfect opportunity for them to practise. It also saved me doing my least favourite part of CPR.

The engineer came round quickly. It turned out he hadn't tried to kill himself. He'd taken a nap and his heater had leaked carbon monoxide. It was a close one. Had a generator not broken down, no-one would have come looking for him until the following day, by which time he would certainly have been dead. I was relieved to escort him to the airport a week later and say goodbye.

One afternoon my Afghan fixer warned me quietly that the guards were growing restless. They hadn't been paid for three months now. He feared they planned to strip the compound of its valuables: camera equipment, generators, satellite dishes, computers, vehicles. My main concern was what they had in store for us if that were to happen. I asked him to reassure the guards that the money was coming. Everyone knew the new bureau chief was on his way with the bureau's cash. He landed at Kabul airport a couple of days later and I was there to greet him.

Kabul International Airport was a gloomy 1960s structure that had been built by the Soviets. I met the new chief in the arrivals hall. He wasn't hard to spot. He could've passed for Elton John in his late 50s.

I thought he looked a little unwell. I decided his dark ginger hair was dyed. As we walked into the baggage hall to collect his suitcase, I surreptitiously offered to take charge of his small backpack, assuming it contained the bureau's cash. I wouldn't have put it past our Afghan staff to organise a robbery since they all knew he was the money man. He said he was fine carrying it.

I leaned forward in the crowded baggage hall and suggested

AFGHANISTAN

in a low voice that it would be a good idea if I took responsibility for the money. He nonchalantly told me the money was in the suitcase we were waiting for. Surprised, I asked when he'd last had the case in his hands. He said he'd not seen it since London and that it had been automatically transferred between flights in Islamabad. That was high-risk since in this part of the world bags routinely went missing or were ransacked by baggage handlers and customs officials. Forty or so minutes later, we were the only people left in the baggage hall, gazing as several suitcases continuously trundled around on the rickety conveyor belt. His wasn't among them.

The new chief was vexed by the bag's disappearance. I didn't want to tell him just yet that the implications were far worse than he could imagine. I left my fixer to see if he could track down the suitcase, though I had little hope. I didn't tell him the money was in it, allowing him to assume, as I initially had, that the chief had it safely in his hand baggage.

I needed to buy some time before the staff found out. As we drove to the bureau, all I could think of was the guards' reaction when they learned they were not going to be paid as promised. I was furious at the chief's stupidity, but there was little point in venting. I had a crisis looming. I considered evacuating the CNN staff to the safety of a friendly NGO house while the guards went ahead with their threatened ransack.

As we sat having a cup of tea in the dining room I started to broach the subject, but the chief interrupted me with a pressing problem of his own. He placed a medicine bottle in front of me. It contained a couple of pills. He asked if I could source more of them, as he'd accidentally left three months' supply back in London. I didn't recognise the name on the bottle. He explained they were for an enteric problem and asked if I could keep it confidential. Virtually any pharmaceutical drug could be acquired in Kabul, but it would most likely be an Indian or Pakistani knock-off. They even copied the packaging in fine detail, making it difficult for the layman to tell the difference between the counterfeit and the real thing. It was risky to take these fake drugs. They would either be too weak, too strong, or the wrong thing altogether.

I asked how important the pills were. Very important, he said, looking troubled. I called AKE Hereford on my satellite phone to speak to our 24/7 doctor. When I read out the name of the drug, the doctor warned me it was medication for a serious condition. I asked how serious it would be if we couldn't get a fresh supply. Very serious, he said. I asked for a three-month supply and for Ops to get them to anyone travelling to Kabul asap. The chief must have kept his illness secret from CNN or they wouldn't have let him come to Kabul. My priority was to keep the bureau personnel safe but I also had a responsibility to do everything I could to keep things operational. The challenges were mounting.

I put the pills to one side and explained the threat posed by the guards now there was no money to pay them and the other staff. Just then my fixer walked in grinning broadly and carrying the bureau chief's suitcase. It transpired that while he had been at the baggage collection offices trying to locate the case, a call came in from the Saudi Embassy. A Saudi official on the same flight had brought a dozen suitcases with him and his porters had picked up the chief's in error. It wasn't until they'd arrived at the embassy that they realised they had one case too many. My fixer drove to the embassy to find it standing alone in the hallway by the front door.

AFGHANISTAN

We took it into the privacy of the bureau to open it and I was mightily relieved to find the $70,000 wrapped in brown paper among the chief's clothing.

That night I received a call from AKE telling me a security manager for another news group was flying into Kabul in a couple of days and would have the chief's pills with him. I poured myself a large whisky in celebration and the chief eagerly joined me.

The new chief was a highly experienced CNN reporter and had been sent to Kabul for a specific reason. Atlanta had decided to drastically slim down the bureau because the story had become less newsworthy. Within a few weeks of his arrival the other reporters and assistants had gone, including the new engineer, and the local staff was slimmed down to one cook, a fixer, driver, cleaner and four guards. The house was a much quieter place. And no more parties.

The chief was going to be a one-man band: producer, reporter, cameraman, editor and engineer. It was a CNN experiment, not just to cut costs but also to improve efficiency. The only problem was it didn't work, not in a country where electricity and communications were unpredictable. I watched him set up his stand-ups position, which meant acquiring the satellite signal, setting up the camera, sound, lighting if needed, updating his report and, for live broadcasts, establishing a communications link with the Atlanta desk to coordinate his slot. But the comms frequently dropped out, as did the sat signal, and on occasion the generator would waver or stop all together.

I stepped in to help out where I could and it immediately became my full-time job, along with all of my other responsibilities. I would ensure the camera was on him, talk directly with the Atlanta desk to coordinate the broadcast, keep an eye on the sat signal and maintain the generator. It wasn't the first time I'd been roped in to help out with that side of the business. Months before, in a crowded Bethlehem square, I was with famous CNN camerawoman Margaret Moth, who'd been shot in the face in Bosnia a few years before. It was a Christmas report.

Margaret and I became separated from the reporter and producer, who were looking for stories. I always stuck with the camera-person since they were the most vulnerable and usually loaded down with equipment. Margaret was a tough, highly experienced woman. After losing patience with the absent reporter and producer, she shoved a microphone in my hand and ordered me to start interviewing people while she filmed. And so I obeyed, asking Palestinians the most topical question of the day, which was how they felt about Yasser Arafat not being permitted to attend the ceremonies while the IDF kept him locked up in the Mukataa in Ramallah. Many of my interviews ended up being broadcast that day. I could add CNN reporter to my CV.

Dinner at the Kabul bureau usually consisted of the chief and I sitting at either end of the large dining table that only weeks before had seated 10. The room was lit by candles because we didn't use the generator when we weren't working. It might have been romantic under other circumstances. Here, it was more like something out of the Addams Family.

The chief was good company and shared many of his reporting experiences with me. But there was a side to him that I was initially unaware of. During our third or fourth dinner he informed me that, although he was Australian, his heritage was

AFGHANISTAN

100% Irish – republican Irish, he emphasised. I knew where the conversation was headed and sure enough it was only a matter of time before he brought up the subject of Northern Ireland. I think he'd been burning to talk about it ever since he arrived and learned I was former Brit SF. I didn't hide the fact I'd operated in NI.

He declared he was a passionate supporter of the IRA. I suspected he'd never actually met an ex-member of British special forces before. He wasn't being aggressive. I sensed no animosity. I don't know what he expected to get out of the conversation. I couldn't care less what his politics were. I'd long since grown cynical about politics and religion, what was supposedly right and wrong, lawful and unlawful, fair and unfair. The only thing I was certain of was that humans were constantly evolving and that we had a long, long way to go.

One morning the chief decided to take a brisk walk. He was far from the athletic type and I put it down to one of those spontaneous moments of guilt at being overweight and out of shape. The only place to walk locally was up to the old British fort. I'd paid it a visit shortly after I'd arrived and found it to be a fascinating monument to the Afghan-British wars of over a century and a half ago. It was a narrow, dilapidated two-storey structure of dirt and stone some 150 yards long, littered with rusting weaponry from the more recent Soviet occupation. A slice of history gradually being eroded by the weather. I couldn't let him go alone of course, so I donned tracksuit and trainers and tucked my pistol into its holster. It never occurred to me that I would need it.

The chief set off at a brisk pace which, to my surprise, he maintained along the 400m-500m looping track all the way to the top. He was pretty knackered by the time we reached the huge, original wooden double doors that hung open. The terrain was sand and gravel without a speck of flora. The crumbling ramparts towered above us. There were thousands of empty artillery casings lying around. A broken, rusting artillery piece sat inside the entrance, its barrel sticking through a hole in the wall, aimed at the city. On my previous visit an old Afghan man had greeted me with a polite nod and toothless grin. I took him to be the caretaker since he appeared to live outside the main entrance in a small brick structure with a corrugated roof, smoke trickling from a chimney.

As we left the fort to return to the bureau, a young Afghan stepped from the old man's dwelling. He wore a camouflage jacket over traditional baggy trousers and scuffed sandals. His hair was thick and dusty and his expression decidedly unfriendly. There was no sign of the old man.

The chief gave him a nod and a smile as he kept on walking. The young man's dark eyes bored into me as I passed him. I followed the chief, turning my back on the man, and seconds later a rock struck me hard between my shoulder blades. I spun round, ready for an assault. The Afghan's menacing eyes never left mine as he crouched to pick up another rock. A second young man of similar appearance emerged from the hut and joined his colleague. He held a machete. The first man raised his arm to throw the rock at me. It was obvious where this was headed. Afghans were generally brutally aggressive in these scenarios. A charge would follow the rock, then the machete man would join the fray. They could inflict a great deal of damage.

Before the first man could release the rock I yanked out my

pistol and aimed it at his chest. He froze, but kept his arm cocked ready to launch. He was a ballsy bastard. I was pointing a gun at him and he was still contemplating stoning me. His colleague had halted his advance though he still held the machete menacingly.

I knew the drill if I shot either of them, even in the leg as a warning. I'd have to get myself on the first flight out of there. Law and order barely existed in the city but a westerner shooting a local would attract a great deal of interest. If I was arrested, I'd spend who knew how long in police custody awaiting trial. There was every chance I'd end up in jail, where I'd doubtless survive as long as an Englishman might expect to, which wasn't long. But at that moment I didn't have much of a choice. On the positive side, we were in a remote location. The nearest houses were a few hundred yards away skirting the bottom of the hill and no-one would be able to see exactly what was going on.

The Afghan holding the rock wasn't quitting. I took a step forward and shifted my aim to his crotch. The threat of losing his manhood might be more persuasive. I looked him in the eye with an expression of icy calm that I hoped would convey I had no qualms about pulling the trigger. The man's expression remained full of malice but he lowered the rock, although he didn't drop it.

I told the chief to get going. He looked stressed. He told me later he was horrified when he saw the machete and even more so when I produced a pistol. He didn't need to be told twice and hurried on his way, stumbling on the gravel, looking back every few steps to gauge the threat.

Keeping the pistol aimed at the Afghan, I took a few steps back. Then I lowered it and walked on, my eyes still boring into his. The track curved around and below the two Afghans, who moved to keep us in their sights. The one with the rock never took his eyes off me. I expected him to throw it any moment, but he just watched me until I was out of range.

The chief and I maintained a brisk pace down the hill until we disappeared between the houses.

Over dinner that night, I couldn't resist asking the chief how he felt about having his Fenian arse saved by former British Special Forces. He was not amused.

My last week was quiet. I spent time with the SAS lads, often visiting them in Camp Souter, the British Army base on the other side of the city where they lived. They took me into the countryside to their training area, where I fired various weapons and joined in with their contact drills, acting as the client, getting dragged out of the car and hurried to safety while under fire. The lads occasionally popped into the bureau for a drink, much to the chief's chagrin – he didn't take kindly to being surrounded by British soldiers who took every opportunity to wind him up about the IRA, recounting completely fabricated stories about assassinations and torture. I don't think any of the 21 lads had even been to Northern Ireland.

There was a battered old long-wheelbase armoured Land Rover parked in a corner of the bureau compound under a tarp. It had been with CNN since they first arrived in Afghanistan six months earlier and had been a significant asset during the war, not only as transport but as a refuge during fierce fighting and accommodation when there was nowhere else to go. It looked as if it had stories to tell with its chips and dents, a couple of bullet holes, and evidence of many paint-jobs during its lifetime. Its current livery was a black base with random green, purple,

AFGHANISTAN

red and yellow blotches, suggesting a crude attempt at camouflage for an unspecified environment. Andrew Kain had called to ask if I could assess how feasible it would be to transport this vehicle back to the UK. The Land Rover weighed a couple tons and the engine was on its last legs, as was the suspension. I doubted it would make it out of the compound. Because of its sentimental value from the early days of the war, CNN wanted to put it on display in their corporate museum in Atlanta, and had asked Andrew to arrange its delivery. Andrew had personally driven the 'Pizza Wagon', as it was known, on several CNN operations in Afghanistan and shared the news teams' fondness for it. It was an interesting challenge. I had little else to do, so I set about researching.

The obvious option was to transport it by air but after several phone calls the cheapest quotes I could get were $45,000 to the USA and not much less to the UK. I called Andrew to ask him if that price-range would be acceptable to CNN. He told me the museum was as yet unbuilt and unfinanced and no money was available. Andrew was basically asking if there was a way I could get the two tons of junk home for free. Now there was a challenge indeed.

We had maritime contacts and there was a chance a cargo ship could take it to the USA. But that meant getting it over the border on the back of a truck to Karachi. The Taliban controlled the roads and I would need someone with major clout and connections to oversee the vehicle's transit onto a ship. I certainly couldn't do it myself. The poor old Land Rover looked destined to spend its final days rotting in Kabul.

But there was a twist to come.

I was due to leave Afghanistan in less than a week when the

FIRST INTO ACTION AGAIN

SAS lads invited me for lunch at Camp Souter. Officially, I wasn't permitted inside the military barracks. I was a civilian, regardless of my background, and the fact I worked for CNN didn't make me any more desirable. However, the lads simply let everyone assume I was one of them.

While having a brew in their quarters, we were joined by an army captain on a social. The SAS lads introduced me by my first name only. During the conversation the officer revealed he was responsible for transporting British Army cargo in and out of Kabul. I couldn't resist quipping if he fancied flying my armoured Land Rover back to the UK for me. The lads chuckled, knowing my story. The officer nonchalantly replied that it wouldn't be a problem. There was an element of bravado on his part. He was a bit of an SF groupie.

A couple of the lads raised their eyebrows at me, wondering if I'd bite. I didn't miss the open door. It was madness to even contemplate, of course. There would be huge ramifications if the British Army flew a civilian Land Rover, owned by CNN, out of Afghanistan. I'd be hung, drawn and quartered for starters. The conversation should have ended there and then. But the naughty little devil that has been my constant companion throughout my life couldn't resist pushing the subject a step further.

I asked the captain what I needed to do. He asked when I was looking to ship it. As soon as possible, I replied. He got to his feet and said with a theatrical air, 'Follow me.'

I glanced back at the lads as I left the room. Most were grinning. One was shaking his head, warning me not to do it. He was no doubt concerned about the possible repercussions for them. If the bubble burst, questions would be asked about me. Who, in fact, was I? But it was too early in the game to consider that. It was impossible for me not to take it to the next stage, and I would continue until it came to a natural halt.

The captain led the way into the HQ building and up a flight of stairs to a security door. He tapped in the access code and entered, holding the door open for me. This was the operations centre, the nerve centre of the camp. By entering I was pushing my luck way further than I had ever anticipated. Things were happening fast.

I casually followed him inside. He told someone behind a desk that I was with him and led the way through the busy operations room with its various cubicles, cells, and rows of monitors displaying maps, asset locations, communications systems. It had been a while since I'd been inside an army ops room but it was still familiar.

The captain stepped into a small office, sat behind his desk, opened a filing cabinet and pulled out a waybill with multiple duplicate coloured pages, which he handed to me. I was to fill it in and get it back to him asap. As I left alone through the ops room, everyone glanced at me, my unkempt civilian appearance informing them I operated beyond the wall. I was used to such looks from my years in SF and as an undercover operator, when I occasionally had to wander through a regular military camp for one reason or another.

With practised ease I coolly ignored them, not catching anyone's eye, eager to be out of there. On this occasion I just hoped no-one had the temerity to challenge me about my purpose there.

Back at the bureau, I filled in the form. The final destination and UK contact details were required. It was time to talk with AKE.

FIRST INTO ACTION AGAIN

I called the Hereford office and spoke with the duty ops officer, Mick, a former SAS warrant officer who'd recently left the regiment and would have had a lot of experience transporting vehicles around the world. I explained what I was doing and, without missing a beat, he suggested I assign the vehicle to the SAS HQ, Stirling Lines, Hereford. I wondered if that wasn't problematic.

He explained that since it was certainly an irregular vehicle, addressing it to SAS HQ would give it credibility and no-one would question it. The trick would be to intercept it at RAF Lynham. Hereford wouldn't be expecting it and so nobody would be there to collect it. Of course, we didn't want it to go to the SAS camp. We just needed to ensure it got picked up from RAF Lyneham as soon as it arrived.

Mick knew several SAS lads in the final stages of their leaving programmes. Although already working in civvy street, they retained their SAS ID cards for a few more weeks as they were technically still in the military. Mick would get one of them to access the air base and pick up the vehicle. He suggested I put the AKE office ops phone number as the consignment contact.

It was all very tidy. With added confidence, I delivered the waybill the following day. The captain saw no problem with any of it and said it could take a week or so because there was suddenly a lot of movement.

As I left the camp I felt I'd reached the end point of my endeavour. I'd be leaving in a few days and I couldn't ask my replacement to take over the risk.

As I drove through the city I received a call from AKE asking me to head over to the United Nations HQ and prepare an insurance report on a robbery that had just taken place there. I

AFGHANISTAN

was exclusive to CNN but I could fit in the occasional side job for AKE as long as it didn't interfere with my media responsibilities.

I met with the head of the UN Kabul security team to get the details of the incident. It was an interesting one. Every month the UN received a cash delivery of many thousands of US dollars to pay its running costs. The money was flown to Kabul International Airport and driven to the UN compound where it was placed in a large safe on the first floor of the main administration building. A month prior to the robbery, the head of security hired a new Afghan guard commander after the incumbent had mysteriously disappeared. The new commander then promptly set about firing the Afghan guard retinue, replacing them with members of his own clan. He'd convinced the head of security that the previous guards couldn't be trusted and, being from a different clan, they wouldn't be loyal to him.

The night after the money arrived, the new gate guards gave a lorry access to the UN compound. Inside it were a dozen Afghans and, along with the new guards who all left their posts to assist, they proceeded to drag the safe out of the office, down the stairs and onto the back of the lorry. Everyone left with it, including the guard commander, never to be seen again. It was a slice of Kabul life and nothing new for the UN, who appeared to get robbed with monotonous regularity.

The following day I was surprised to receive a call from a corporal at Camp Souter asking if I could get the Land Rover to the camp within the hour. A flight was leaving for the UK that day and a cancellation had opened up a space. Talk about timing. I was due to fly out the following day. I told my fixer to meet me outside Camp Souter and hurried out of the office. I felt a mixture of concern and exhilaration that I might just pull it off.

The Land Rover was a temperamental beast to start and it took several attempts before it roared into life. It steered like a cow as I manoeuvred it through the front gate. I could feel all of its two and a half tons as I eased it onto the street. The engine was out of whack, the cylinders misfiring. I wasn't confident it would make the five miles across town to the camp. But all I could do was press on. If it died, I would have to leave it where it was.

I left the residential area, turned onto a main road and joined the city traffic. The engine continued to misfire. There were a few scary moments when I thought it was going to die completely. I kept the revs up and willed it on. Thankfully, traffic was light and I didn't have to keep stopping and starting. The journey was uneventful until the last big roundabout.

It was a big one for the city. There were a couple of cars on it but mostly mopeds and cyclists. I took a tight line, aiming to exit the opposite side. The heavy vehicle felt like a lumbering cargo ship as it leaned into the bend. I should've been going slower. I suppose I was impatient since the camp was so close. Suddenly, to my horror, the lock on the armoured passenger side door, which had a thick bullet-proof window and must have weighed half a ton, suddenly snapped and the door swung open. I was between several cyclists and the door slammed into the back of one of them like a cricket bat going for a six. He disappeared from view with a clatter. The door-hinge straps had long since broken and the door kept swinging forward, bouncing off the front wheel arch as I continued the turn. Through the open door I caught a glimpse of the luckless cyclist rolling on the

AFGHANISTAN

road. I steered frantically to avoid more cyclists and took the exit without slowing. The vehicle lurched over to the other side, the suspension grinding in agony. To my relief, the door swung back, slammed shut and miraculously locked.

If I'd stopped I would've found myself quickly surrounded by an angry mob demanding immediate compensation, more so because I was a westerner. The police would eventually arrive and I'd end up at the police station with the victim and his family baying for my blood (or a fistful of cash). Fleeing the scene was a case of self-preservation. I only hoped no-one was in pursuit.

The Land Rover was hardly a getaway car. I accelerated as fast as I dared while keeping an eye on my rear-view. The left turn to the camp soon came up and I took it. Within minutes I was safely inside the camp checkpoint. I made it through the entrance without anyone arriving behind me and drove to the depot. Leaving the keys with the admin clerk, I walked out of the camp to avoid meeting anyone and continued down the street until my fixer arrived to pick me up.

A few hours later the captain called to let me know the vehicle was on the flight and bound for Blighty. I thanked him but didn't feel completely relieved when I put the phone down. That would only happen when the Rover was safely with AKE and there was no follow-up from the army.

Things didn't go smoothly at the other end either. The Land Rover made it to RAF Lyneham but wasn't picked up soon enough by Mick's mate. Mick received a call from Stirling Lines a day or so later. It was the SAS Regimental Sergeant Major. He knew Mick, having served with him for many years, and asked if he knew anything about a knackered, armoured, civvy

Land Rover that had arrived at RAF Lyneham from Kabul. The RAF had contacted Stirling Lines requesting it be picked up. This the SAS duly did, assuming it was theirs, but when it arrived no-one had a clue who it belonged to.

After some investigating, including a close inspection of bits of rubbish found tucked away in crevices, it was deduced the vehicle belonged to AKE. Mick was most apologetic. The RSM told Mick that someone had better pick up the damned thing sharpish before any more questions were asked. The embarrassment for the army would hopefully outweigh any satisfaction derived from nailing those responsible for the deception.

The vehicle was taken to the AKE garages, which were only a few miles from Stirling Lines, where it remained until CNN Atlanta could convince the powers that be to provide the funding to ship it to the States, where it would be preserved for posterity as a piece of CNN history.

I flew out of Kabul with several boxes of rugs, pashminas, assorted trinkets and the rifle and cavalry sword I'd bought after getting permission from the local museum. I returned to Afghanistan six years later, but not for CNN. I smuggled half a million dollars in cash into Kabul from Dubai to facilitate the release of Mellissa Fung, a Canadian Broadcast Company journalist who had been kidnapped. We were staying in the Gandamack Lodge and I remained to witness Mellissa's release, which was very tense.

The Canadian CIA was threatening the CBC with all sorts of punishments if it defied government policy and paid any ransom. The CBC editor told the Canadian CIA to fuck off. The Afghan intelligence services then turned up to ask the CBC not to pay. The editor told them to fuck off too. All he wanted was Mellissa back. The kidnappers had come down from millions of dollars to around $350,000. The Afghan IS explained why they didn't want the money to be paid. The head kidnapper, an Afghan, was hiding out in Pakistan just over the border, out of reach of the Afghan authorities. The Afghans had devised a cunning plan. They kidnapped the kidnapper's mother and told him she'd remain in prison until Mellissa was released. The plan worked. Afghans are very close to their mums.

As I left Kabul on that first trip for CNN, I was initially warned I'd be going into Iraq with the first wave of coalition forces, a journey I looked forward to immensely. But as I touched down in the UK I got a call from AKE about a change of plans. I was not going to Iraq. Not right away at least. I was headed for Liberia, west Africa, where a war was about to break out. I was, literally, to be right in the middle of it.

7

LIBERIA

I ARRIVED IN ACCRA, GHANA, to join an eight-man CNN team who would be flying into Liberia to interview its notorious president Charles Taylor. Trouble was brewing in the west African state. I've had tasks over the years that I look back on and ponder how fortunate I was to survive. This visit to Liberia remains high on the list. A full-on battle was about to break out, and my CNN team and I would find ourselves on the front line, caught between two opposing armies. We were certainly First Into Action on that day.

There were two correspondents in the team to begin with: Brent Sadler and Jeff Koinange. The rest of the crew was made up of two engineers, a young Aussie producer, two cameramen and editor Neil Hallsworth, who was also our back-up cameraman.

Liberia was unique among African states. It was created in the 1820s to allow former African slaves from the USA and Caribbean to resettle in their ancestral continent. Almost 20,000 ex-slaves made their homes there. It was hoped they'd

LIBERIA

have a greater chance of prosperity in Africa than America. Unfortunately, it didn't quite work out that way, not least for the indigenous people who had to make room for the newcomers. The former slaves were the root of the problem. They regarded themselves superior to the locals in every way, and although fewer in numbers, they seized the reins of power and ended up governing the country. Liberia's internal strife and rollercoaster politics continued into the 1900s, leading to a coup in 1980 and eventually civil war. The low point came when Charles Taylor gained the presidency. Taylor's official list of war crimes included rape, murder, terrorism, slavery, kidnapping and torture. The unofficial list was longer. He looted his country, increased his infamy by creating an army of child soldiers, and was accused of harbouring members of Al-Qaeda wanted in connection with the bombings of the US embassies in Kenya and Tanzania. Under his rule the country became an international pariah.

We arrived to interview Taylor a month after he'd been officially indicted by the Hague for war crimes. Taylor was battling two rebellious factions that between them controlled two-thirds of the country – LURD in the north and MODEL in the southeast. We arrived during a pause in the fighting and planned to stay long enough to interview Taylor and record some opinions and slices of life in the capital.

My brief, as usual, was to manage safety and security and assess the operational risks. Liberia was a dangerous place for sure. Full-scale war could kick off at any moment. Poverty was everywhere, utilities unpredictable, there were food and fuel shortages, the average wage was US$1 a day, and there was an outbreak of cholera in the capital.

FIRST INTO ACTION AGAIN

We chartered an aircraft and flew to Liberia's international airport 30 miles from the capital Monrovia. For safety reasons, we kept our CNN identities hidden. News people were welcomed by some and despised by others. One could never be sure of the prevailing mood until one had spent time among the people. We were staying at the Mamba Point Hotel in the capital, a stone's throw from the beach, and my first objective was to get us there without incident.

Monrovians hoped the US would send a peacekeeping force to prevent an invasion of the city by LURD. I don't know where they got the notion that the Yanks were coming to protect them. As far as we knew, and we were pretty well-informed, the US had no intention of sending troops. The Americans didn't have enough manpower in the region anyway. The US was applying pressure on neighbouring African countries to provide their own peacekeeping forces, but none were willing to help.

We set off from the airport in three 4x4s and soon arrived at our first government military checkpoint. I told the officer in charge that we were a world news crew and didn't elaborate. Several international news organisations had already arrived, with many more on their way. Taylor and the conflict had become a topic of interest to the world's news media.

The soldiers weren't hostile but neither were they particularly welcoming. After taking their sweet time, they let us through. Ten miles on we came to another checkpoint where we received the same apathetic treatment.

At the next checkpoint a few miles further on, our vehicles attracted the attention of passing locals as we waited to be processed. We were still 10 miles or so from the outskirts of the city. Our producer was working on his laptop, a CNN device

LIBERIA

with the company's distinctive logo as a desktop background. One of the onlookers spotted it through the window and cried 'CNN!' Others clustered round our vehicle, grinning, waving and chanting 'CNN! CNN!' We were celebrities.

Although few Liberians possessed a television, they were passionate about soccer and almost every village had a bar with a satellite TV. When it wasn't showing football or a soap opera, CNN was the default international news channel, mainly because it had been covering the troubles in Liberia.

It seemed the belief was that if CNN was in town it meant the US military was on its way. Why else would the US network be here?

We always carried CNN logo cards and I immediately stuck some on the windows of all the vehicles. The checkpoint guards appeared to share the sentiments of the crowd and let us through without further ado. From that point on, we were greeted with waves and cheers as we made our way into the city.

After settling into the hotel, Brent Sadler and I paid a visit to the US Embassy. Making friends in places of influence was always a wise first move when arriving in a new country. A journalist could source information about stories, while a security manager could gather intelligence that might alert him to any threats – as well as make contact with potential safe havens.

We met with US Ambassador John Blaney, who was most welcoming and brought us up to speed on the situation. The ambassador's attaché was also helpful and he and I exchanged cell phone numbers. He was keen to establish a two-way information flow – we would be on the ground gaining local knowledge while he could share the embassy's intelligence on the rebels. The attaché was particularly concerned about a

LURD attack since it could necessitate an embassy evacuation. The attaché would turn out to be an important contact for me over the coming days.

Charles Taylor was out of the country when we arrived so we spent the first few days driving around the city pursuing 'life' stories and looking for anyone willing to talk frankly about the conflict and politics. Come evening we'd return to the hotel, where Neil Hallsworth would edit the footage while the journalists wrote their pieces. Brent might do a live stand-up report from a position we had been allowed to set up in the hotel grounds. We had brought a large satellite dish with us for the purpose.

Over the coming days the hotel gradually filled with media people from all over the world. Like everyone else in Liberia, they were waiting to see if anyone was going to do anything to help these people. All the big US networks were represented including CBS, ABC, NBC and Fox. The BBC was there, several European outfits, and Chinese and Japanese networks too.

The hotel bar was packed in the evenings, overflowing to the outside restaurant and patios where staff set up extra tables. The stout Lebanese owner was no doubt delighted with the increased cash flow. Every room was taken and the media folk, on expenses and per diems, ate and drank heartily.

When Taylor returned to Liberia we were at the airport to record his arrival. A day or two later Brent was permitted to interview him in his palace. Taylor arrived in the presidential chamber accompanied by his usual retinue of male and female bodyguards, all doing their best to look intimidating in dark suits and sunglasses. His sudden entry took us by surprise. I

LIBERIA

happened to be lounging on his golden throne with my feet up. There wasn't much for me to do while the team were setting up. Taylor gave me a cold look as I got to my feet. I put on a nonchalant act, whistling cheerfully as I pretended to help the cameraman with something. Had I not been with CNN, I might've been skinned alive for my transgression. Taylor had apparently done that to one of his predecessors.

After the interview, we spent the next few days touring with the United Nations and various ambassadors. It was a classic media circus, with dozens of vehicles in convoy, escorted by the Liberian military, visiting hospitals and refugee camps. Clamouring reporters, photographers and TV cameras gathered at every stop to record the events and interview dignitaries.

Meanwhile, 40 kilometres to the north, the rebels were stirring.

After the initial hullabaloo, with nothing further of interest happening, the story was in danger of drying up. News crews were expensive to keep on location and CNN wasn't getting its value for money in Liberia. I expected the plug to be pulled at any moment. Brent was anxious to get to Iraq, where it was far more exciting. The following morning he left with his cameraman and our team shrank to seven, with Jeff Koinange taking over correspondent duties. Jeff was keen. He saw it as an opportunity to shine and perhaps even scoop that elusive Emmy award. For that, something exciting needed to happen. Jeff was to get much more than he bargained for.

Having covered the city thoroughly, including the Freeport, its small sea port, we decided to explore the countryside. Up until then we'd not experienced anything particularly dramatic

– apart from the refugee camps packed with orphans, and the hospital beds overflowing with cholera sufferers and those wounded in the conflict. On local trips I usually took just the one vehicle with Jeff, his cameraman, the producer and Neil.

We were driving along a jungle road a few kilometres from the city when we came upon a gang of heavily armed child soldiers blocking our way. We stopped immediately a short distance from them. We were too close to attempt anything rash such as reversing out of there. There were a dozen or so of them, aged between seven and 15. They were like a bunch of schoolkids hanging around with nothing better to do, except they were armed with AK47 assault rifles. They were drinking beer and smoking thick roll-ups of marijuana, which grew on the side of the roads like every other weed.

Their outfits were bizarre, as if they'd raided a charity shop and went for all the fancy party clobber. They were all boys but some wore wigs, bras and mini-skirts. I don't think the cross-dressers were trying to express gender fluidity. I'm pretty certain they either didn't know it was female clothing or they were too high to care.

The scariest thing about child soldiers, why they are so dangerous, is that they have zero accountability for anything they do. That includes shooting someone dead, a complete stranger or one of their own. Add drugs and alcohol to the mix and you have some very dangerous children. No-one cared about them and they repaid the favour. They had been coached from their earliest days to shoot people and to revel in it. It was their norm. They took what they wanted or needed and killed whoever tried to stop them, or simply for their own amusement.

As we sat looking at them my mind raced to figure out how

to handle this situation. We needed to get away without being shot.

I told the others to wait while I climbed out of the vehicle. I took a deep breath, smiled broadly and ambled over to them, hands in my pockets. All eyes were on me. The boys were unsmiling, but I detected curiosity. Whites were uncommon in Liberia. It's possible some of them hadn't seen one in the flesh before.

I asked how they were doing. One of the taller boys, the leader I assumed, asked me in a deep, slow, ominous voice who we were. He looked 14 or 15 going on 40. By the way he leaned back watching me and the way he talked, it was clear he'd lived a hell of a life in the few years he'd been alive. I told him we were CNN, hoping it would do the trick, but he didn't seem impressed. As I walked over I looked to see if the safety catches on their rifles were off. The AK is one of the few weapons whose safety catch is visible on the outside of the working parts housing. They were on full automatic, ready to fire. I couldn't tell if they were loaded but I assumed so.

The trick to surviving such situations, faced with people who couldn't care less if you lived or died, is to show you have some kind of value to them. It can be anything, as long as you have it and they can't just take it from you. One method was to try to form a bond, but I certainly couldn't relate to these kids in any way.

The boy in the mini-skirt started a funky dance routine around me which seemed to vaguely entertain some of the others. I got a little nervous every time he went behind me, twirling his rifle like a baton.

Then I had an idea. We should do what we were there to do. I asked the leader if we could film him and his friends. He wasn't sure what I meant. I explained that we'd like to put them on TV. He looked intrigued again.

I signalled to the others to join me. Within a few minutes a camera was rolling on several of the boy soldiers in full swing, dancing and hamming it up. Those who didn't join in appeared to be amused. The cameraman did a great job of moving about, looking for different angles, keeping tempo with the lively flow. After 20 minutes or so we wrapped it up and I told the leader that if he watched TV in the next couple of days to look for CNN and he'd see himself. His cold expression didn't change but I felt as if I might have made a connection. If he wanted to see himself on TV, he had to let us go on our way.

We waved and climbed back into our vehicle. The kids no longer looked aggressive. Some of them were still dancing about. We drove away, looking back at them. It was sad on so many levels. Perhaps there had been nothing for us to worry about. They might not have intended us harm. Who knew what was going through their minds?

I don't know if CNN broadcast the footage we shot that day.

Back at the hotel that night there was once again talk of us leaving the country, perhaps the following day. I called AKE to warn them and the ops room asked if I'd be okay with transferring directly to Iraq, where things were heating up. Saddam Hussein and his two sons had disappeared, and news crews were running all over the country in search of stories, several getting themselves killed in the process. I was up for the challenge and looking forward to something more exciting than this place.

Next morning it was confirmed we were to leave the following day. A commercial flight was coming in from Ghana and we were booked on it. There was nothing else planned so the rest of the day would be lazy.

A few hours later my phone rang. It was the embassy attaché. He'd heard that LURD might be on the move, heading south towards Monrovia, but he couldn't confirm it and wondered if we knew anything. I'd not heard any such rumours. The attaché let me know one of his concerns. The government troops were low on ammunition and an expected resupply had been delayed. If LURD was aware of this – and the attaché believed it had numerous spies among the government troops – now would be the perfect time to strike.

I informed Jeff and he suggested we head north to look for signs of an advancing army. If LURD was advancing I expected significant government military activity. They probably wouldn't allow us to get close to the front. There was only one road directly north and it would be crawling with troops. Jeff was super keen to go, and my job was to find a way of safely achieving his wishes.

The five of us divided into the two vehicles, each with our local driver: Jeff, his cameraman and the producer in one, Neil and myself in the other. The engineers stayed in the hotel. We set off along 'Embassy Row', where the US, British and French embassies were located, across the Gabriel Tucker Bridge, north along United Nations Drive and over the Saint Paul River Bridge. The landmarks were familiar to us by then.

Things looked normal as we headed into the northern part of the city. People were going about their daily lives. By the time we reached the Brewerville Junction nine miles from our hotel, the streets were noticeably less crowded than a few days before. The market stalls were practically empty of produce. As this came from the north, it suggested the farmers had not come south to deliver their goods for some reason. The tinkling of an alarm bell rang in my head.

We left the outer city buildings behind us and continued north on an orange dirt road through dense jungle with swampland on either side. The entire region was swampland, which made the roads so essential. There was no skipping across country to outflank the city defenders. Any confrontation would be head-on. Neither LURD nor the government had an air force or navy. Bridges would be key defensive positions.

Every mile or so we'd pass through a village or small town. They all seemed very quiet. I decided to keep going to the Po River Bridge, five miles north of Brewerville. The bridge was the most significant choke point for any force heading directly south to the city and where I expected the bulk of the defending government forces to be entrenched, if indeed LURD was on its way. We passed occasional small pockets of government troops and a few army vehicles, but nothing very different to what we'd seen on previous trips up the same road.

As we pressed on, the only locals on the road were moving south towards the city, many carrying bags and suitcases. One man was balancing a rolled-up mattress on his head and appeared to have his entire family in tow, including grandparents. We stopped to ask what they were doing and the answers were emphatic – LURD was coming.

I couldn't understand why we'd seen so few government soldiers. It's possible the locals were just responding to the rumours that had been circulating for weeks and were finally moving to the city. No-one had actually seen any rebels.

I decided to keep going, expecting each turn in the road to

reveal a comprehensive defensive emplacement of Taylor's government forces. At that point we'd pull over, see if we could find a senior officer willing to be interviewed on camera, and find a place to shoot some stand-ups.

The road soon became completely deserted and I told the driver to slow down. We kept our eyes fixed ahead as our uncertainty grew. Villages and dwellings had been abandoned. I started to feel we should stop proceeding until we knew more. I was at a familiar metaphorical crossroads, one I would confront many times in this business: where to draw the line between getting the news and getting to safety, because they were not always in the same place. CNN employed me to make those decisions. I was supposed to be better than these civvies at assessing the dangers in conflict zones.

There was something else I found curious. The hotel was full of news people – print, radio, TV, big players from all over the world – yet none of them were out here, sniffing the same rumours as us, unless they were ahead of us, which I doubted. We were ahead of them all. It was something I was to grow accustomed to, working with CNN. We were often the first into action. And that had a lot to do with AKE and its risk managers.

We passed through a village called Voyou which was also a ghost town. My map showed a soft bend up ahead followed by a long straight that led to the Po River Bridge. I wouldn't go beyond that for sure. The bridge was my crucial point where, if I was the military, I'd try to stop LURD's advance. If the government believed LURD was coming, they'd be there in force. And if not, then perhaps LURD wasn't coming.

My driver was visibly nervous. When I asked if he was okay,

he insisted he was. One of the rules I had for taking teams into potentially dangerous situations was that every member had to feel up for it. If one wasn't, then I'd pull everyone out.

I asked the driver to ease around the bend. When the road straightened I brought the vehicles to a stop. The Po Bridge was 800 metres ahead, out of sight due to a gentle bend just before it. There was also lots of jungle either side.

I turned off the engine, climbed out and signalled the other driver to kill his. Jeff joined me as I watched and listened. Nothing but the usual jungle sounds. No government forces, but no LURD either.

I decided to leave Jeff and the others here and proceed alone with one of the vehicles to check out the bridge.

My driver's name was Pad. He was still nervous but in control of himself. When I told him I'd take the vehicle to the bridge myself, he insisted on driving me, reminding me it was his responsibility. I accepted that. After telling Jeff's driver to turn his vehicle around and stay at the wheel in case they needed to get out of there sharpish, Pad and I set off down the road at an easy speed. I told Pad to be ready to turn around quickly if we needed to. He nodded, eyes wide with concentration.

I could make out the entrance to the bridge as we eased into the bend. There was no sign of life. It was possible government forces had secured a position even further north, but I doubted it. A wall of sandbags had been stacked a metre high at the nearest end of the bridge for a checkpoint guard to hide behind, but that had been there when we came through a few days earlier.

A hundred and fifty metres short of the bridge, the forecourt of a disused fuel station came into view. Half a dozen govern-

An eternity ago: My first military operation at 19 years old in 1976 *(left)*

Training days: Pass-out parade, Commando Training Centre, Lympstone in 1975 *(right)*

Suited up: Getting ready to free-fall *(above)*

HM Submarine Orpheus: During Exit and Re-entry 1983 *(right)*

Free falling: HALO training, Brize Norton in 1978 *(left)*

The Det: During my days in the 14th Intelligence Detachment *(right)*

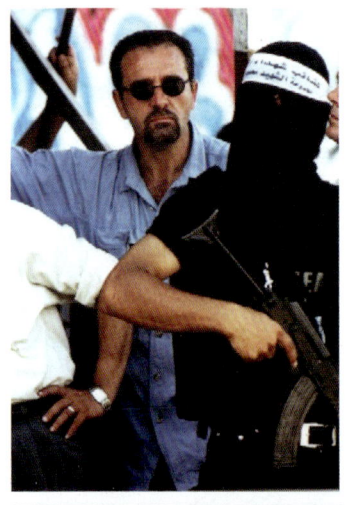

Gaza: I spent about three months in Israel and Palestine, Christmas in Bethlehem, and made several trips to Gaza *(above left)*

Border control: A Peshmerga officer at a Kurdistan Iran border checkpoint *(above right)*

The QE2: Undercover on board with a friend *(left)*

HALO: On a C130 just prior to a HALO jump

My poacher hunters: Nigerian Rangers of Kiangi National Park *(above)*

Baghdad: There was plenty of loot to be had in Baghdad: art, jewellery and gold, precious artefacts and lots of cash

Gaza: With Hamas attending a funeral

Certified: Third place award for Liberia civil war adventure

Nigeria patrol: In Nigeria, heading out on a poacher hunting patrol *(below left)*

City view: On the roof of the Al Hamra Hotel, Baghdad

Close call: Al Hamra Hotel, Baghdad bombing. My room just above my head *(left)*

Mentor: I spent a pleasant week working with Bob Shepherd and couldn't have had a better mentor for my purpose and responsibilities in Israel and Palestine

Liberia: A full-on battle was about to break out, and my CNN team and I would find ourselves on the front line

Yemen: I'd never been to Yemen before. It was a hot, sleepy desert of a place

Greenpeace: I was sent to Colombo, Sri Lanka to spend a week on board the Greenpeace vessel Esperanza, advising on how to deal with Somali pirates

Nigerian Delta: With CNN to interview militant group, MEND

High-profile tasks: Kofi and Nane Annan in Palestine. This turned out to be one of the most stressful tasks I've ever run

Bourdain in Gaza: He was a greatly troubled man, but very entertaining to share a few private hours with

CM Training: In Jakarta lecturing media organisations on Kidnap and Ransom

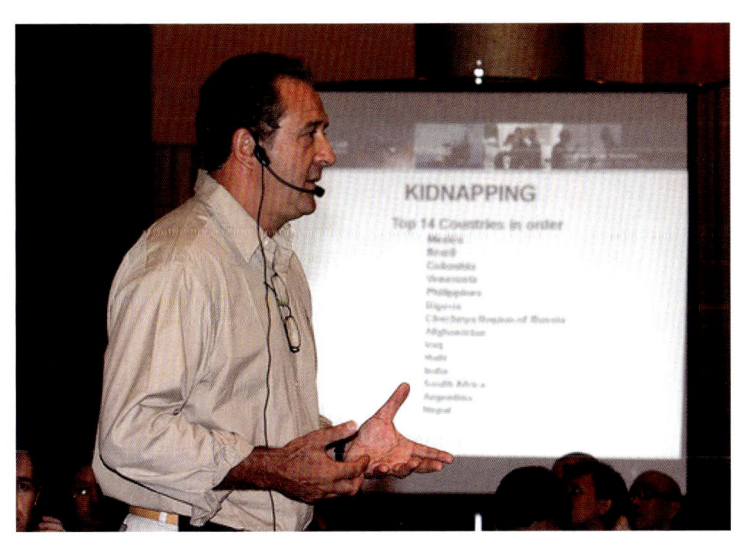

Ramallah: Getting a CNN news team through the IDF defenses to interview Yasser Arafat was a challenge

The Congo: The destination was deep inside the unstable Democratic Republic of the Congo (DRC) and the client was CNN's top domestic anchor and journalist, Anderson Cooper

China: Lecturing Chinese shipping companies on maritime security

ment soldiers were gathered there in their familiar black jackets and berets.

They looked surprised to see us as we drove in and parked beside a small structure that had been the forecourt kiosk. I climbed out. The commander, a fat, squat man, came over to meet me. He looked cheerful. We shook hands. He'd seen our CNN card in the window and remarked on it.

He explained he was a general in charge of defending the bridge. It wasn't uncommon in Africa to meet a general in the field in charge of only a handful of soldiers, since general was often a euphemism for boss. I asked how many troops he had. He said there were some by the river keeping watch. So not many. There were no vehicles suggesting they'd been dropped off.

I asked about LURD. He was quite casual when he said they were coming. I asked if he was expecting reinforcements. He didn't know. I asked if he intended to blow up the bridge. He shook his head firmly at the suggestion. There were two possible reasons for that. Road bridges were precious – they were built by foreigners and couldn't be replaced to the same standard, if at all. The second reason, and the more probable one, was that they had no explosives.

While we were chatting, I heard a distant sound that was familiar though I couldn't quite place it. A faint metallic clunk or pop. Whenever I recall that moment, standing with the general on the forecourt, it frustrates me that I didn't recognise the sound quickly enough. I should've thrown myself to the ground immediately. It came again a second later. A couple of seconds after that there was an explosion 50 metres to my left among the dense foliage as I faced the bridge. The soldiers dropped flat to the ground. The familiar sound had been a mortar firing from its base plate less than a kilometre away.

For whatever reason, I don't know why, I was filled with that foolhardy bravado that we are sometimes afflicted by. I suppose it was brought on by the soldiers diving in desperation to the ground. I refused to do the same. You often hear stories of soldiers in the midst of battle who refuse to even flinch, let alone take cover. I had one of those moments. It's not bravery or fearlessness at all. It's self-important arrogance. I stood there, unflinching, as a second shell exploded to the right of me, not far beyond the kiosk. My vehicle, with Pad curled up in a ball on his seat behind the wheel, was fortunately this side of it. The third explosion was 40 metres in front of me, close to the river, again in the dense foliage. The fourth and final mortar of that particular set landed 70 metres behind me on the edge of the road.

The soldiers scrambled away and I walked smartly to my vehicle. LURD was definitely on its way.

I jumped in beside Pad, who was visibly shaken. He needed no further instructions as we screeched out of the forecourt and onto the dirt road, wheels spinning as we accelerated back the way we'd come.

I kept looking back, expecting the rebels to appear any second, but as we took the bend I saw nothing on the bridge.

We hit the straight and I could see Jeff standing beside the vehicle up ahead. We came to a sharp stop beside them. I suggested we get going and Jeff asked if we had time to do a stand-up. I shouldn't have been surprised. He was as anxious as the rest of us to get away but the opportunity could not be missed.

LIBERIA

The road was still clear back to the bend. Perhaps LURD was taking its sweet time to secure the bridge. We would have a good lead on them as long as we sped away the moment they came into view.

'Emmy, Emmy, Emmy,' I said, referring to the award I knew Jeff coveted. He smirked. It was to become a running joke between us throughout the rest of the adventure whenever he prepared for a stand-up.

'One take only,' I insisted.

Jeff agreed. The drivers sat behind their steering wheels ready to go, engines running. While Jeff stood in front of the camera and said his piece, I kept vigil, staring towards the Po bridge, wondering about the fate of those government soldiers. I didn't doubt they'd already fled into the jungle. That's when we heard the shooting.

We piled into the vehicles and drove away at speed.

A mile down the road we finally met the government response to the invasion. We'd been half an hour ahead of the army. A dozen military vehicles and a couple of hundred troops were clambering to set up a defensive position on the entrance to a town.

The soldiers waved us through as they set up machine-guns and took up firing positions, aiming down the road we'd just come along. We carried on into the town and as we got to the other end of the large market square I told Pad to pull off to the side of the road so that we could see what might develop.

Jeff was clamouring to do another stand-up. There was no stopping him. More troops were arriving. A battle would make a dramatic backdrop for his report. We still appeared to be the only news people around. I assumed the government troops could hold off any attack, for a while at least. I was so wrong.

The cameraman set up his tripod while Jeff rehearsed his piece. As he faced the camera and opened his mouth to make his introduction, all hell broke loose. LURD, it seemed, had been tearing down the road in a host of vehicles not far behind us. They arrived at the government defensive line like a herd of rampaging elephants. They hit Taylor's troops with everything they had. Heavy vehicle-mounted machine-gun fire tore into the defenders, followed by rebel footsoldiers pouring from their vehicles.

LURD crashed through the defensive line with ease. As I stepped from our position to see what was happening, bullets splattered along the road in front of us. Some soldiers crouching by a shipping container metres away were shot to pieces, the heavy-calibre bullets ripping through the container with a deafening staccato so loud it had us all dropping for cover. We were instantly in the thick of battle.

I yelled for everyone to get into the vehicles. Nobody needed to be told, except for the producer who for some reason was trying to crawl beneath one of them. I pulled him out, repeating my command as I climbed in beside Pad. The opposite side of the road was under intense fire. To drive off was potentially lethal but to remain meant we'd surely be butchered along with the soldiers.

Pad tore out onto the road, wheels spinning, and floored the accelerator. I couldn't take my eyes off the other vehicle tight behind us, willing it not to get hit. If one of us got stopped, the other would have to stop too.

Explosions began hitting the marketplace, LURD's mortars

engaging. I don't remember seeing a single rebel in those few seconds. Everything happened so fast it was a blur. If any soldiers survived it would only be because they ran off into the swamps.

We were soon around a bend and out of the line of fire. I talked as calmly as I could to Pad, getting him to slow down a little. I didn't think LURD would pause for long in that village. They'd want to keep the momentum going all the way to the city.

We passed several military vehicles packed with soldiers heading north. The poor bastards were driving to their deaths. As we crossed the Saint Paul River Bridge the city came into view. Handfuls of civilians were on the streets outside houses as if curious about what was happening. They could hear distant gunfire and explosions. Oddly, they didn't appear to be in a panic. I couldn't fathom it. Run, for fuck's sake. Hide. We kept going at speed.

A mile further on we passed the Freeport, Monrovia's seaport. The two long concrete bridges into the city were coming up. As we closed on them I was astounded by what I saw. The road, a broad one, houses and businesses tightly together on either side, was literally packed with people. Hundreds of them, coming over the bridges. As we got closer, my estimate grew to a thousand or more. What was even more extraordinary was their behaviour. Instead of fear, I was astounded to see them filled with jubilation. Cheering, riotous, euphoric. It was utterly bizarre. Behind us, just out of sight, was a juggernaut of death, a bloodthirsty army of heavily armed rebels intent on destroying their city, and these people were surging towards it, rejoicing as if they were at a gospel gathering.

FIRST INTO ACTION AGAIN

We had no choice but to stop as the mob reached and encircled us, banging joyously on our windows as it flowed past. A solid mass of humanity was coming over the bridges like an unstoppable river of lava. They passed us singing, grinning broadly, inviting us to join them. Armed government soldiers were among them. It was extraordinary. The atmosphere was positively carnival. We had no idea what was going on. They surely couldn't be welcoming the rebels. There could be no doubt of their fate when LURD arrived. Thousands would die. There'd be raping and pillaging on a huge scale. Was it some kind of delusional belief that their sheer joy might turn the evil tide? My entire team, drivers included, were mystified.

I opened my door and stood on the seat to get a better look. People packed the bridges as they came our way. The city was emptying. Everyone was delirious with joy, jiving, butt-bouncing, fist-pumping, singing, their hands aloft as if in prayer.

Unable to go forward against this tide of humanity, we climbed out of our vehicles. Jeff and I looked at each other. Our blank expressions said it all.

I was mobbed by revellers. A young woman threw herself at me, screaming, in tears, repeatedly thanking me. She hugged me but was so overcome by emotion she couldn't stand and slid down my legs, sobbing with relief. It was as if I was a super-celebrity of some kind. Jeff caught the moment on camera.

A young man was thanking me profusely. I asked him what he meant by it. He cried repeatedly: 'The Americans are coming! They have arrived at the Freeport to save Monrovia. It's a miracle. God has saved us!'

I was being mobbed because they thought I was one of the American liberators, having come from the direction of the port. It was utter madness. There were no Americans. We'd just come past the port. We hadn't seen any troops or US warships. If they were coming, the embassy attaché would certainly have told us. Somehow, wishful thinking had turned into rumour and then fact. The news had spread that the Americans were here and people ran from their houses, converging on the port to greet them, despite LURD.

There was nothing we could do. We were in the midst of uncontrollable mass hysteria. Nothing I could say would influence the crowd. We watched helplessly as people continued to surge past us towards the port. I could see smoke on the horizon in the direction we'd come from.

As Jeff and I were discussing what to do next, a stand-up foremost on his mind of course, an explosion ripped into the crowd on the broad main road, 50 metres away in the direction of the port. I spun around in time to see several bodies flung into the air.

The crowd stalled, stupefied. The cheering quickly abated, to be replaced by the sound of gunfire in the distance. Seconds later, another mortar exploded among some nearby buildings.

It was as if a switch had been flicked. In an instant the crowd went from jubilation to panic. People who'd been dancing and cheering seconds earlier turned and ran screaming back towards the city.

A few seconds later, bullets tore into the crowd. Screams filled the air. I stood on my seat again to see bodies lying on the ground. More bullets smacked into the crowd.

The people surrounding us lurched back towards the bridge. I shouted for Pad to get going and we moved along with the human mass. Those still coming from the city collided with those desperately trying to get back. Soon everyone got the same message from the explosions and gunfire.

We moved along with the crowd, trying not to run anyone over. We were soon on the bridge and making our way to the other side. I phoned the embassy attaché to report what was happening. He told me LURD was also attacking the city from the north-east. If they succeeded in pushing through to the sea, they'd cut the city off from the airport.

We reached the south side of the Gabriel Tucker Bridge and pulled over. Jeff needed that stand-up. Everyone pulled on their body armour and helmets. The gunfire and explosions were concentrated on the other side of the bridge where we'd been moments earlier. As Jeff faced the camera and began his report, I concentrated on the bridge, looking for signs of LURD coming across it. It looked like enough government troops had finally arrived to stall LURD's advance. Civilians were running for their lives back towards the city. Hundreds must have died already. The numbers coming over the bridge soon dwindled. People stood scattered around on our side, catching their breath, confused, distraught, some of them wounded. Many must have lived on the Freeport side and were now wondering where to head for, since they were homeless and without their belongings.

Government forces finally arrived on our side of the bridge in numbers and began to entrench, while others headed across to support their colleagues where the fight was raging.

Jeff managed to complete his stand-up despite the constant interruptions from people begging us for help. All we could do was urge them to move away into the city and direct the wounded to the hospital, which was surely overflowing by now as it had been full when we visited it a few days before.

Bullets began to reach our side of the bridges, slapping through treetops and into nearby roofs. It was time to move out.

As we climbed into the vehicles, a woman came up to us, holding out a young boy in her arms. He was covered in blood and struggling to breathe. There were wounded people all around us, slumped on the ground as if they'd lost all hope.

The producer urged me to do what I could for them. That was frankly ridiculous. He was just saying it because he felt he should. We only had enough medical supplies to dress a few wounds.

I was keenly aware that we might soon need them ourselves and were lucky not to have needed any already. It was ruthless of me, but I couldn't abandon the team to set up a medical centre administering aid to all and sundry in the middle of a battlefield with a handful of dressings. LURD could storm over the bridge at any moment. Most of the wounded were beyond my meagre skills and equipment anyway. We had to get out of there or we were all dead.

As if to underline the urgency, more bullets struck a nearby building. People screamed, scrambling for cover. I shouted for the others to get into the vehicles. I climbed in beside Pad and we sped away, leaving the wretched woman and her dying child to watch us go. Playing the callous protector was a harder role than I had ever expected.

We sped through the streets, climbing a steep hill in the direction of our hotel which was on the other side of a ridge that ran east-west through the middle of the city. This meant that the south side wasn't in a direct line of fire from the north where the two bridges were located. But according to the attaché, LURD had 82mm mortars with a range of up to seven kilometres. That meant the entire city would be in range even if LURD didn't cross the bridges.

One of my responsibilities on arrival in a hostile environment was to create an Emergency Evacuation Plan or EEP. There were four options when it came to evacuations: escape by land, air or sea, or to stay put. Liberia was clearly too dangerous a place to stay put. Nobody would be safe if LURD broke into the city. I was equally worried about the government soldiers once they'd run out of supplies.

A road escape with the aim of crossing a border would require driving through rebel territory as well as along unknown and poor-quality roads. So that was out.

I initially had high hopes for a sea evacuation. I'd paid a visit to the Freeport the day after we arrived and took a walk along the jetty inspecting various vessels, fishing boats in particular. It wasn't long before I found several captains who, for $1,000, would take us and our equipment to Freetown in Sierra Leone, 270 miles along the coast. But the port was now in the hands of LURD so that was out.

When we first arrived at the airport I made a point of making contact with the person in charge and getting his number. The airport was now our only option.

Serious as the situation was, we weren't quite at the point of evacuation. We still had a job to do. This was big news and we were in the heart of it.

When we got back to the hotel there was pandemonium. A number of news teams had been caught out in the city when LURD attacked. Many were still out there. Everyone had stories of death and destruction. There were rumours that reporters had been killed or captured. The air was filled with the constant sound of explosions and gunfire. Nowhere was safe.

We remained in or close to the hotel over the next few days. Everyone was anxious about how things might develop. The big question was whether the government troops could keep LURD from sacking the city. Some reporters and photographers ventured out but the story remained the same – lots of dead and wounded, but LURD was being held off from breaking into the city proper.

I called AKE Hereford to warn them that my evacuation options were, for the moment at least, compromised. One of the ops guys knew of a private Russian helicopter charter company in Sierra Leone and gave them a call. The head guy, a Ukrainian, said he could send a Mi-8 Hip to pick us up and fly us to Sierra Leone. The pilot didn't seem to mind that the pick-up would be in the middle of a war zone. All he needed was a time and place and $40,000 in cash. We had enough dollars to pay him but he wanted it up front, in his hands, cash or gold, otherwise he wouldn't leave Sierra Leone. CNN Atlanta didn't want us to leave just yet, but they gave the green light for AKE to send someone to Sierra Leone with the money in case we had to.

For the next week we lived in a city under siege. The government troops continued to prevent LURD from crossing the bridges in the north or entering from the north-east, but by all accounts it was a tenuous hold. Mortars constantly rained down on the city. The body-count mounted daily. We were hearing figures in the many hundreds. The few times we ventured out, we came across destroyed homes and body parts in the streets. The mortar explosions were random but continuous. Four or five an hour on average. Fires burned day and night and the smoke-filled air never cleared.

Nowhere in the city was safe from mortars, including our hotel. Most of the building was on the ground level, with a tin roof. If we were hit there'd be no protection and it was purely down to luck whether we were hit or not.

One evening we were having dinner in the garden patio when a mortar landed close enough to blow away the palm fronds that decorated a bamboo framework above the table. The mortar had landed below us on the other side of an embankment, close to the beach road. Five people in a hut were killed, pieces of their flesh landing in the restaurant garden. A couple of metres short and it would've landed on us. We went back into the hotel, shocked at the near-miss, but it didn't really matter where we hung out. The bar seemed as good a place as any.

A girl reporting for the BBC arrived in an emotional state after spending several hours on the streets looking for a story. She was a shaking, babbling mess and described how there'd been a sudden burst of machine-gun fire and an explosion. She took cover behind a tree and something struck the branches above her. She looked up to see a mortar stuck nose-first in the 'Y' of the trunk. Had it detonated, she would've been killed. Everyone had a story to tell of a close call. Most would have left the country by then if they could. But as long as the last junction to the airport road remained in the hands of LURD, everyone was stuck in the city.

As the days ticked away, the threat of LURD breaking through remained. And with it the fear that if LURD didn't kill us they'd loot our equipment, leaving us unable to report the story. The news was getting repetitive anyway. Bullets, bombs and bodies, followed by more of the same.

I called AKE to find out how the Russian helicopter option was coming along. The Russians had raised the price to $65,000 on account of the increased danger and, although CNN had agreed to the price hike, we were still waiting on our man with the cash to arrive in Sierra Leone.

The following day I saw a helicopter fly past, low over the sea. It was a Mi-8 Hip. I called AKE, who called the Russians, who told them the deal was off. They had two helicopters and the American Embassy had paid for the exclusive rights to both. Since the Americans had no helicopters of their own in the region, they hired the Russians to fly in a cadre of US Marines from Sierra Leone and to remain on call. My helo option had closed. If it came to the point where I had to get the team out, I couldn't. There had to be another option.

In the meantime the locals had turned resentful towards the Americans for not defending them against LURD. Hope had turned to rage. They began piling dead bodies against the walls of the US Embassy. A rumour going around the hotel was that Ambassador Blaney was making plans to evacuate the embassy. I didn't want to call the attaché on it. If it was true and he didn't want to confirm it, it would compromise what little relationship we had. If true, it would suggest LURD was getting the upper hand. But then, if the embassy was thinking of bugging out, it would be the best place to be. A new perspective might also refresh the story.

I phoned the attaché to ask for sanctuary for my team. I felt justified. CNN was a US network. I didn't tell him I was the only US citizen in the seven-man team, an honour I had been granted during my Hollywood days. The attaché was resistant at first but then decided to kick that ball upstairs. He got back to me an hour later with permission from the ambassador to allow us in, as long as we didn't bring any locals with us.

I put it to Jeff and the producer, who were immediately up for it. We loaded our gear on two of the vehicles. The embassy wouldn't let us set up a satellite dish so we left it packed in our third vehicle at the hotel along with our drivers.

I passed through the hotel lobby, which was full of media people hanging around, generally looking forlorn, trapped in the city like we were. The embassy was a much safer option and I suddenly felt guilty not sharing it with them. Perhaps one or two might want to join us. I climbed onto the bar and called for everyone's attention. I announced that CNN was evacuating to the US embassy and anyone was welcome to join us. The attaché was only expecting the seven of us, but I was confident I could squeeze in a few extra.

Twenty minutes later, I left the hotel and headed along the beach road to our CNN 4x4s. I was stunned to see some 20 more vehicles parked behind them, ready to depart. I walked down the line to get an idea of how many people there were and counted 50 or so.

Shit!

I winced at the thought of telling the attaché. I had to call him to let him know. He was horrified and told me there was no way that many people could enter the embassy.

I didn't have the courage to tell everyone their invitation had been rescinded. They'd packed their bags and checked out of the hotel, like us, ready to go.

Fuck it. I decided not to say anything and leave it to the

attaché to send them away. The mortars appeared to have paused for the occasion. As I walked down the line of vehicles, ensuring all were ready to depart, I felt like some kind of Wild West wagon train boss, whipping the pioneers into line before heading off into the unknown.

When we finally got going, I led the convoy at 10 miles an hour. The Pied Piper of Liberia, someone joked. The embassy was less than half a mile away but I wanted to keep the vehicles tightly together. We crawled along the practically empty streets, up a steep incline and halted outside the main vehicle entrance to the embassy. I was hoping the gates would be open and the guards waiting for us, but there wasn't a soul outside. The dead bodies had been cleared.

I climbed out and banged on the main gate. No-one answered. Everyone in the convoy was looking at me. Perhaps the attaché had decided to ignore us completely. The mortars started up again but on the other side of the city. The rhythmic boom and clatter of distant machine-guns was an ominous backdrop. I knocked again.

A small hatch in the gate opened and, like some 1920s speakeasy, I was asked what I wanted. They had to be kidding me. I explained what I was doing there and that the attaché knew we were coming. The hatch closed. A moment later it opened again. This time it was the guard commander and I had the same conversation with him. The hatch shut again

I waited patiently, forcing a reassuring smile back towards the convoy. After several minutes a door in the gate was unlocked and creaked open. The attaché stepped out onto the street to look at the convoy for himself. He seemed vexed. The end of the line of vehicles was out of sight. He wanted to know how many there were. I told him. He was silent for a moment then said there was no way they were all getting into the embassy. I asked him how many could enter and who he would turn away. The poor guy was just saying no because this was all new ground to him. He went back inside and the door closed behind him.

The ABC correspondent decided to record a stand-up about the situation. I was part of the report. Several producers and reporters ambled over to ask me what was happening. I told them to be patient and return to their vehicles. I had no idea what was going on. The mortars continued but still on the other side of the city.

Some 20 minutes passed before the door in the gate opened again and the guard commander emerged onto the street. In his dry manner, he said that the ambassador had invited us all to enter. I was relieved. He explained that every vehicle was to be searched. There must be no weapons, no locals, no contraband. Any failure to comply would result in rejection.

It took at least three hours for all the vehicles and personnel to pass through the security checks. The mortar fire continued throughout but nothing landed nearby.

Come early evening we were congregated in the main bar/restaurant area, which is where we were to stay. Army camp beds and meals were provided, and the bar was open. The Yanks were very hospitable, as per usual in my experience. We gathered to listen to a talk by the US Marine commander, a lady, Major Sandusky, who gave us a brief on the rules and regulations. She was exactly what you would expect from a female Marine major, coarse and tough as old boots. She didn't attempt to hide her disdain for the media. I presented myself as the point of contact for the group. Everyone was pleased to hear that the embassy's focus would be on getting everyone out of there.

The following day the first mortar round entered the embassy grounds, exploding near an administration block, causing several injuries but no fatalities. It made the news of course. There was little else to report. A rumour circled that the mortar had been fired by Taylor's troops to convey their displeasure that the US hadn't arrived to assist them. I suspect the rumour started in the embassy bar. I felt the criticism would have been better directed at ECOWAS (the Economic Community of West African States), which had pledged to send support to Liberia but had failed to. The mortar was a concern since the roof of the bar where we were living was no more than corrugated metal sheeting. We were no safer against mortar attack than back in the hotel.

I wondered how the embassy would respond if LURD banged on the doors demanding entry. I'm sure the embassy had war-gamed such a scenario, along with others, which is why they flew in the extra Marines.

The following day the ambassador kindly made the Russian helicopters available to fly everyone to Freetown, Sierra Leone. The shuttle run would take several days. As people began lining up, my team gathered in the bar to discuss whether they should leave right away or not. Jeff pointed out, quite passionately, that the story was still popular and reporting it was why we were there. Brent Sadler's engineer voiced his concern about leaving the sat dish. We wouldn't be able to get it on the chopper. But no-one else gave a shit about Brent's dish.

In order to accurately report what was going on in the city, we needed to see for ourselves. I offered my usual pros and cons. Bottom line was I didn't think we should be in town if LURD arrived and the embassy was evacuated. We still had a day to mull it over.

I had identified a possible way of venturing out into the city in relative safety. The embassy had a civilian armoured 4x4, but what was interesting was the guy who drove it. I'd noticed him walking through the grounds, a sturdy, confident, intelligent-looking man, long-haired, always in adventure clothing, with a carefree attitude. He always looked alert. Everything about him cried 'Spook' or Special Forces.

The next time I saw him I took the opportunity to intercept him. I came straight out with my pitch, revealing I was former UK Special Forces. He didn't skip a beat as we walked on, merely asking if I was Hereford or Poole. It confirmed he wasn't the embassy janitor. He was smart enough not to try to bullshit me with some cover story. I'd worked enough with our US cousins not to feel like an intruder. Nor did he make me feel like one.

I explained my job with CNN and asked if he'd take us out in his armoured 4x4 for a few hours. He chuckled at my audacity. But after some chat he decided that, although we couldn't use his vehicle, it would be okay if we followed him on one of his reconnaissance drives. He'd take point since he was bullet-proof. He was being exceedingly generous.

The following day Jeff, his Kenyan cameraman, Neil and I jumped into our 4x4 with me at the wheel and the Spook led us out of the embassy. He was most considerate of our soft skin as we cruised through the city and was clearly a man of experience. Machine-gun fire and the occasional boom of a mortar were constant. He approached each junction carefully, inching into it, and when he was happy he'd pass through and I'd follow.

The streets were largely deserted, rubble and trash everywhere, the occasional dead body. There were a lot of destroyed homes. Smoke filled the air. There were no other cars moving and we drew attention from locals as we drove along.

We turned into a broad street where several youths were gathered at the side of the road. As we passed them, something struck the vehicle. At first I thought it was a stray bullet. Then I realised it had been a stone. Another followed, accompanied by gestures and verbal abuse. We were being punished because we were CNN. Our crime: failing to bring in American soldiers. Heroes one day, bad guys the next. We removed the CNN cards from our windows.

The Spook paused at a junction. After nosing slowly into it, he suddenly reversed out of it and halted. Bullets were flying in random bursts through the junction into the buildings beyond and he almost caught some. We were at the crest of the ridge. The junction was in the line of direct fire.

The Spook backed up alongside us to tell me the junction was the limit of our journey. We were safe where we were so Jeff wanted to do a stand-up, using the flying bullets as a dramatic backdrop. Emmy, Emmy, Emmy! The Spook agreed to wait for us. It seemed he didn't have much else to do that day and was somewhat interested in our work.

Jeff's cameraman was a pleasant, softly spoken young lad who hardly engaged with us but, so far, had done his job to Jeff's satisfaction. His only experiences were African assignments but it was clear he was new to conflict zones. What we didn't know, and what he'd successfully hidden from us so far, was that he was utterly terrified. There we were, in the midst of this madness, explosions and gunfire all around us as we went about our daily routines, and all the while it had been gradually driving the boy to the edge of a breakdown.

While we were preparing for the stand-up, with mortars falling in the distance and bullets randomly spitting through the junction metres from us, he finally cracked. He picked up his camera and started walking at a casual pace towards the deadly junction. Neil noticed him first. I only realised something was wrong when I saw Neil hurrying towards the lad, calling his name. The boy was unable to hear because his mind had blocked out all contact with reality. He stepped into the junction. Neil ran after him. It was an incredibly brave thing to do. A burst of gunfire could come at any moment. Neil grabbed the unresisting boy and firmly guided him back.

We got him back to the vehicle. He didn't respond to our questions. His expression was blank, his eyes hollow. He had no idea where he was or what was going on around him. It wasn't my first experience of traumatic stress syndrome but I'd never seen anyone do something like that before, the equivalent of calmly walking off a cliff. Neil sat with him in the vehicle as Jeff and I hurriedly packed up our gear. The cameraman's condition was a medical emergency. That changed the dynamics of our mission.

While we'd been gone, the embassy had been evacuating all non-essential staff. The two Russian Mi-8 helicopters maintained constant round trips to Sierra Leone, stopping when darkness fell.

That evening the bar was much quieter. The rest of the staff and media would get out over the next couple of days. We

LIBERIA

would be leaving with them. The cameraman was responding to questions by bedtime but it was clear he could lose it again at any moment.

Neil had meanwhile compiled an exciting and informative piece from our day out and sent it to Atlanta. We sat at the bar, watching the TV, sipping beers and waiting for the broadcast. CNN began with a report on Saddam Hussein's two sons, who were barricaded in a house in Mosul, refusing to surrender to the thousands of US troops surrounding them, while the world waited to see what would happen. The next big story was a fire on top of the Eiffel Tower. It was nothing spectacular, just a lot of smoke that was quickly brought under control. The news flipped between these two stories and others. Our producer arrived to let us know our Liberia story had been cut. There was no room for it in the slot. We were taken aback. We'd risked our lives that day for nothing.

It was definitely time to leave.

We packed everything in readiness to go. The engineer grumbled on about the dish back at the hotel. Jeff was taking the broadcast snub personally, moaning that he hadn't pushed the story enough for Atlanta to put it on air. It was a miserable evening.

The following morning the Russian helicopters didn't turn up. No reason was given. Every other major news network had left.

The battle for the city continued. Mortars were still landing dangerously close to the embassy. Several fell in the sea just off the beach, which made interesting viewing from the bar, which was the only place we could hang out.

I grew concerned about us not getting out at all. The airport was our only option. It was safer than the embassy, even if there were no flights. I just needed to know who had control of the last crossroads. If it was the government, it should be a simple case of driving through it.

I telephoned the airport operations officer I'd met when we first arrived. He was an amiable chap and explained the airport had remained safe throughout the conflict. A commercial flight had arrived from Ghana that morning and was due to return in the afternoon. I asked if there were seats on it and he chuckled that it was practically empty. He couldn't say when the next flight to Liberia would be after that. I asked him whether he would be able to hold the Ghana departure for me if I paid for seven first-class seats, in cash. He thought that buying seven first-class tickets would certainly encourage the airline to wait, although he did stress that the pilots would want to depart before the light started to fade.

News of the flight was encouraging. I set about trying to find out what I could about the last road junction to the airport. Apparently it had changed hands between LURD and the government several times. Taylor's troops still maintained control of the 30-mile-long airport road. Since the airport was surrounded by swampland, the road was the only way LURD could get to it. The obstacle was that last junction. The only way to find out who had control of it was to see for ourselves.

I put it to the team that the airport might be our only option for weeks. It also meant we could take the satellite dish. The engineer was keen. So was everyone else apart from Jeff, who remained ambivalent but agreed his cameraman had to get out asap.

As we loaded up the two vehicles in the embassy car park,

the producer dropped his money box. It burst open and $70,000, mostly in $100 bills, spilled out. I helped him retrieve it all, thinking how fortunate the mishap had occurred inside the embassy grounds and not on the street where we would have been lucky to rescue any of the cash. I collected around $20,000 but when I held it out to him he asked if I'd keep hold of it for him. He hated carrying all that money around. I had to pay the drivers when we were done anyway. It turned out to be fortuitous.

As I stuffed the money into my pockets I saw the Spook heading across a lawn towards his vehicle. I intercepted him and outlined my plan to get to the airport, hoping he might know something about the last junction. He said he was heading that way and would be happy to run point for us again. That was fabulous news. I explained we had to pick up the satellite dish from the hotel and he agreed to meet us there in half an hour.

We quickly loaded up our gear. As we drove out through the main gate the guard commander warned us that the embassy wasn't a hotel – leaving its grounds cancelled whatever sanctuary it had offered and we were not to come back. This really was to be an all-or-nothing run to the airport.

At the hotel I remained on the beach road with the two vehicles and our PTSD patient while the others went off to collect the rest of the gear. The Spook, accompanied by Major Sandusky in her Marine fatigues, arrived in their vehicle.

It started to rain heavily. I was soaked within seconds. Several mortars landed uncomfortably close. It had been quiet until we got there. Sandusky was impatient and shouted that she needed to get going. Armoured cars weren't proof against a direct mortar hit.

FIRST INTO ACTION AGAIN

I signalled for her to wait a moment as I hurried up the steep ramp towards the entrance, wondering what was taking so long.

I saw the team huddled under the hotel porch. As I got closer I could see they were engaged in a heated discussion. Jeff was having a change of heart about leaving, believing the story was still worth covering and was trying to persuade Neil to be his cameraman. Jeff couldn't stay without the producer, who wanted to leave. This was a crazy time to start a debate about a decision that had already been made.

A shout came from behind me. Sandusky was standing there in the rain, yelling at me to 'get my ass moving'. I begged a few more minutes. She replied with an expletive, declared that I was wasting her time, and climbed back into the armoured vehicle. Then she and the Spook took off.

I was now pissed off. I stormed over to the news team and interrupted their debate, explaining that the cameraman needed to get out of the country before he lost his marbles entirely. I added that there was no question of the team splitting up, with some going and some staying, because I was responsible for everyone and couldn't be in two places at once. The conversation was over. We headed for the vehicles as the rain continued to pour down. There was more drama to come.

We had a number of drivers with us, all desperate to escape the city along with their wives and girlfriends. The vehicles were fully loaded and with the extra bodies the tyres looked like they might burst. I shouted that any driver who wasn't behind a steering wheel couldn't come with us. I told them to get out of the vehicles, along with their families and belongings.

Their response took me by surprise.

One of the drivers knelt on the road in front of me in the

downpour, hands clasped in prayer, begging me not to leave him behind. A couple of others joined him, looking at me with sorrowful expressions. I'd never experienced anything like it in my life. Their heart-rending cries showed just how traumatised these people were. It was incredibly harrowing. I was no-one to be prayed to. They made me feel like a monster. The rest of the CNN team were looking at me. Of course I had no problem taking them. But the cold pragmatist in me had calculated that if I let the drivers and their families come with us it would jeopardise everyone's safety on the 35-mile ride to the airport, assuming we could get through the junction.

But how do you refuse a bunch of people on their knees, hands clasped tightly, pleading with you in sheer desperation?

I caved, having absorbed their misery for weeks, and told them to get back into the vehicles, families included. On condition, I added, that if we had a flat tyre they would move like lightning to fix it. They leapt to their feet, swearing to do everything they could to ensure we all made it to the airport.

It was madness. We were screwed.

After a swift redistribution of weight everyone was aboard. I stood back to look at the tyres and shook my head in despair. There was no way we were going to make it. But there was nothing else for it. There were no other vehicles I could commandeer. No time to look for extra tyres. This was it. We set off for the dreaded junction.

The mortars and machine-gun fire seemed to get heavier as we headed into the east side of the city. Nothing landed close to us but they always seemed to fall just up ahead. The first flat tyre came within a mile of leaving the hotel. I had to hand it to the guys. They replaced it like a Formula One race team. Half a mile further on, we had another. We had one spare tyre left and we weren't even halfway to the junction. To call the situation stressful would be an understatement. We had no choice but to press on and hope the gods were with us.

As we closed on the ominous junction, the sound of bullets flying above our heads grew louder. The ground had levelled out this far east and we'd lost the protection of the ridge. The bullets weren't aimed at us but were coming from a battle raging somewhere to the north.

I stopped the vehicles, climbed out, and told everyone to stay put while I went ahead to take a look at the junction. The rain had stopped. There was sporadic gunfire but I couldn't see a living soul.

I crouched as I moved forward. A bullet zinged off the road nearby. It was a horrible walk. The road was lined by trees on my left and houses on my right. There were a few parked cars, all of them riddled with bullets or shrapnel. I moved forward, using them for cover when I could. Fifty metres from the vehicles I could make out the junction the same distance ahead. I moved beside a tree to take a good look at it. Still no sign of life. Several vehicles were abandoned around the junction, some sandbag firing positions had been built. But no people. I would've expected someone to be there, given the significance of the position.

My phone rang in my pocket. I looked at the screen. To my surprise, it was the Spook. I quickly answered. He'd driven through the junction a few minutes earlier and said it was currently in nobody's hands, but would be snapped up by one side or the other soon enough.

There was no time to waste. I ran back to the vehicles, shouting

LIBERIA

at them to start up. If we had a flat on the way, they were to keep going – everyone was to get out and push if needed. We had to get through. They were all wide-eyed, tense and well aware of the significance of this next stage of the journey.

We drove towards the junction at an easy speed. Smoke drifted along the road and the gunfire remained constant. My eyes were everywhere as we arrived. The junction was indeed empty. We rumbled through, nose to tail, taking the turn towards the airport. I looked back at the other vehicles anxiously, willing everything to just keep moving.

A few hundred metres beyond the junction my vehicle began to shudder. We had a flat and came to a stop. The other vehicles stopped behind us. The guys raced into action once more and replaced the tyre in record time. It was our last spare but at least we were on the home straight.

Just then a 4x4 headed towards us from the direction of the airport. It was the Spook and Sandusky. He gave me a smile and a wave as he drove past. Sandusky was po-faced, of course. I grinned and waved back and he was gone. I never saw or heard from him again.

Whoever you were, wherever you are now, many thanks!

With the tyre fixed, we jumped back in the vehicles and off we drove. Apart from the threat of another flat tyre, there was one more obstacle to overcome. The government checkpoints. I never saw them as a major threat, more of an unknown quantity. They could wave us through, or be a pain and make life difficult for us. All I was thinking of was whether the aircraft would still be waiting for us.

The first checkpoint we came to, the soldier on duty was an arse. He asked all kinds of stupid questions: Where were we going? Why were we going to the airport? My patience had worn thin. I reached into my pocket, pulled out a wedge of cash, probably about $1,000, and threw it into the air above him. His buddies, sitting on their backsides nearby, leapt up and joined him in grabbing the bills off the ground. We drove away.

I didn't even bother talking to the next checkpoint guard, just threw dollars in the air as soon as we arrived. The producer was in the vehicle behind. I don't know if he approved or not. He never mentioned it. I thought it was a fair use of our funds.

We arrived at the airport and I was relieved to see the large Ghanaian commercial aircraft still waiting at the terminal. We didn't hang about. The producer hurried into the terminal to buy the tickets and the rest of the team got the 30-odd equipment boxes loaded onto trolleys and into check-in.

I gathered the drivers by the vehicles in order to pay them. Despite having reached the safety of the airport, they were all fearful for their futures. I owed them a couple of hundred dollars each. I still had a load of cash, minus whatever I had chucked at the checkpoint guards. It wasn't my money. The drivers needed some good news so I handed it all over. A thank you from CNN. If they were careful, the money would keep them and their families in food and shelter for a long time. They were overjoyed.

After saying our goodbyes, with lots of sincere hugs and best wishes, I made my way to the terminal. I felt immense relief, although I'd save my celebrations for when we were out of Liberian airspace.

We sat in the first-class lounge sipping chilled bottles of Heineken, classic elevator music playing in the background, waiting to be called to the aircraft. We were the only ones there.

LIBERIA

Despite the widespread desperation to escape the city, there were few passengers on the flight, a testimony to how difficult it was to move around.

The silence in the room was oppressive. I could see the last three weeks etched into every face – except for the Kenyan cameraman, who looked quite cheerful, perhaps because he had no idea where on Earth he was. I think everyone was reliving their worst moments, scarcely able to believe we had all made it out unscathed.

We boarded the aircraft and, as I walked down the aisle towards the front of the plane, I passed Pad sitting by a window in economy class. He'd used his share of the money to buy a ticket to Ghana to see if he could make a new life for himself. All he had were the clothes on his back, but he smiled with confidence. We shook hands firmly, grinning at the adventure we'd shared.

I sat in my seat, the engines rumbling, and managed to get a cellphone signal. I messaged AKE, letting them know we were on our way. Monrovia's mobile phone network worked perfectly well throughout the conflict for the simple reason that both sides relied on it for their communications. Neither bomb nor bullet passed anywhere close to the main mast, the ground beneath probably the safest place to sit out the battle.

The AKE operations manager had no idea what we'd been through and wanted to chat about when I might be ready to roll out on ops again. He needed me in Baghdad asap. I lived in Hunstanton, Norfolk, at that time. I was looking forward to getting home to my lady and baby daughter more than anything else… but the thought of heading into the war in Iraq did sound exciting.

FIRST INTO ACTION AGAIN

The plane rumbled along the runway, took off over the jungle and climbed steeply. I could see Monrovia but no sign of the devastation that was taking place. Pretty much the same view the rest of the world had of it.

A year later CNN sent me a National Headliner Award certificate for 'Continuing Coverage of a Major News Event – Crisis in Liberia'. For the purposes of the award, I was classed as a technician. I won third place.

8

IRAQ

AS THE GULF WAR THAT brought down Saddam Hussein was coming to an end, the only way into Baghdad for a civilian was by road. CNN had set up a bureau at the Palestine Hotel in the heart of the city. Fox News, soon to become an AKE client, had taken a floor in the Sheraton Hotel, the biggest in Baghdad, in the same compound as the Palestine. Most international media were accommodated in one or the other.

The two main routes to Baghdad were from Turkey or Jordan. The latter, the most popular with us, began in Amman after arrival by plane. This was followed by a four-hour drive to the border at Trebil, which could take minutes or hours to cross, depending on traffic. We swapped our Jordanian vehicles and drivers for Iraqi ones and drove another four hours along Highway 10 to Baghdad. Other than a collapsed flyover that forced a short cross-country detour, the roads between Amman and Baghdad were in great condition. The only hazards were the bandits who began operating along a 200km stretch west of Ramadi soon after the route was opened.

FIRST INTO ACTION AGAIN

Initially, the Ali Babas, as they were called, targeted local tradesmen or fleeing civilians carrying all their earthly belongings. When westerners began pouring in – private security personnel, businessmen and media people – it was obvious they all carried US dollars since it was the only currency accepted and there were no banks or credit-card facilities. For the bandits, it seemed like open season. Iraq was utterly lawless, with no police or internal security forces. Like the early post-war days of Kabul, it was the Wild West. The coalition forces did little to police the country, still busy hunting down pockets of resistance and reorganising. The bandits were a growing problem for the rest of us.

AKE had always had a 'no weapons' policy when working with the media. We sought to mitigate risk using non-lethal solutions. We endured the risk of bandits initially because it was assumed that, once the war was over, life would return to some level of normality and an internal security system would emerge. The assumption was flawed. Iraq, Afghanistan and later Syria, would force us to change our weapons policy.

The motorway between the Jordanian border and Ramadi ran through wide-open, generally flat, stony desert – 250 miles of sand and rocks with the occasional turn-off and fuel station. During one of AKE's early trips along that highway, two operators, both former SAS, were pulled over at gunpoint by four Iraqi thugs. A couple of the bandits pushed the boys into the sand to search them while the other two went through their baggage. The lads managed to deck one of them and escaped on foot into the desert.

The bandits drove in pursuit, caught them and gave them a beating. They forced them to kneel with pistols against their

IRAQ

heads and told them they were to be executed. The lads were fortunate. Although the bandit they'd punched insisted on killing them, the gang leader chose to let them go. Up until then no westerner had been killed by the bandits. It was only a matter of time before something would snap. The bandits were never going to fare well against some of the types of men increasingly taking that stretch of motorway.

It wasn't hard to find weapons in Iraq at the end of the war. Guns were lying on the ground in places. An AK47 in good condition could fetch little more than $25. After the bandit incident, the next time an AKE member drove down Highway 10, he carried a pistol and an assault rifle. This was without the official consent of Hereford or CNN Atlanta. The lads had asked for permission but it had been denied, despite the motorway incident and warnings of worse to come. It was a classic example of the powers that be sitting back in the comfort and safety of their homes while failing to grasp the realities of the environment they were sending employees into. CNN was clinging to an outdated moral high ground.

Despite 9/11 and many other atrocities committed in the name of Allah, many in the West remained in denial about the ruthlessness of Islamic extremism. Those of us on the ground, in Afghanistan and Iraq, could see what was happening. A classic power vacuum was unfolding, first filled by criminals, then by religious and/or political zealots. We couldn't hide the weapons from our CNN staff, but they were grateful for the protection and kept the guns a secret from Atlanta.

A week before I arrived, an AKE lad, former SAS, was being driven to Baghdad by a CNN Iraqi driver when a couple of bandits pulled alongside, waving their pistols and signalling the driver to pull over. The AKE lad, a no-nonsense veteran of Northern Ireland and Oman who was fluent in Arabic, regarded the bandits coldly. I knew him from many years before, having completed a three-week survival course with him in Hereford. He was a private individual who didn't mix easily with others. A loner. Calm and competent. He showed little emotion, rarely smiling, and was quite ruthless.

He wound down his window and shot both bandits in the head. I don't imagine his heartbeat changed much as he wound his window back up. The bandits' car careened off the motorway behind him and rolled into the desert. It was his driver who told the story. The lad wouldn't have bothered.

It was not to be an isolated incident. AKE wasn't the only private security company tooling up. Several bandits suffered similar outcomes. The bandits kept at it for a while because they needed to make a living. These were hard times. They altered their tactics, took a more cautious approach. They became more aggressive, firing warning shots, shooting tyres, working in teams. The private security teams responded by coordinating convoys, utilising mutual support, communicating between vehicles. The bandits took to ignoring vehicles that looked like they might be private security and focused on soft targets such as a family on its own.

CNN eventually accepted there was a need for us to defend ourselves and gave its blessing to carrying weapons – for AKE personnel only of course.

I arrived in Iraq after Liberia, about the time bandit activity was peaking. I must've done the run between Amman and Baghdad a dozen times and never encountered a single highwayman. I also enjoyed many trips to the Turkish border via

IRAQ

Mosul and Kirkuk, a longer drive but more scenic, especially in winter when the mountain routes were covered in snow. It was also safer. The Kurds maintained a strong military presence throughout this region, taking full advantage of the war by becoming autonomous with an eye on independence. There were many military checkpoints along the route and the Kurd soldiers were always courteous. One could stop in towns and have lunch in restaurants without fear of attack, although the option became less secure as the insurgency progressed.

The journey in and out of Baghdad became more convenient when commercial flights to the city resumed, initially from Amman. We were glad to see the back of the long drives. But it wasn't long before flying became a dangerous option. The insurgents were getting bolder and more organised. The air attack we'd anticipated eventually happened when a cargo plane was struck by a missile above Baghdad International Airport. The plane managed to land safely but the incident brought commercial flights to a halt until a solution was found. It didn't take long before flights were resumed, but not in a way anyone was used to.

Jordanian Airlines, which ran the only commercial flights into Baghdad in those early days, was told by the US military that it could no longer fly into Baghdad airspace in the usual manner. The standard procedure on approach to the airport was to gradually lose height from miles away, the wheels passing close to rooftops before crossing the airport boundary fence to touch down on the runway. This method clearly left aeroplanes vulnerable to ground fire.

The new procedure was for the aircraft to maintain a height of no less than 25,000ft as it arrived above the runway and then spiral down in a corkscrew pattern, pulling out at the last moment to land. Jordanian Airlines didn't have pilots qualified to execute such a manoeuvre so they hired a bunch of South African former air force pilots exclusively for the Baghdad run. I must've done that journey a dozen times and it never got old. I'm certain the pilots got a kick out of scaring the hell out of everyone, first-timers in particular, when the plane suddenly nosed-dived as if shot down, circling tightly several times before pulling G-force to level out at the last second to hit the runway with a screech of wheels.

When the war ended there was a period of several weeks, and months for some, when UK SF, mostly SAS, hung around the city with little to do. It was that period of calm just after a war when forces needed to reorganise while at the same time employing caution and not removing pieces off the game board too soon.

But idle SAS men abroad always brought with them the risk of misbehaviour. They were by nature independent and adventurous types. And the British national character has always tended towards the naughty. The underlying philosophy of the common or garden British military person can be summed up by a well-known navy saying: 'If it moves, salute it. If it stays still, paint it. And if it ain't bolted down, nick it.' The SAS, on occasion, had its fine reputation tarnished because of a little extracurricular activity of the dodgy variety by the very few. Such as the occasional post office robbed just south of the border in the Republic of Ireland during the Troubles. Or poor defenceless SAS troopers who, during the First Gulf War, insisted that their emergency evacuation coins – gold Krugerrands worth thousands of pounds – had been stolen from them

IRAQ

in the desert by merciless bedouins who otherwise didn't harm them or take anything else for that matter.

There was plenty of loot to be had in Baghdad. When Saddam did a runner at the end of the conflict, he ordered millions of US dollars to be secreted around the country, presumably in the hope they would be used to finance a guerrilla war against the invading forces. To give an example of how much cash there was, when his main palace in Baghdad was captured, there were many underground tunnels and rooms that needed to be cleared. US troops searching the area found a dark narrow stairwell that descended for several flights. At the bottom they broke down a door and found themselves inside a cavernous hall in complete darkness. Their flashlights revealed a vast, ornate ballroom with dozens of white marble columns topped by gold Corinthian capitals supporting a vaulted ceiling hung with chandeliers. But something even more resplendent caught their attention. Spaced out neatly on the marble floor of the vast ballroom were dozens of pallets, stacked several metres high and wrapped from top to bottom in clingfilm.

As they approached the towers of pallets, their torch beams revealed bundles of $100 bills inside the plastic covering. Thousands and thousands of them. The troops had stumbled upon one of Saddam's largest cash hoards. The estimated amount of money in the ballroom was apparently $15bn. The soldiers could be forgiven for becoming distracted from their immediate responsibility, which was to report the find. They promptly emptied their backpacks and ammunition pouches and stuffed as much cash into them as they could. The following day a team of CIA agents entered the ballroom to find the pallets intact – except for one corner which had been torn open as if by rats and a chunk of money removed. They also found items of US military clothing on the floor, with the owners' names on the labels. The hapless soldiers were soon located and their booty confiscated.

Word soon spread about Saddam's hidden caches. There wasn't just money to be found: art, jewellery, gold, precious artefacts and many other valuable items had been left behind in shops, homes, offices and museums by the fleeing population. The US military was understandably anxious to secure these riches to prevent them being used to fund the insurgency. The first wave of westerners to enter the city were faced by many such temptations. These were initially soldiers, obviously. Then came the civilian support to the military such as logistics suppliers, caterers and so on, swiftly followed by utilities engineers, the media and the private security contractors protecting them all.

Many SAS teams were free to roam the city and several came across stashes of cash. Much was dutifully handed in, but apparently not all. One story was that the Mercedes and BMW dealerships in Hereford ran out of their top-range cars soon after the first squadron returned home. I doubt that was true but it was a good chuckle to pass around.

A story I heard first-hand from one of the SAS lads on the ground was apparently typical. I have no idea how true it was. It could have been nothing more than a tall tale, but it is a good example of the stories going around at the time. He described how his four-man team had been hanging around the city for a week or so, living in abandoned homes and waiting for orders. Rumours abounded of other teams getting rich by engaging in a little discreet looting, but so far all their efforts to join the party had yielded nothing. There were millions of dollars secreted about the city and time was running out to get their hands on a share.

Banks were an obvious place to look and were not difficult to find. The SAS team found one that had been severely damaged by a large bomb. The lads were unsurprised to find a single US soldier standing guard outside, a testimony to the shortage of manpower at the time. The streets were quiet and mostly empty. Snipers had been operating up until recently and people were still nervous about stepping out into daylight. The SAS lads rocked up, armed to the teeth, sporting beards and long hair, with green and black keffiyehs carelessly draped around their necks. They looked more like irregular Arab militia than British soldiers.

They told the lone American guard that they had come to inspect the building. The soldier, clearly nervous and intimidated, explained that his orders were to prevent anyone going inside. The lads commended him, urging him to keep up the good work as they ambled past him into the damaged building. The US soldier doggedly followed them into the rubble-strewn lobby, politely asking them to leave. They continued to ignore him.

They eventually came to a room where part of the floor had collapsed, leaving a large, dark hole. They crawled to where they could shine their torches through a narrow gap into a cavernous room below, where they could make out bags and boxes behind twisted, broken bars. All indications were that it was a vault.

They had a rope with them but they were fairly big lads and the gap into the vault was narrow. Being wily individuals and not keen to pothole, they called over the American soldier, who was slight compared to them, and explained they needed him to assist in their search of the premises. I can only assume the Yank was a gullible type or that they made a deal with him, because they soon had him stripped down to his T-shirt and shorts. He was lowered into the hole, the rope tied under his arms. They waited patiently, sharing a smoke, while the soldier climbed through the twisted bars to inspect the bags.

'They're full of cash,' he finally called out.

'What currency?'

'Dollars, man,' he replied.

Jackpot. And judging by the number of bags, there was enough to empty Hereford's Porsche and Jaguar dealerships too.

At that moment they heard a vehicle pull up outside. The heavily armed SAS lads didn't have a great deal to fear in the city, but that didn't mean they were completely safe. Criminal elements were also scrounging about and a bank was worth fighting for.

The lads left the soldier in the hole calling to them, and made their way back to the entrance. A man in civilian clothes was climbing out of a US Army humvee, clutching paperwork and a map. The lads ambled over to him. He was surprised to see them but remained cool despite their fearsome appearance. A couple of US soldiers climbed out of the humvee to stand behind their boss.

He asked the lads who they were. British Army, they replied. He announced he was CIA. When they failed to display the submissive awe he was accustomed to, he repeated the famed acronym in case they hadn't quite heard.

'Yeah, you said,' one of the lads replied dryly. There wasn't a military or intelligence outfit in the world that would unduly impress anyone in UK SF.

The agent explained the bank was under the charge of the US government and they needed to vacate the premises. The lads asked him if he could come back later. He was stunned by their lack of deference. Several more humvees arrived and a dozen US soldiers climbed out.

It was a most disappointing development for the lads. They couldn't possibly recover any of the money under such conditions. Deciding it just wasn't their day, they strolled past the agent and down the rubble-strewn street. My thoughts went to the poor US soldier still down in the vault in his shorts and T-shirt.

After an uneventful day, in late afternoon the team selected one of the many abandoned houses to spend the night. After spending an obligatory few hours searching for booby-traps they made themselves at home. The house had ample water in the storage tank. They carried their own rations and there were mattresses and furniture to relax on.

They enjoyed a brew while overlooking the large, dusty back garden that had a square brick building in the middle, the size of a garden shed. It had a tin roof, there were no windows and the rickety wooden door was secured by a padlock. It was the sort of structure that invited booby-traps and none of the team fancied poking around inside to look for any.

They had been in the house for a couple of days when several humvees rolled up outside and the US military climbed out. An officer checked the house against some paperwork he had with him, and came inside. He explained to the lads that they were conducting a general search of the area.

FIRST INTO ACTION AGAIN

'Fill your boots,' was the response he received.

The American soldiers went directly through the house to the garden. The lads watched with curiosity as a couple of EOD (Explosive Ordnance Disposal) guys produced equipment to detect explosives. They poked around the little building in the garden for several hours until they felt confident enough to cut into the side of the roof, allowing them to lift up a corner. After further inspection it was deemed safe to open the door.

The EOD guys continued their work inside the structure and after an hour or so the lads heard sounds of celebration. The lad telling me the story said he wandered down to see what all the fuss was about. Inside the brick structure were four large steel containers. It turned out they were filled with $100 bills with an estimated total of $450m. The US soldiers packed the money into crates, placed them in the back of the humvees. By evening they had cleaned out all the cash and went on their way.

The SAS lads could only stare forlornly at the empty steel containers and imagine what might have been had they ventured inside when they had the chance.

A few days later the team was ordered to report in and shortly after flew back to Hereford. A couple of years later the SAS lad told me the story as we sat having a coffee in the Sheraton Hotel. He'd left the Regiment shortly after returning from Baghdad in order to get back to Iraq as a private security contractor and make himself some money. It was a familiar story.

It was a 20km drive from Baghdad International Airport (BIAP) to the hotel. In the early days it was a straightforward enough trip along the BIAP road (known as Route Irish by the coalition forces). The first mile from the airport, which had no exits, was used exclusively by coalition, Iraqi military, government personnel, airport staff, private enterprises and security services.

Basically, anyone on that stretch of road was in some way or other aligned with the West and therefore a legitimate target for insurgents. That stretch became the most dangerous mile of highway in the world and held the title for many years. What started off in the early days as a simple drive soon became a roll of the dice as to whether or not your vehicle would be attacked. The ground was generally flat either side of the motorway for miles. Vehicles were easy pickings for the insurgents from a distance.

Hundreds of people met their end on that highway, either by machine-gun ambush, snipers, roadside bombs or vehicle suicide bombers who drove along looking for a target to detonate beside. I nicknamed it 'the Lonely Mile' because much of the time we were the only cars on it. Whether leaving the airport or passing that last junction on the way towards it, when there was no-one in front or behind, was a tense journey. I was on the motorway heading for the Lonely Mile when Edinburgh Risk, a British security company, had two cars with eight or so guys pinned down by machine-gun fire from half a mile away.

The cars were fired on for five to 10 minutes. The guys were rolling around, trying to find cover behind the wheels, engine blocks or any dip in the sand they could find. Bullets were ripping through the vehicles, bouncing off the road. Hardly a round was returned. Two lads bled to death from bullet wounds shortly after the shooting stopped. Others only survived because their buddies managed to get them to the US military hospital in the Green Zone. A group of Polish security guys got caught in a complex ambush from several different directions and only escaped because they tossed hand grenades to cover them as they abandoned their vehicles at the run.

Within a week of hearing about that attack, we acquired grenades too. They were US Army issue, a couple of hundred dollars each. The added peace of mind was well worth the cost. We never revealed the grenades to CNN staff or to AKE Hereford. We would happily risk being sacked if we ever had to use them to escape an ambush. We also had the latest lightweight body armour and helmets that were AK47-proof. All in all, we were well tooled up when we went on the ground, with lots of spare ammo and smoke grenades, a far cry from a few years before.

I must've been up and down the BIAP road 100 times over the years I spent in Baghdad and although I often heard explosions and machine-gun fire ahead or behind me, and drove past the smoking remains of recently attacked vehicles, I somehow managed to avoid a direct contact. I personally knew half a dozen people who'd died on that godforsaken stretch of tarmac, a few ex-Bootnecks among them. Its fearsome reputation was well-earned.

During those early days CNN's bureau was on the ground floor of the Palestine Hotel. There were two or three CNN teams plus the bureau chief, and four to six AKE operators, depending on what was going on. The rotating AKE teams were mostly former Special Forces: SAS, SBS, Aussi and Kiwi SAS, US Navy Seals and some Paras, Bootnecks and a Green Jacket. We were kept busy but there was always time for the gym and relaxation.

The US military often offered to host a news team on routine patrols. They weren't always as safe a bet as they seemed. I was in the ops room one night monitoring a cameraman who'd joined a US Army humvee patrol. His job was to film some footage to add to a report, but he got more than he'd hoped for.

A sat call came in around midnight from our cameraman, talking softly and sounding desperate. His patrol had come under intensive fire. He and the soldiers evacuated the humvee and scurried for cover as bullets and RPGs flew about lighting up the night sky. Unfortunately he missed the recall signal and was still hugging the bottom of a ditch when the humvees sped away. Apparently none of the soldiers noticed he was missing, or they assumed he'd jumped into another humvee.

He had no idea where the hell he was. Fortunately his sat phone could send us a GPS location. When we found his whereabouts on the map, we didn't fancy going into that village, especially considering what had happened to the US patrol. I urged him to leg it out of there while it was still dark and gave him a direction to go in, across open ground for a mile to a road where we would meet him.

We managed to pick him up without incident. He left Iraq a few days later, vowing never to return.

As the months went by, insurgency attacks on westerners and coalition forces intensified. Suicide bomb vehicles became more common. Every few days we'd hear of a security company or military vehicle struck by a suicide bomber detonating alongside. Roadside bombs were also increasingly popular.

Katyusha rocket attacks against hotels were a fad while stocks lasted. The Palestine and Sheraton hotels were favourite targets due to the large number of westerners who lived in them. We'd get hit by a rocket at least once a month. The US military ended up placing a machine-gun team on the mezzanine roof of the Sheraton. It was a conspicuous position, visible from the street. But that didn't deter one bunch of insurgents who'd been sent to attack the hotel. They parked a lorry right in front of the machine-gun team one sunny afternoon, 200 metres away, and set about preparing several Katyushas for firing. The machine-gunners watched in disbelief. They didn't open fire immediately because they couldn't believe anyone would be so stupid. The insurgents even set sentries armed with AK47s either side of the lorry, not under cover, just kneeling down beside the wheels in the road. The Yanks finally opened up and wasted them all. If there had been a Dumb and Dumber Award for the stupidest insurgent attack, those guys were certainly contenders, but they wouldn't have won. Not by a long shot.

Several months before that particular attack, a group of insurgents led three donkeys, each towing a rickety wooden farm trailer, to a piece of open ground 600 metres from the Sheraton. On the back of each trailer were three Katyushas, making nine in all, each with long igniferous fuses. The insurgents carefully lined up the trailers so that the Katyushes were aimed at the pyramid-shaped hotel, which was certainly a big enough target from that distance.

They lit the fuses and retired to where they could watch the hotel be decimated along with its hundreds of guests. One could only marvel at the genius who came up with the plan. Nobody had considered how the donkeys might react when the rockets fired.

Since the rockets were individually ignited, they were not synchronised and so the firings would be random. When a Katyusha ignites, there's a short delay while the burning solid-fuel propellant builds enough thrust to activate the launch. During those seconds there's a furious burst of flame from the rocket's tail that stretches several metres. The first rocket's flame completely engulfed the poor donkey. Needless to say, it flew into an utter frenzy as the rocket screamed from the trolley and shot past the Sheraton. The other donkeys didn't remain idle once they saw what had happened to their mate. They bolted away with their trolleys in tow seconds before their own rockets launched, engulfing them in their own fireballs.

It was utter mayhem. Rockets were blasting off in all directions as the hysterical donkeys ran aimlessly, crashing into each other and everything else in their path. When Iraqi security forces eventually arrived on the scene about 20 minutes later, the poor, smouldering beasts were still in a frenzied state. One was so badly burned it had to be shot immediately and another was put down later that day. Miraculously, one of the donkeys survived despite its wounds. I heard years later it was living on a farm near Mosul, doing well, with a notice on its fence warning people not to light a cigarette anywhere near it. I never learned if that was a sick joke or fact.

If there had been a Dumb and Dumber Award for media people, it too would've been heavily contested. Journalists were turning up from all over the globe, many of whom, I suspect, could not have found Iraq on a map before the war. The finalists achieved their ranking with displays of stupidity that took us all by surprise. Runner-up was a French journalist who must remain nameless.

I left my room in the Sheraton Hotel one afternoon and as I walked to the elevators I was surprised to see a dozen or so Iraqi hotel workers, all males, crowded together, their faces pressed against the large plate-glass window that provided a panoramic view of the city. It also looked down onto the hotel's pool area, which was the focus of the staff's attention. The elevator was taking an age, as usual, so I decided to walk down to the lobby.

As I turned the corner of the stairwell I saw the corresponding panoramic window on the floor below was also crowded with Iraqi staff, straining on tiptoe to look steeply down. When I arrived at the next floor down, that window was also mobbed. Curiosity got the better of me. I joined the staff at the window and was stunned by what I saw. Lying on a sunbed by the pool was an attractive lady in a bikini. That was an unusual enough sight in a conservative Islamic city that was in the midst of a brutal fundamentalist insurgency. Hotel guests weren't here on holiday. No-one sat by the pool for relaxation. Anyone who sat there would normally be surrounded by paperwork or in serious, private discussion. On this occasion the woman was the only person by the pool. But what was even more bizarre, incredible even, was that this lady was topless. She had a fine pair of tanned breasts, unashamedly on full display. Most Arab boys never got to see a pair of breasts, or any part of the female anatomy for that matter other than hands and faces, until they were married. A pair of tits flagrantly displayed for the entire hotel to enjoy was the stuff of legend. As I watched, a gang of hotel managers dashed across the patio and hurriedly threw a towel over the lady, snapping her out of her snooze as they delivered a severe admonishment for her disgraceful exhibition.

The contest for the Dumbest Fuck Award was hard-fought. As far as I was concerned, the clear winner was a Japanese journalist a few months later. While most people walking the streets, journalists included, kept an eye out for anything of value – it

IRAQ

was a journalist who found a gold-plated AK47 belonging to one of Saddam's sons – this guy happened upon a high-explosive hand grenade lying somewhere. Most people would've given it a wide berth or at least reported it to the military. He not only decided to pick it up and take it back to his hotel room, through at least one military checkpoint where he could've handed it in, but also thought it would make a great souvenir. When the day came for him to leave Iraq, he put the grenade in his suitcase and took what was then the usual drive across the Jordanian border, intending to fly home via Amman's international airport. His baggage was scanned at the border and a suspicious object was detected. A security officer opened the case, removed the grenade and as he inspected it, clearly quite thoroughly, it exploded, killing him instantly.

I believe the Japanese reporter might still be in jail.

Nearly all of my tasks for CNN in Baghdad were successful, and there must've been hundreds of them. By successful I mean we achieved the two main aims of every task – the journalistic objective, and making sure no-one on the team died in its pursuit. I did have several close calls, though.

One of my more memorable failures with regard to the first aim, and very nearly with regard to the second, occurred in the dreaded Sunni Triangle. One morning I learned I was to take Nick Robertson, one of CNN's top correspondents, to the town of Fallujah. During the night, soldiers of the US 82nd Airborne Division had ambushed a group of Iraqi police vehicles, believing them to be insurgents. Eight police officers were killed and many wounded. The police, who had been trained by the Americans, had been chasing criminals when the US patrol opened fire.

FIRST INTO ACTION AGAIN

Tensions between the locals and the Americans were already high in Fallujah, but this incident had many Iraqis baying for blood. The injured were in a hospital on the outskirts of the town and Nick was keen to interview them. I rated Nick as the finest journalist I'd worked with in Iraq. His enthusiasm made him prone to impulsive decisions that sometimes tested the boundaries of acceptable risk, which was something I could relate to. I never felt he was driven by a yearning for fame or by peer pressure, so I tended to give him a little more latitude than I might give others. I wasn't keen to travel through Fallujah, as I had done several times in the past. It was fast becoming a dangerous place for westerners to even set foot in. But since the hospital was close to a dual-carriage highway on the outskirts of the town, I felt the risk was within our boundaries of acceptability.

The rest of the team consisted of Joe Duran, our colourful Spanish cameraman, a female Lebanese producer, a Lebanese fixer, and our trusty driver, the softly spoken Ahmed, a former Iraqi soldier who was a rock of reliability.

We operated mostly in single vehicles in those days. As long as we remained within reasonable reach of our bureau, we deemed it safe enough to operate with one 4x4 per team. Within a few months, we wouldn't go anywhere without a backing vehicle.

The Fallujah objective was straightforward enough. We were to drive to the hospital, interview the surviving policemen, then return to the bureau. It was to be one of the most dramatic single-day tasks I was ever to undertake.

Everything went to plan, right up to leaving the hospital after a couple of hours filming and interviewing, and turning onto the highway back to Baghdad. As we passed by the end

IRAQ

of a major road that led through the middle of Fallujah, Nick craned to look along it and asked the driver to pull over. He explained the mosque we could see a few hundred metres away was where the funeral procession for the dead police officers would commence, ending at a cemetery half a mile away.

Nick asked if we could do a pass of the mosque so he could get a look. The detour was not part of the plan. Venturing inside Fallujah had not been included in my risk assessment. I had a lot of experience covering Islamic funerals in Ramallah and Gaza. Emotions always ran high, particularly when those being buried had been killed by occupying or enemy forces.

The mosque was on a broad boulevard. Apart from a handful of people outside, the street was quiet. Our Lebanese fixer, whose job it was to inform us of potential stories as well as warn us of problems, supported Nick, assuring me it was completely safe to visit the mosque.

As we weren't far from the highway back to Baghdad, I saw little reason not to allow it and gave our driver Ahmed the nod. We pulled up outside the mosque and Nick, the fixer in tow, marched inside in search of the mullah in charge. I hung around outside while the producer stayed in the car and Joe prepared his camera in case it was needed. More local men turned up but showed little interest in us. Half an hour later the crowd had grown to 100 or so. I began to feel uneasy.

Nick finally came out of the mosque and reported that the mullah had assured him it would be okay for us to cover the funeral. That was unexpected. The pressure on me went up another notch. I hadn't prepared to cover a funeral march. The cemetery was half a mile away. I had immediate flashbacks to the volatile Islamic funerals I'd attended in Gaza and

FIRST INTO ACTION AGAIN

Ramallah. They needed special attention – plans if things went wrong, such as an emergency rendezvous in case the team got split up. I would never have brought a female producer along since women weren't permitted at Muslim funerals. As usual with correspondents, it became a negotiation and we settled on Nick covering the formation of the funeral march without joining it once it moved off. It was the best I could agree on.

I didn't want to be parked outside the mosque so we drove a few hundred metres further along the boulevard towards the town centre and pulled over outside a line of shops. They were classic Middle Eastern single-room stores with large shutters that rolled down across the entire front when closed. I waved to a bunch of old boys sitting outside their shops, smoking and drinking tea. They waved back. Those friendly gestures were to be a significant connection.

In the short time since we'd arrived, the crowd had grown to more than 500 men. We kept by the vehicle at first, unsure about the situation as the noise level rose. A loudspeaker piped up and began whipping up the crowd's fervour. Someone in the crowd fired a rifle into the sky and was quickly joined by others. Rifle-fire at gatherings such as weddings and funerals was traditional in Iraq. Every household was permitted by law to possess one rifle.

Nick called out to a young man he recognised who was carrying an AK47 and making his way across the boulevard toward the mosque. The man, who was accompanied by a couple of others, looked pleased to see Nick and approached us. He was the mayor of Fallujah's assistant whom Nick had met while interviewing the mayor some months previously. He greeted Nick warmly and welcomed us to Fallujah. Nick

IRAQ

wanted to confirm it was okay for CNN to be at the funeral and the mayor's assistant insisted it was perfectly fine. Anti-American feelings were running high because of the killing of the policemen but the media was welcome. He went one step further and assured us that we in particular could consider ourselves officially invited by the mayor's office. Arab protocol ensured that an invited guest was guaranteed safety. The invitation gave me some comfort as we followed the young assistant into the crowd. The fixer stuck by Nick as interpreter while Joe endeavoured to film. I kept close as we wriggled our way in between the men. Guns were firing into the air all around, making a deafening cacophony.

The crowd had grown to several thousand. The boulevard in front of the mosque and for 100 metres in both directions was packed. Someone tugged on my arm and I quickly turned to see it was Ahmed, our driver, looking troubled. He shouted above the din that there was a problem to do with the Lebanese producer. I followed him out of the crowd to see her standing a little away from the vehicle in her tight jeans and sweater, with no headscarf. There were no other women to be seen. She must have known she was breaking a serious protocol. Men were giving her disapproving looks. I hurried over, escorted her back to the vehicle and asked Ahmed to drive further down the street as if he was leaving.

I had now lost sight of Nick and Joe. I climbed onto the raised pavement in front of the shops, which stood a metre above the road, to get a better view. All I could see was a sea of men, rifles endlessly shooting into the air. The team getting split up was one of my concerns when it came to such gatherings. Nick would be fixated on his interviews. I was acutely conscious of being a white man in this crowd of Arabs. I caught the occasional look that was not friendly. I was relieved to see other news crews arrive that included white westerners.

I didn't know it at the time, but a Reuters team had chosen to film from the roof of a house overlooking the boulevard. A few days later they would send us footage showing how close one of us came to being murdered.

I caught a glimpse of Nick not far away and was about to make my way to him when I saw several motorbikes arrive with two men on each. They were fedayeen. Unmistakable because they wore red and white keffiyehs wrapped around their heads leaving slits for their eyes, carried AK47s slung over their shoulders and the passengers were holding RPG-7s.

A couple of them stopped their bikes on the edge of the crowd, climbed off and began to strut around. Fedayeen were troublemakers. Their arrival had an ominous effect on the mood of the crowd. They were agitators and had influence. The mob grew more boisterous. The risks had just increased and we needed to go. I pushed my way through the crowd in Nick's direction.

Despite the deafening gunfire, Nick was interviewing someone while Joe did his best to film it amid the jostling mass of people. As soon as Nick was finished I grabbed him and shouted that we should get out of there. He was hesitant, keen for more interviews, but he followed me to the edge of the crowd where he could see the fedayeen.

I pulled him close to me and, referring to the changing mood, asked him, 'Do you feel it?'

Nick nodded. It was time to return to our vehicle. Joe was a few metres away filming the guns shooting into the air. I shouted that we were going. He acknowledged me. And that's when it all went terribly wrong.

Nick and I moved away from the crowd towards our 4x4, which was some 50 metres down the street. Ahmed was standing by it, looking anxiously at us.

Joe then made a fatal mistake. He lowered his heavy film camera, letting it hang from his shoulder by its strap, then pulled his small stills camera from his pocket and aimed it at the fedayeen. Most people will wave and say "hi" to a large TV camera but pointing a small camera at them can induce the opposite effect and even trigger a violent reaction.

One of the fedayeen went ballistic. He pointed at Joe, screaming at the top of his voice. I turned to look. Joe stood frozen, camera in hand, staring at the howling fedayeen. I've never seen anything quite like what followed. The crowd obeyed whatever order had been given and surged as one toward Joe like a tsunami of human fury. The front line crashed into him and he was instantly swallowed up. The mass of enraged people continued towards us, pushed by those behind. Nick and I sprinted towards the vehicle. This was all about our survival now. Ahmed leapt in and started the engine. Nick and I scrambled inside. The fixer appeared and jumped in to join the female producer. I hoped Joe would emerge from the crowd but there was no sign of him. As Ahmed pulled away from the kerb, one of the fedayeen crouched and levelled his AK47 at us.

'Grab your armour! Get down!' I yelled. Everyone grabbed their protective gear off the floor and either struggled to put it on or held it behind their heads. I held my helmet behind Ahmed's head. As we accelerated away the fedayeen kept his rifle aimed at us but didn't shoot. I can only suppose they were not yet mentally ready to shoot any westerner they encountered. That was to come. And not long after that day.

Ahmed swerved into the first side street that appeared and sped down it, screeching around the corner at the end. All I could think was that Joe was still back there and that something terrible was happening to him.

I told Ahmed to pull over in the quiet backstreet. I looked at Nick and the others.

'What we should do now is drive back to Baghdad and the bureau,' I said. 'But I have a real problem with leaving Joe behind.'

I wanted to stay and find him. Acting quickly and remaining close by was Joe's best chance if he was still alive. But I needed the team's consent.

Without hesitation Nick agreed we should try to find Joe. The others nodded. It was brave of them.

Nick suggested we head for the mayor's office since he knew the man, and the mayor's assistant owed us after his assurance we'd be welcome. The mayor's office was on the same boulevard as the funeral gathering, a couple of hundred yards from the mosque. It would mean heading back towards the crowd and the fedayeen.

We drove to where we could nose out onto the boulevard to get a look. There was no passing traffic due to the enormous gathering filling the road, guns blazing skyward accompanied by fervent chanting. We could see the mayor's compound between us and them, a large two-storey building surrounded by a high wall with a gated entrance.

We drove towards it at an easy pace and pulled into the entrance. After a brief chat with the police officers manning the gate, we were permitted to enter. We parked around the back of the large compound and Nick and I hurried inside the main building.

We soon found the mayor's assistant and Nick explained that our cameraman had been kidnapped. The assistant was initially stunned and then became furious. He grabbed his gun and, along with a couple of his men, hurried down to the courtyard and onto the street. His response was encouraging. Ahmed volunteered to mingle with the crowd and find out what he could. He was wily and smart and would be safe.

The rest of us sat in the courtyard at the back of the building, out of view of the gated entrance. There was nothing else we could do but wait and hope.

The shooting and chanting went on. I wondered where all the ammunition was coming from. The crowd had continued to grow and now reached the gates of the mayor's compound. An hour later the mayor's assistant returned to tell us there was mention of our cameraman but he'd been unable to locate him or even confirm his fate.

I found that frustrating. There must have been hundreds who witnessed the incident. The mayor's assistant was befuddled by it himself and left again, determined to find out what had happened to Joe.

Some time later, while we were sitting out back keeping a low profile, our Lebanese fixer appeared. He told us the compound police had warned him that they would not be able to protect us if the crowd decided to invade the mayor's office. The police were merely being pragmatic – there were only nine of them on duty.

I hadn't considered we might be at risk in the mayor's

compound. But there was nowhere else we could have gone to mount a search for Joe. I was risking the many for the sake of the one, who was probably beyond help anyway.

I was reminded of the many scenarios I created for media crews during hostile environment training when I was an instructor, putting teams into challenging situations with no obvious solution. One such scenario I created was in Toronto for the Canadian Broadcasting Corporation. My students were mostly senior producers and reporters. I split the class into four teams with four men and one woman in each. Each news team was required to drive through a make-believe conflict zone where they would be stopped by hooded, armed terrorists. I hired four off-duty Toronto policemen to play the terrorists and they turned out to be scarily convincing in the role.

As the first team drove through CBC HQ's vast underground parking garage, the 'terrorists' stopped their vehicle and ordered them to get out. After some bullying, threats and shouting, the men were ordered to get back in their vehicle and drive away, leaving the woman behind. When the men refused, the terrorists put guns to their heads and told them they'd die if they didn't leave. All four news teams went through the same scenario and each time the men eventually drove away, leaving their female colleagues behind to potentially suffer rape and execution.

When I conducted a debrief at the end of the day I encountered a very depressed-looking bunch. They'd had time to digest what had happened and it had left scars. Before I could begin, one of the senior members got to his feet. Sombre and angry, he described how disgusted he was with himself. He felt physically sick after driving away, leaving his female partner to her fate. One of the students tried to console him by explaining they had no choice. To stay meant to die.

'You damned fool!' the unhappy man shouted. 'This was a play, with actors, in our garage, and I should've acted brave and refused to leave. No-one was going to kill me. What I must now live with is that I have sent a message to everyone in the CBC that I will desert them to die if my own life is in danger.'

He sat back down, gave me an accusatory look, and put his head in his hands.

And now here I was living my own scenario.

I had the keys to the vehicle. We were parked near the rear entrance to the compound. I told Nick that if the crowd entered the main gate we'd hurry into the vehicle and I'd crash through the rear gates to make our escape. Nick agreed. What I didn't explain was that if the mob was in the narrow street on the other side of the gates I'd drive through them in order for us to survive.

An hour after the mayor's assistant left for the second time, he returned without any promising news. When Ahmed returned, he too had no good news to report.

Joe was gone. Depression descended upon us.

As darkness fell, lights flickered on in the building. The sound of engines joined the cacophony beyond the walls. Buses and trucks were arriving. The crowd was moving to the cemetery. At one point the mayor's compound was completely surrounded, the streets packed with people and slow-moving vehicles. A bus slowly drove past. There were people on the roof who could see into the compound. We all ducked for cover.

As the crowd moved on, the noise went with it. I received a message that an AKE vehicle with several operators was waiting on the outskirts of the town in case we needed them. The lads had tripped into special forces mode and were heavily armed.

As the last stragglers left the boulevard, the mayor's assistant returned again, this time with hopeful news. Joe had somehow been rescued by some shopkeepers. They had taken him to the nearby US military base, the home of the 82nd Airborne, the unit that had killed the Fallujah policemen.

Enthused by the news, we piled into the vehicle, eased our way out of the main gates and onto the now empty boulevard. We drove at speed to the US base, a large isolated camp in the desert a couple of miles from Fallujah.

It was always dangerous approaching military bases in Iraq. Soldiers on sentry duty were nervous about civilian vehicles approaching in case they were suicide bombers. Daytime was bad enough when they could see clearly. Nighttime was extremely dangerous for unannounced visitors.

I pulled off the main road and drove slowly over the hard-packed sand through a series of chicanes towards the towering fortress wall, a couple of hundred metres long and dotted with spotlights. As soon as my approaching headlights swept across the camp defences, rifles and machine-guns would be aimed at us. I had no number I could call.

I stopped well short of the first checkpoint, turned off the headlights and flicked on the inside cabin lights so the sentries could get a better look inside our vehicle. They would be watching us through night vision systems but my actions hopefully conveyed I was trying to be as visible as possible.

My next move was to ease out of the vehicle with my hands in the air, turn full circle and open my shirt to reveal my T-shirt which I pulled up to show my bare torso. I'd heard of guys stripping virtually naked to prove they didn't have explosives strapped to them. I lowered my hands and waved cheerily in the hope someone would challenge me. After a long minute there was movement at the checkpoint behind the lights. A voice boomed over a loudspeaker asking who I was. I shouted that I was a US citizen, with CNN, and that I was looking for one of my guys who'd been brought to the camp. They couldn't hear me properly and asked me to move closer. I was relieved that we were at least talking.

I was ordered to stop halfway and repeated why I was there. It went silent while they had a confab and then the voice said our guy was at the camp. It was another 20 minutes before a lone figure walked out of the lights towards us carrying a TV camera. Seeing Joe able to walk on his own was a relief.

He was in a sombre mood as he climbed into the vehicle and as we headed for Baghdad he described what happened.

When the crowd engulfed him he found himself being punched and pulled by countless hands. He went into panic mode and pumped his legs in a desperate effort to escape, trying to protect himself against the blows while refusing to let go of his camera. When Reuters sent us footage of the incident the following day, taken from a roof overlooking the crowd, Joe could be seen desperately swimming through the crowd while fists rained down on him. What he never saw, and the footage clearly revealed, was that at one point a large knife appeared and hovered above him. As the point descended, someone deliberately blocked it, inches from Joe's head. Joe kept moving with no idea where he was going. He managed to reach the edge of the crowd where the pavement stood a metre above the road in front of the shops. As he struggled to climb onto the pavement, a couple of elderly shopkeepers yanked him out of the crowd and dragged him into a shop. Some men tried to scramble after him but the shopkeepers swiftly pulled down the metal shutter and locked it from inside.

Joe was emotional as he relived the experience, describing how the crowd pounded on the shutter so violently it looked like it would break. The old shopkeeper pleaded with him, trying to tell him something. Joe didn't speak Arabic. The shopkeeper persevered, miming his message until Joe realised the men outside wanted his camera. Joe quickly ejected the tape and the shopkeeper raised the shutter just enough to shove it outside. The banging ceased.

When the crowd began to move on towards the cemetery, the shopkeeper smuggled Joe into his car and drove him to the US camp. The old shopkeeper was incredibly brave, approaching the 82nd Airborne camp entrance, climbing out of his car, headlights full on, wearing his keffiyeh and flowing robes. And then Joe climbing out beside him carrying his camera, which could easily be mistaken for a weapon in the poor light.

Losing the videotape was a blow. We were relieved to have Joe back in one piece but the entire day's filming, including the hospital and funeral interviews, had all been on that one tape. The day was a total loss.

The killing of the policemen invigorated the Fallujah insurgency and attacks against US military assets increased. Five months after the funeral incident, the mayor's office and several police stations were attacked in a coordinated offensive. A month after that, a convoy of private security contractors working for a US company called Blackwater was ambushed in the city. Four were shot dead, their bodies dragged through the streets, set

IRAQ

on fire and the charred corpses hung from a bridge over the Euphrates. The US military was determined to apprehend the killers. When Fallujah refused to cooperate, the US attacked in force. After a stalled initial campaign, the US military took control of the city. Over 800 Iraqis were killed in the operation.

9

THE CONGO

I WAS TAKING A BREAK with my family in the south of France for a few months when I got a call from AKE ops asking if I'd be interested in a particularly challenging task. In my business, challenging was often a euphemism for dodgy. The destination was deep inside the unstable Democratic Republic of the Congo (DRC) and the client was CNN's top domestic anchor and journalist, Anderson Cooper. I'd never been to the Congo, which made the job attractive, but I wanted to know what was challenging about it.

The task was to find General Laurent Nkunda, a dissident Congolese Tutsi warlord who was holding out with a force of 5,000 soldiers in the Masisi Forests high in the Northern Kivu region. Nkunda had been accused of a long list of war crimes including murder, rape, pillaging and abducting children to serve as his soldiers. The UN accused him of sacking a town, massacring 160 people and abducting and beating two UN investigators. He'd also been indicted by the Congolese government. Nkunda claimed he was innocent of all charges.

THE CONGO

Anderson Cooper wanted to personally hear the general's side of the story.

The following day I caught a train to Paris and then a flight to Kigali, Rwanda, the most convenient airport for the part of the Congo we were destined for. My task was to get the team there and back in one piece. The main challenge was 60 miles of bandit country before the 40 miles of mountainous jungle up to Nkunda's camp. And we had to come back the same way. Nkunda had promised we'd be safe once we reached his territory beyond the town of Masisi. But the bandit-infested section of road was no small problem.

The DRC had recently come to the end of a brutal civil war in which four million people had died and two million more had been displaced. That was four years ago but the country was still suffering from the repercussions. Starvation, poverty and disease were killing around 1,200 people a day. Militant groups wrestled for control of various areas. Rape and murder were a daily occurrence. There was a lot to fight for – the country was rich in cobalt, diamonds, copper, gold and other rare minerals. But no single leader had managed to tame the militants enough to exploit those riches to the full. Just about every road outside of every major town was claimed by one rebel group or another. Robbing towns, villages and travellers was the main source of income for the rebels and they were ruthless in their work. They mostly operated in small scavenging parties but on occasion they got together to form more potent forces for larger prey. They weren't afraid to take on the occasional UN convoy of armed soldiers. A small western news team with its phones, cameras and laptops would be a most attractive prize indeed.

FIRST INTO ACTION AGAIN

I landed in Kigali and was looking forward to meeting the team in the hotel. As I queued to pass through immigration, I ran into my first security hazard. I'd bought a leather butt pouch while in Nairobi airport's duty-free zone during my stopover from Paris. It was wrapped in a plastic bag and I happened to be holding it as I shuffled towards one of the immigration kiosks. I clocked a man in a dark suit on a far landing watching me intently. He looked like a store detective eyeing a known shoplifter. He didn't try to hide that I was his object of scrutiny. I could only wonder why he was so interested in me.

I was almost at the kiosk when he made his move, walking down the steps and across the hall towards me. He had the confidence of a police officer confronting a jaywalker.

'Good day, sir,' he said.

'Good day,' I replied.

'What are you holding?'

I held up the package. 'It's a bum bag,' I said.

'I'm talking about the sack.'

I was baffled. 'Sack?'

'The plastic sack,' he said, as if I was holding the lead pipe that had been used to murder Professor Plum in the library.

I looked at my plastic bag, now thoroughly confused.

'Do you know it's illegal to bring a plastic sack into Rwanda?' he asked.

I didn't. It wasn't in the brief I'd received. He explained that by bringing in the plastic bag I was committing an offence. I removed the butt pouch from the bag, which I offered to him. He took it, warned me not to do it again, and casually walked away. When I reached the kiosk, the immigration officer didn't look amused either.

THE CONGO

Plastic bags were indeed outlawed in Rwanda, and with good reason. Colourful, small, light as air plastic bags were the bane of Africa. In countries that didn't ban them, every shop in every town and village used them to wrap anything and everything. Millions a day were freely handed out. When discarded, the wind carried them until they were caught by a fence, hedgerow or tree branch, where they remained, hanging like bunting, until they eventually decayed, which could take years. But not in Rwanda. Sitting in the back of my taxi on the way to the capital, I was impressed by how clean the countryside was. Perhaps it had something to do with the majority of Rwanda's elected politicians being women. Rwanda was a small, very crowded country, and the locals were determined to keep it neat and tidy.

I was pleased to see a familiar face when I arrived at the hotel – Ingrid Formanek, a CNN international producer of renown. I'd worked with Ingrid in Baghdad and other places and knew her well enough to bum a smoke and share an evening libation. Apart from being an experienced professional, she was good company with no shortage of enlightening anecdotes.

Anderson Cooper arrived that evening and was as he'd been described: unassuming, low-key, polite and pleasant. He turned out to be the most easygoing correspondent I'd ever worked with. He was accompanied by Charlie Moore, his producer, another excellent lad. It was, for a security risk manager at least, a dream team.

After a day in Kigali organising three 4x4 vehicles and supplies, we set off on the first leg of the journey to the Rwanda/DRC border and across into the city of Goma. We were a large team by normal standards. Along with Ingrid,

Charlie and Anderson, we had a cameraman, a technician, a guest print writer, a United Nations advisor, a fixer and three drivers.

Goma was a sad town that for decades had been soaked with the blood of its people. Situated on the border on the northern shore of Lake Kivu, it had suffered greatly during the Rwandan genocide and then didn't catch a break from the First and Second Congo Wars that rapidly followed.

On top of that, there were the endless battles between the various rebel and guerrilla groups, all fighting for control of the town and region. As if that wasn't enough misery, an active volcano overlooked the town. Mount Nyiragongo had erupted four years before we arrived, sending a kilometre-wide lava flow through the town and into the lake. Fortunately most of the inhabitants managed to flee the lava's path but many properties were destroyed.

Our meeting with Nkunda was set for day three. I'd pondered the obstacles we might encounter on our journey and wasn't satisfied with the options I had to mitigate them. The bandits were the main problem but not the only one. Breakdowns would be a challenge. We could just about cram everyone and everything into two vehicles, but if we lost them we'd have to find some way of ferrying people between safe locations. If that happened on the outbound leg, it could jeopardise the entire task. There were several towns and villages en route but we couldn't count on much in the way of support. The owner of a garage in Goma agreed to pick us up in the event of an emergency. I offered to pay him a tidy sum if we needed him. I'm certain he prayed we'd require his services. I had phone numbers for the local UN military, an Indian outfit, but I

THE CONGO

had no idea how reliable they'd be, nor did our UN advisor. Another challenge was accommodation. We might not be able to complete the journey to Nkunda in one day but there were no hotels that we could book ahead. Thankfully, that wasn't my responsibility.

The bandit problem took up most of my time. Local intelligence, which included the Goma police and our UN advisor, reported that bandits had recently been active on our proposed route. A week before we arrived, an armed UN vehicle had come under attack and although it got through unscathed it highlighted the seriousness of the threat. We would not be armed. It didn't exactly make me keener to undertake the trip.

I was certainly used to cancelling such adventures, although always reluctantly. When I was team leader for Fox News in Baghdad, a post I held for several tours, the news teams would come to me, usually on a daily basis, with suggestions for tasks across the city and beyond. I would assess the risk and decide if the team could proceed or not. Baghdad was a seriously dangerous place in those days and I had little choice but to reject the majority of the proposed tasks.

This one was different. Apart from the fact that a great deal of money had been spent on getting the team to Goma, Anderson wouldn't even consider calling it off. He was well aware of the risks. But he had his objective and it was my job to make it happen. I didn't fancy telling him and Charlie that I thought it unwise. I gave us a broad 50-50 chance of getting through without meeting bandits. Those weren't great odds. If we were stopped by bandits it wouldn't be pretty. They'd strip us of everything for sure. If it happened on the outbound we'd be unable to interview the general, and if it happened on the way back we'd lose all the recordings. Kidnappings for ransom were apparently uncommon, but the threat of bodily harm was significant.

I needed to increase the odds in our favour somehow. I asked for a UN escort but was turned down. There was no local military or police I could engage. In Nigeria by contrast, where I ran several CNN operations, hiring armed military or police was a simple matter.

Subterfuge was an option. Any bandits would most likely employ spotters on the route to give advance warning of our approach. At such short notice one would expect to encounter only a small group of bandits. I needed the spotters to report that we were a force to be reckoned with – one that would require more than a handful of thugs to take on. I therefore had to create the illusion that we were well-armed. All I could think of was one of the oldest tricks in the playbook. I bought several wooden broom handles and painted them black. When we were clear of Goma we'd poke them out of our vehicle windows to look like gun barrels to an undiscerning local. If there was a large group out there looking for a fight, we were screwed anyway.

I would normally have been obliged to discuss the seriousness of the risks with Anderson and Charlie, and if not them at least with Ingrid. But I decided not to.

When Charlie casually asked if we were all set, I replied confidently, 'Let's do it.'

The first 30 miles of road were tarmac and good going. I was surprised how few potholes there were. Traffic was light, mostly carts and bicycles with the occasional truck. We drove through several towns and villages. There were plenty filling stations and no shortage of fuel to ensure our tanks never dropped below half-full. The next 30 miles to Masisi were a mixture of dirt and tarmac, very winding and steep with sections washed away by the rains. I spent the entire journey looking for signs of bandits. I felt completely helpless. I didn't expect to get much of a warning. They'd be on the road waiting for us. If we tried to push through, guns would be fired and people were going to get hurt. I'd bring the vehicles to a halt and take whatever deal the bandits would give us. If we came through it without anyone getting hurt, it would be a major plus.

The miles went slowly for me and I was mightily relieved when we finally arrived in Masisi. We'd passed through the worst of it.

We stopped at the Médecins Sans Frontières house for a coffee and a chat, Anderson hoping to add some texture to the story and me to gather local intelligence. It wasn't encouraging. They described how just days before, a doctor and his local assistant had left the town in a vehicle heading for Goma and several hours later they returned to Masisi, on foot, completely naked, having been stopped by bandits and robbed of literally everything, including their footwear. The doctor considered himself lucky on that occasion because the bandits wanted his vehicle intact and therefore stopped him without firing a shot. On a positive note, the doctor believed the worst road for bandits was behind us. The road ahead would soon be in Nkunda's territory where bandits feared to operate.

We pressed on and, as expected, the roads became decidedly worse. They were so uneven and undulating, with tightly twisting uphill turns, that they threatened to roll the vehicles at times. We averaged five miles an hour on that leg.

FIRST INTO ACTION AGAIN

We decided to spend the night in a small town in the Masisi forest, the name of which escapes me. It was in the middle of a tall, dense, humid jungle. We came across a hand-painted hotel sign, stopped the vehicles and walked along a concrete path through thick vegetation to investigate. The dilapidated reception was empty and so we explored the accommodation for ourselves. We found a collection of single rooms with connecting paths, the dense, rotting foliage encroaching from every direction. The walls of the rooms, inside and out, originally white, were coated in thick black mould. The single beds consisted of damp, filthy mattresses on concrete shelves. The showers were equally dirty and produced a dribble of water, the toilets mere holes in the ground. I suspected we might catch some kind of respiratory disease if we spent the night there. Most international news crews are used to roughing it but we would rather have slept in the vehicles than this place.

We set off again, not particularly confident of finding a bed, but we didn't have to go far. At the end of the village was a tidy building in manicured grounds with a large wooden entrance gate. It was a monastery. It was Anderson or Charlie's idea to ring the bell and ask if they'd take us in for the night. To our delighted surprise, the monks were most welcoming. They would of course be well paid by Charlie for their hospitality. The accommodation was simple, the showers clean and hot, and the food was good.

The following day we made the final leg of the journey, with steep climbs over lush hillsides into Nkunda's territory. We soon began passing sentries and observation outposts. The heavily-armed soldiers didn't try to conceal themselves as they coldly watched us pass by.

THE CONGO

The camp was a sprawling, largely grassy area with pockets of tall trees. There was a small parade taking place on one green, a group being drilled in weapon-handling on another, and a hundred or so men seated in the shade of several trees attending lessons on tactics. The soldiers were more presentable than I would've expected of men living in the bush. Their uniforms were clean and in good condition, as were their weapons and equipment. They were disciplined, calm and well-organised. I don't doubt much of this was laid on for our benefit, although Nkunda had a reputation for commanding well-trained and orderly troops. When he arrived to greet us, he was immaculately turned out, as befitted a genuine general.

Anderson conducted several interviews with Nkunda, moving between various locations that demonstrated the depth of his organisation. At the end of our visit we were treated to a traditional dance and singalong involving several hundred soldiers with Nkunda joining in. The atmosphere was quite relaxed and jovial.

It was most interesting, observing Nkunda and his army. Highly disciplined, quite immaculate considering they were living in the jungle, ordered, organised, well fed, fit. Their weapons were clean and treated with utmost respect. I was quite taken by surprise. Coming from the British military, the Royal Marines no less, it has always been easy for me to criticise the military machines of other nations in comparison. Every other African military I'd ever seen verged on the comedic. I have no idea what these men were like in combat, how effective they were, but from what I saw I would advise respect if going up against them on their home turf. Considering Nkunda's obsession with control and organisation, his ambitions and obvious passion, I felt that many of the accusations of unruliness and undisciplined brutality levelled against him had a tinge of incongruity about them. Anderson was certainly right not to dismiss him as just another maniac.

After several hours, Anderson was satisfied he'd got what he came for and was keen to drive non-stop back to Goma. That suited me. It was mostly downhill and the going would be much quicker. It also meant we'd reach the section of road prone to banditry at night when I felt there was less chance of an attack. Bandits in that area seemed to keep banker's hours.

The broomsticks went back through the windows and we had an uneventful drive back to Goma, stopping only to refuel. We spent the next few days doing local interest stories, which included climbing down a mineshaft to observe miners at work. We were also in *Gorillas in the Mist* country and couldn't pass up the opportunity of doing a piece on the famed animals.

Driving back to Kigali airport three days later, I was keenly aware we'd been lucky not to encounter any difficulties, criminal or mechanical. I had, once again, taken the correct fork in the road.

I was eager to rejoin my family, having left them soon after my daughter's fourth birthday. But I would not be with them for long. My next assignment, a couple of weeks later, was one of the most extraordinary and stressful of my career. I was on my way to Moscow to uncover a dark secret that involved the president of Chechnya and Vladimir Putin. It was one of those tasks that, had I known what I was getting into, I might never have taken.

10

RUSSIA

A WEEK AFTER REJOINING MY family in France I received an urgent call from AKE's number two, Tim, a former SBS operator, asking if I was up for a special task. I should've said no and ended it there, but the word 'special' had me hooked. I'd probably had more than my fair share of exciting adventures but there were never enough.

'Where is it?' I asked.

'I don't know,' he replied.

'How long's it for?'

'I don't know.'

'Well...what's the task?' I asked.

'Sorry, but I have no idea.'

'Is this a joke, Tim?'

'It's not.'

Tim had a sense of humour, to be sure. He wouldn't have lasted long as a Bootneck without one. But when it came to business he was always earnest.

'Do you know when it might start?' I asked.

'Probably right away.'

'Can you say who the client is?'

'Human Rights Watch.'

'I didn't know they were a client.'

'We've been confidentially advising them for several months.'

'Are you calling me because everyone else is busy or turned it down?'

'You're my first call… I have a feeling it might be right up your street.'

'By that you mean you think it's dodgy.'

He said the client sounded stressed, that it was urgent, and they couldn't discuss it over the phone. He went on to explain that HRW were not the flappy sort. They were used to things getting nasty and managing on their own. If they were concerned enough to call AKE for help in this matter, it suggested it was serious.

I pondered.

You see, although I enjoyed the variety and unpredictability of my work, as the years went by and my resumé of successfully completed tasks grew, I became more cautious about the risks. It wasn't that I was becoming more risk-averse. Not at all. I just wanted more accuracy in assessing the risks of tasks prior to accepting them. In the early days, I assumed the operations manager and his staff assessed each task for its risk rating, deciding how safe it was before accepting it and passing it on to an operator. But I'd come to realise that due diligence was not always exercised, nor was it always possible since the risks of many jobs couldn't be accurately assessed until boots were on the ground. But that could sometimes be too late. This task was a perfect example. No one had a clue how dangerous it was. As it turned out, I don't believe even the client truly grasped the terrible implications.

I'd never worked with the Human Rights Watch before. The organisation was often exposed to high-risk situations, gathering sensitive information in order to build cases against individuals, organisations and governments. They often operated in dangerous locations, conducting investigations, clandestinely meeting with whistleblowers, gathering evidence in the shadows. Threats against personnel included harassment from repressive governments, revenge violence, criminal violence, sexual violence, and environmental and health risks. AKE had conducted a security review for HRW a few months prior which suggested improvements to all of its operating procedures: communications, IT security, crisis management, task-planning, reporting, equipment, office/accommodation/personal security, personal awareness, self-sufficiency, et cetera. An exhaustive list but no different to just about any organisation I've ever assessed for security risks. Like many organisations, they functioned satisfactorily under normal conditions, a relative term, but when things went wrong, especially seriously wrong, essential components cracked or failed to function effectively. Our job was to support the four main pillars of operational organisation: duty of care, business continuity, reputation and litigation management. These were the fundamental guidelines I would preach in later life when I became an international crisis manager.

I called the HRW London office, keen to find out more. They insisted I come to the office to meet them in person. They refused to divulge any aspect of the issue over the phone. I asked if there was anything they could tell me, such as the location. They categorically refused. I suggested an encrypted message and again they said no. It was extraordinary.

And so I caught a flight to London. I met two very pleasant ladies who began by telling me they still couldn't reveal the gritty details of the problem. All they would say was that it involved their office in Moscow. They provided me with the contact information of the director, Allison. I would only find out the true nature of the situation from Allison in Moscow, and they needed me there as soon as possible.

I'd had issues in the past assessing risk due to lack of information but this was ridiculous. I asked if they could at least tell me whether or not it was life-threatening. They glanced at each other as if unsure if they could even say that much, which made it clear to me that it probably was. I asked if there had been any violence to date with regards to the incident. They acknowledged there had not been any as yet. I asked how many personnel were involved. All they'd say was that it was hard to give a precise answer because there might be another office in danger by association. I asked how many people were in the Moscow office. It was five in all, plus the occasional part-timer.

My task, if I chose to accept it, was to get to Moscow as soon as possible, assess the situation, and take it from there.

I couldn't refuse. I was never going to – it was far too intriguing. They were clearly concerned. I was familiar with parts of the old Cold War Russia. Not as a soldier but earlier in my risk manager career. I climbed the Potemkin Steps in Odessa one evening on my way to an opera house wearing an Armani suit and carrying a Sig P220 semi-automatic pistol in a shoulder holster. No, I wasn't a spy and neither was I on a hit. The reason is somewhat embarrassing and I'll never tell unless heavily

RUSSIA

laden with drinks and in the mood to illustrate what an idiot I could be.

I returned to France and had one night with my family before flying to Paris and the Russian embassy to collect my visa. That process went smoothly and I flew to Sheremetyevo International Airport, Moscow, arriving early evening. I passed through immigration without a problem, made my way to the taxi rank and showed the driver the hotel address in Cyrillic, which I couldn't read. After a 40-minute drive in heavy traffic, we arrived at a gloomy, somewhat seedy-looking neighbourhood, I climbed out with my bag and the taxi pulled away. I checked that the Cyrillic address corresponded with that on the front of a shoddy hotel in front of me. It appeared to. AKE had an efficient travel department but also an annoying habit of looking for budget accommodation to save clients money. This was well-intentioned but could sometimes create inconveniences. I was used to low-standard accommodation in dodgy neighbourhoods. It was more often than not the case in my business. I'd had higher expectations on this trip since it wasn't a conflict zone and the general dynamics of the organisation and environment suggested it might be a tad more civilised than I was used to. I was sadly disappointed. I mentally prepared myself to spend the night in a roach-ridden room with plenty of drunks and druggies for neighbours.

Before heading inside I decided to call Allison, the Moscow HRW director, and let her know I'd arrived. She picked up immediately. Her American-accented voice sounded warm and pleasant. I began by asking if she wanted to get together that evening. She was at home with her husband and child and settled in for the night, but suggested we meet at the office the following morning. Whatever the emergency was, it could obviously wait a few more hours. I asked her the best way to get to the office. She grew concerned when I gave my location, asking why I'd chosen it. I explained it was a random choice since no-one in the AKE office had any knowledge of Moscow. Allison told me to hail the first taxi I saw and get out of there. Apparently it wasn't safe. She'd get back to me ASAP with a better hotel.

She was very efficient. By the time I found a taxi she had called back with a new address. Apparently there was a shortage of hotels in Moscow and the only one she could find at such short notice was of the more expensive variety. I was impressed as we pulled up outside the five-star establishment. This neighbourhood was plush compared to the previous one. My luxury room a dozen floors up overlooked the Moskva River. I dumped my bag and went for a walk to find a restaurant and a spot of dinner.

That night would be the last time I felt safe during my stay.

I was up bright and early the following morning, looking forward to visiting the HRW offices and getting to the bottom of the dark mystery. It was a 15-minute walk across the river using the Krymsky Bridge to the Park Kultury metro. All the station names were in Cyrillic of course and I made my way through the underground system by comparing the Cyrillic symbols on my map to the station names on the platform walls as I passed through them. I alighted at Krasnye Vorota and followed the map for a five-minute walk to the offices off Staraya Basmannaya. Entering the small four-storey building, I was greeted by a pleasant elderly man at the foot of a narrow staircase. He doubled as receptionist and caretaker and therefore wasn't

RUSSIA

always in attendance at the entrance to the building. I made a mental note of this porous access control.

HRW shared the building with a couple of other companies and some private apartments. I climbed the stairs and entered the compact office, which consisted of three modest rooms and a kitchen, all shared by five permanent staff and a handful of interns and assistants.

My general assignment was to evaluate the safety and security of the staff offices and accommodation in the city, assess data security and management, operational procedures and capabilities, conduct an overall threat assessment, and scrutinise the evacuation plans and crisis management policies and procedures. Not a small task for the five days I'd been given. I would gather the information and write the detailed report when I returned home, as was often the case.

My starting point for such tasks was usually a chat with the team, a Q&A to familiarise myself with personnel, policies, procedures and so forth, followed by an inspection of the facilities and local area. The main players were Allison the director and Alexander, a Russian, whom everyone called Sasha. He was a quiet, unassuming man, mature in years and, I was to learn, the most important member of the team and the key to the entire mystery.

I didn't want to leap straight in with '*So, what's this all about then?*' We all got cups of tea and coffee and sat together informally, exchanging small talk. Despite the friendly reception, I could feel the anxiety in the air.

Allison kicked off with some background, describing how the authorities didn't make it easy for them to operate. There were endless bureaucratic obstructions such as operating licences and visas for cross-border movement. As the team became more comfortable with my presence and saw how open the boss was being, they became less stilted.

The office had been broken into several times over the years, the last time a week ago. The culprits didn't appear to have been common or garden burglars. They were very selective. Valuable items had been ignored. A phone and laptop had been examined but not taken. Computer monitors were left untouched but hard-drives had been inspected. The team believed the purpose of the break-ins was to steal data. They also suspected they were under surveillance. Several felt certain they'd been followed, and recently too, particularly Sasha. He lived outside the city in a rural housing estate, didn't have a car and took an overland train to and from the office in the morning and evening.

HRW had a satellite office in Tashkent which had experienced similar intrusions. When I telephoned Andrea, the girl running the Tashkent office, she described how a surveillance team often followed her whenever she left the office. I asked her why she thought she was being followed by a team. She said they were very obvious, as if they wanted her to know they were watching her. That was quite possible – the Russians had a fondness for intimidation.

I sat patiently, waiting to hear what this was all about. Finally Allison leaned forward, lowering her voice, her expression conspiratorial. It was the big reveal.

I want to pause for a moment to explain in simple terms how HRW gathered information about human rights abuses. In order to find the victims and perpetrators, HRW conducted its own investigations but it relied a great deal on victims or whistleblowers volunteering details. Much time was spent confirming that sources were genuine. Information certainly is power – it can bring down individuals in high places and even whole governments. If powerful people find out others possess information that could threaten them, things can get very dangerous.

Sasha sat quietly, watching with a sombre expression as Allison and the others huddled together.

'We have a source,' Allison said, 'who says they know who's behind the killing of Anna Politkovskaya.'

'Stop!' I said immediately, preventing her from continuing, even though she was speaking softly.

I took a moment to digest the news. 'When's the last time you had the offices electronically swept?' I asked.

They had never swept the office for bugs, despite suspecting that devices had been installed. Conducting a technical sweep was not as easy as walking around the office with a phone app pointing it at things and waiting for it to beep. A lot of equipment was required, especially in those days. You wouldn't want to use a Russian security firm because they'd all be former members of the military or intelligence services and therefore untrustworthy. The only secure way would be to employ a team from the UK or USA, but they might be prevented from bringing in their equipment.

Knowing who killed Anna Politkovskaya at that time put one's own life at risk. She had been murdered in Moscow two weeks before I arrived. Her killing had attracted worldwide media attention. She was a Russian journalist who campaigned vociferously against her country's conduct of the war in Chechnya. She'd written a critical book that documented widespread abuse of civilians by Russian troops throughout the campaign. She was a major thorn in Vladimir Putin's side and had received many death threats. On one occasion she had to flee the country for several months when a Russian police officer threatened to murder her after she accused him of committing atrocities. A couple of months before her death thugs tried to break into a car her daughter was driving. She was an incredibly brave woman to take on Putin. But as the world has come to learn, there is nowhere safe for anyone who criticises the Russian president. Anna was mercilessly gunned down, shot in the back and the head as she entered the elevator in her Moscow apartment block.

I didn't want to take the chance that Allison's whispers would be overheard by a nearby bug, so I got to my feet and suggested we all go for a walk. Allison's revelation had cast a sombre shadow over the meeting. Everyone grabbed their coats and we headed out of the office, down the stairs and out onto the street. I asked Allison to find a cafe. She led the way along a narrow pavement. I checked if anyone was following, glancing at parked cars to see if they were occupied. I made a mental note of the pedestrians around us, front and rear, in case I saw them again.

We turned into a street lined with small shopfronts and Allison stopped outside a cafe. It was practically empty and we piled inside. I found a discreet booth and we all huddled around the table, waiting in silence until we were sure no-one had followed us inside. I could see enough of the front door to register if anyone else entered. When I was satisfied, I asked Allison to continue.

She got right to it. The source had called a week ago. The caller specifically asked for Sasha, which was no surprise. Sasha

RUSSIA

was Russian, well-known as a member of HRW, and very experienced. The caller's identity needed to be verified but they claimed they knew who had ordered the assassination of Anna Politkovskaya.

Allison didn't give any more details and I didn't need to know them. I wasn't there as a member of HRW to consider what to do with the information. I was there to assess the risk to the team and its data and suggest solutions. The revelation certainly explained the extreme concern in HRW London and Moscow and why they couldn't tell anyone outside their immediate circle. Whoever ordered the execution of such a high-profile journalist would have no qualms about eliminating anyone who could implicate them. Once HRW verified the source it had to decide what to do with the information. This was the period of greatest risk. The number of people who knew was small and manageable. If the bad guys nabbed any of the office staff and forced them to reveal what was known and who was the source handler, that would sound the death knell for Sasha. He would be kidnapped and tortured until he gave up the name, after which the source would promptly disappear.

The surveillance of HRW staff and the break-ins at their offices didn't necessarily mean they were suspected of knowing something about Anna's murder. It's possible the surveillance was purely precautionary. If the bad guys did suspect, I would've expected them to have already snatched one of the staff to find out what they knew. Allison didn't believe that any HRW data on the subject had been stolen. However, it would be safest to assume the worst, that the bad guys knew everything, and act accordingly. But that would require closing down the office and getting everyone out of the country ASAP. The problem was that some staff, including Sasha, would need visas, which wouldn't be granted. Allison wouldn't desert her office if there was a single member still in country. The only other option was a safe house. But that would mean everyone abandoning their normal lives and loved ones. It would be impossible to sustain for any length of time, if at all.

The only viable option that I could see was to verify the source and, if it was genuine, release the information. In other words, share it as widely as possible in order to take the pressure off the team. The decision wasn't mine to make. It was easy for me to arbitrarily summarise the threats and come up with recommendations, but they had to be practical.

I felt like I was caught in a Cold War espionage ring in the heart of the Soviet Union.

I got back to my responsibilities and spent the rest of the day conducting my security survey, assessing vulnerabilities and interviewing the staff on various safety procedures. It was dark by the time I left.

As I made my way to the underground to catch a train back to Park Kultury station, I was acutely aware I had become one of a select few who possessed dangerous knowledge. I could confirm that HRW had a source who could reveal the identity of the person who contracted the killing of Anna Politkovskaya. From that point on, my life in Moscow changed. I was conscious of my vulnerability as I crossed the Krymsky Bridge, a broad, long, four-lane road between the metro and my hotel on the other side. I was the only pedestrian on it that evening. I looked back every now and then to see if I was being followed. It would be very easy for a car to pull alongside me and a bunch of thugs to either snatch me or toss me over the side. The security

RUSSIA

advisor from the UK might be the first target. I was becoming paranoid.

I always carried a door alarm in my utility bag and that evening I installed it. It would alert me if the door was opened and stop it from fully opening, for a moment at least. My room was high up and had a balcony. How convenient.

The next couple of days I conducted security surveys of the HRW staff homes. Alison lived in a city apartment with her husband and young child. I didn't know until then that Russian front doors opened outwards, unlike ones in the UK, Europe and the USA which open inwards. Opening outwards makes it harder for someone to smash the door in. Helpful if thugs tried to gain entry, less so if emergency services needed to rescue those inside.

Visiting Sasha's apartment in the countryside didn't assuage my paranoia. He'd stayed home that day, so I made the journey alone after leaving the office at the end of the day. It was dark by the time I got to the train station. It was a 40-minute ride into the boonies in an old carriage with an all-wooden interior, the sort of thing one might find in a museum in the West. It was long and empty except for an elderly couple and two young kids who I assumed were their grandchildren. I spent the journey gazing out of the window at passing farms and villages.

I stepped off the train with one other person who took no notice of me as he walked on ahead. Sasha had given me a sketch map. It was a 10-minute walk in darkness, partly through woodland. It wasn't hard to locate Sasha's tall apartment block. The security lighting was poor, leaving shadows everywhere. There was a single elevator with a staircase beside it. He lived in a small corner apartment four floors up with simple furnishings.

FIRST INTO ACTION AGAIN

I suggested the office purchase an emergency escape ladder that he could lower to the ground from his apartment window. It would be a challenging descent for him and his wife, but in the event of a fire on the central staircase they might prefer to take the chance. It might also be useful if thugs were bashing down the door. He was extremely vulnerable. Again, the only solution seemed to be some kind of secret alternative accommodation. I was concerned for him.

It was late by the time I caught the train back. Three large men joined me in the carriage a few benches away. They looked at me briefly then one of them produced a bottle of clear liquid which I presumed was vodka and passed it between them. I was the only person to get off at my station and I walked through empty streets to the metro. It was much busier there.

There were a lot of drunks. Most were young. As I left Kultury Station I saw a dozen youngsters congregated outside, necking large brown bottles of beer. Hundreds of empty bottles lay discarded.

Once again I made the lonely walk across the bridge. I continued to feel vulnerable after closing my hotel room door, acutely aware I had three more days before I could get out of there.

I completed my work in the time-frame and there were no incidents while I was there. My paranoia continued as I made my way through the airport to depart. I ticked off all the stages as I got through them. Check-in, immigration, the gate, boarding the plane. I didn't relax until we took off and the plane was outside Russian air space, beyond the point of no return.

I have no idea what HRW did with the information, not that it was any of my business. I was soon off on another task and

RUSSIA

I put my experiences in Moscow behind me. I would've heard if something bad had happened to any of them. It was several months before I read a news article, no doubt based on information from HRW, that revealed Chechen thugs had killed Anna Politkovskaya. Vladimir Putin's enthusiasm for assassinations at home and abroad wasn't deterred by accusations that she had been killed on his orders.

I rejoined my family in France to finish our vacation. A few days after we returned to England, I was on my way back to Iraq. It would be another two years before I was blown up in the Al Hamra Hotel. The next few years were probably the most dangerous of my life, not helped by the fact that I was becoming complacent. I was getting past my sell-by date and starting to feel I needed a new line of work. But I couldn't decide what that would be. The solution, I decided, was to upgrade.

A new fork in the road was approaching.

11

IRAQ, SAUDI ARABIA, YEMEN

MOST OF MY NEWS CLIENTS maintained a footprint in Iraq for more than a decade after the end of the war that saw Saddam and his regime dismantled. It remained a fascinating and challenging place to operate. But I wanted greater variety. There were other exciting tasks and places in the world. The more time I spent in the business, the more experience I gained. There were other varieties of security risk management to explore. I felt it was time to get into more cerebral disciplines such as crisis management and kidnap and ransom. Dodging bombs and bullets had their moments but I was becoming blasé. That was dangerous in my line of work. There was one memorable turning point in particular. A serious reality check that happened not long after the Al Hamra Hotel bombing.

IRAQ, SAUDI ARABIA, YEMEN

I received a call from ABC, the major USA network, one of my 'advisory only' clients. They lived a mile from the Al Hamra. The bureau chief was growing increasingly concerned about the safety of his premises. They'd been in the same location for several years and had created a walled compound which they shared with other organisations. It was a relatively safe part of town when they arrived in the early days, but of late they were feeling isolated and vulnerable. They had good reason to. The Mahdi Army, a large militia led by firebrand Shiite cleric Muqtada al-Sadr based in Sada City seven miles north, had been flexing its muscles for several months by sending out armed combatants to dominate sections of the city as a show of strength. They wouldn't dare take on any coalition troops and after a few hours would scurry back to their base. But while they controlled a specific location, it was a dangerous place for any western civilians to wander into. It seemed that every few weeks the Mahdi army ventured further afield. The ABC chief's concern was the militia getting closer to his bureau.

I was well aware of the Mahdi army's activities and had warned ABC and others in the area months before to relocate but I was ignored. Nothing new there. I preached prevention but, like many clients, they waited until response was their only option.

I told the chief I'd come and see him, got my gear together, climbed into my battered little car that we used for pottering about in Baghdad, stuck the magnetic taxi sign onto the roof and left the hotel. I was tanned and usually maintained a short beard while in Iraq, doing my best to look like the average Iraqi. Western features were a red flag since the 1920s when the Brits occupied the lands that would become Iraq. On their departure they left behind a few red-headed and pasty-faced kids, and their mothers had some explaining to do. To complete my look I wore a kaffiyeh, but not in the romanticised TE Lawrence manner. I rolled it into a lump and placed it on my head with an end draping down one side, an unkempt, sloppy style I'd noted many old Iraqis sporting.

I put my ops bag on the passenger seat, a locally bought shopping bag containing my map, spare ammo and smoke grenades. The barrel of my AK47 rested on the passenger floor with the butt leaning close to the gearstick within easy reach and covered in a scarf. My taxi was grubby, rusting, with trash distributed across the dashboard.

I thought nothing of the dangers as I left the security gate of the Al Hamra compound and joined traffic heading for Karada Kharidge road. I'd done it so many times before. Obviously I ignored anyone trying to wave me down. As I arrived at the junction of Huriya Square, the traffic slowed to a crawl as it navigated through. It seemed slower than normal. I needed to turn right and squeezed over into that lane. It wasn't until I was 50 metres from the junction that I saw men carrying AK47s up ahead. They were in civvies, so not police or military. I knew instantly they could only be one thing. Mahdi Army. Another of their power moves, this time into Karada, which was a first as far as I knew. There was usually an Iraqi police presence on the junction but they'd obviously fled. This was not good. If they were checking vehicles, which is what they usually did, I had a serious problem. I was stuck between cars and could only drive forward along with them. As I edged closer I could see more armed men spread about the junction, moving between vehicles looking inside them.

IRAQ, SAUDI ARABIA, YEMEN

The militia was of particular concern to us. We ran into dodgy police and army quite often but they rarely messed with private security knowing we were armed and usually had backup. But if these guys knew who I was, especially all alone, they'd take me, and brutally.

A year before, five Brits, four of them private security from a company called Gardaworld, along with their client, a computer programmer, were forcefully taken from the finance ministry in Baghdad. At the time we thought it had been the Mahdi army. It later turned out to be the Iranian Revolutionary Guard. The lads were in the finance ministry when a hundred Iranians drove into the compound in Land Cruisers dressed as Iraqi police and swarmed into the building. It was a planned kidnapping. Gardaworld had made the fatal mistake of setting a routine. There were five British security guards in all, but one of them had managed to hide under some floorboards. He was lucky. The Iranians knew he was somewhere in the building but couldn't afford the time to look for him. I knew the lads, having visited their HQ only a couple of weeks before. They rented out and repaired armoured cars as a side business and we used them regularly. I also knew the finance ministry. I was there a week before the kidnapping with Ade, former SAS, my partner at the time. Ade had business with the ministry, drumming up work, and I tagged along to keep him company. We went back a second time a few days later and, as I hung about outside the building I felt most uncomfortable. It was as if eyes were on me but I couldn't see who was watching. In my business, such senses were honed and we didn't question them. When Ade left the building to join me I asked him how he felt about the place. He also sensed the threat and decided he wouldn't be coming back for the meeting he'd been invited to. The rules for visiting anywhere in Iraq was to arrive unexpectedly and leave soon after. The Gardaworld lads were handcuffed, hooded and whisked away to Sada City, stripped off completely in case they were carrying trackers, kept inside a dark room, then a couple of days later driven out of Baghdad across the Iraqi border into Iran. It was a balls-up by the Iranians because they thought they'd kidnapped a bunch of Americans. The kidnapping was planned in order to trade the victims for comrades being held by the Americans. The Brits stuck by their policy of not dealing with kidnappers and so the Iranians murdered the boys over the next year or so, except the computer programmer who they released as part of a prisoner exchange. The incarceration was the bit we all feared. Death in a fire-fight, blown to bits, they were acceptable. To be imprisoned by those thugs who beat, tortured, starved and violated their victims to death, slowly and painfully, was terrifying to contemplate. I'd shoot myself at the first opportunity. That was not bravado. I'd heard hundreds of stories, described in too much sordid detail over the years, about what those animals did to people. I don't doubt any of the victims would've blown their brains out had they had the chance. The only opportunity for that was just before getting caught while a gun was still to hand. Save the last bullet. The only journalist in Iraq who I knew carried a pistol – I knew because he asked me to show him how to use it – only wanted a couple of bullets in the magazine. He didn't intend to shoot anybody. They were only for him.

As I shunted forward, closer to the junction, I had nowhere else to go but through it. I considered stopping, climbing out and walking away until I heard a shout, then running for all I

IRAQ, SAUDI ARABIA, YEMEN

was worth. The fundamental rule of escape from captivity was to make your attempt as early as possible. The later you left it, the less chance you had of success.

The car ahead of me pealed away and I was at the junction with half a dozen Mahdi army close by. Two of them walked down either side of my car holding their AKs in one hand. One of them put a hand on my roof and leaned down to look inside. If he told me to get out of the car I'd be searched. They'd find my pistol and ID hanging inside my shirt. I'd be grabbed, beaten and taken away. Next stop a prison in Iran most likely. Torture. Abuse. Death. If he did ask me to get out, I knew exactly what I'd do. I'd carried out the drill a hundred times during my 14 Int training days in Pontrilas on the Welsh border near Hereford. We'd rehearse how to respond if, alone in the street or public place, you were suddenly grabbed. The key was total, unbridled aggression. Climbing out of the car, I'd already have my pistol in my hand. I'd brutally shove the person back to create enough space to bring my pistol into position, holding it close to my gut at first and shooting those nearest to me as quickly as possible, turning full circle if need be. Then extend the pistol into the familiar firing stance and shoot anyone else nearby. Headshots preferably but anywhere will do. I'd then run as hard as I could, away from the junction, between the long line of cars, changing lanes so no one could get a bead on me. Every metre away from them was a little safer from being shot. The AK was not an accurate rifle. A shooter would need to be good to hit a moving man at a hundred metres. Running between cars would make it more difficult. I'd keep going to the next junction, then either straight to my hotel, or towards the 14th of July Bridge where the Yanks had a checkpoint into the Green Zone.

I glanced at the guy for a second and looked ahead nonchalantly. He didn't pause for long. The other guy didn't even look in on me and banged my roof to get going. I drove through the junction, turning right, and joined the traffic. My heart must've been going like the clappers at that point. I must've squeezed every bit of adrenalin I had into my system. I had been ready to go. I would certainly have shot three or four of them. Would I have made it out of there, running for all I was worth? Probably not. Thankfully I didn't have to find out.

My kaffiyeh had saved the day. Fuck cultural appropriation.

The incident was a serious reality check for me. I'd been too complacent. I hadn't called any of my own people to let them know I was heading out into the city. Had I been lifted, no one would probably know for a day at least. I was furious with myself for being so lax. It was a warning, a stark one, but not so much to be more alert. I needed to get out of Iraq.

I let Ops Hereford know I needed a break. I found out later they were surprised I'd stayed on as long as I had after the Al Hamra bombing. There were many other tasks to keep me busy and I was soon on the road.

One of my more satisfying tasks was creating Emergency Evacuation Plans (EEP) for companies operating in unstable countries. My first real attempt at executing an EEP had been in Liberia during the war, trying to escape with my CNN team. That had been a useful lesson since it'd been a complete failure. An effective EEP cannot be created by anyone who has not had a great deal of operational experience. It required practical knowledge of land, sea and air transport relative to the country the EEP was intended, investigation, threat analysis, an understanding of the organisation concerned, its business model,

IRAQ, SAUDI ARABIA, YEMEN

policies and risk appetite, the latter having the greatest impact on preparing an EEP. Some companies were keen to evacuate at the first sign of trouble while others preferred to wait until the last minute. Risk appetite was decided at the highest level of a company. The policy makers. Evacuations were costly and often meant a total loss for the company which was why they would try to hold on until the last possible moment. Evacuation triggers needed to be clear and obvious.

Creating an EEP was a great responsibility. The author had to fully appreciate the ground, the people involved, the threats, assets, politics, neighbours and – most often overlooked, the environment – any of which could change at short notice. A plan written for the winter will probably fail in the summer and vice versa.

An example of an EEP is one I completed for a French company, Vallourec, based in Dammam on the east coast of Saudi Arabia. Vallourec wanted an EEP for the same reason everyone else in that part of the world was concerned. Iran, 150 miles away across the Persian Gulf, was producing weapons grade uranium and threatening to build an atomic weapon while remonstrating that Israel should be wiped off the world map. Understandably, the Israelis didn't want them to have a nuclear capability and threatened to destroy the bomb-making facilities. That would potentially trigger a major conflict in the region. Iran didn't get on with many of its neighbours, Saudi Arabia in particular, and if Israel did attack, Iran might go on a retaliatory rampage, shut down the Strait of Hormuz to block the flow of a large portion of the world's oil, and attack Saudi Arabia.

Emergency Evacuation Plans are basically divided into two

main components: preparation and response. What could be put in place beforehand, and what needed to happen when the evacuation was triggered.

Vallourec had roughly 70 personnel in Dammam, 40 or so of them locals. Locals could present a problem. The first question I asked on that subject was which locals should be evacuated and which should be left behind. It usually meant evacuating the employee's entire family. Would that only be technical staff, or include cleaners, cooks and gardeners for instance? You can be sure others will turn up to be evacuated such as distant relatives, and be prepared for friends, other people's children, pets and domestic animals, and they'll all have baggage and probably furniture too.

The company would be responsible for the locals once they got them to the home country and would have to provide housing, jobs, schooling, medical aid, etc. By this time in the conversation the client might be having second thoughts. But then I'd mention the most likely scenario would be that once the authorities learned the evacuation plane included refugees it would refuse it entry into European airspace. So often what began as a magnanimous gesture became a refusal to evacuate any locals at all, unless the company was prepared to charter a second plane and fly them to somewhere that would take them.

It was no surprise that Vallourec, being French, had a high risk appetite and wouldn't flinch until it looked certain the Iranians were mobilising to invade. A high risk appetite might be plucky but it was also problematic. A late departure meant the airports and roads leading to them would already be clogged by those companies and families with lower risk appetites. International airlines would cancel flights, mainly because their insurances

IRAQ, SAUDI ARABIA, YEMEN

would be cancelled. Since Dammam was on the Persian Gulf a seaborne evacuation was out of the question because it would mean passing through the Strait of Hormuz which would be a dangerous place. The only remaining option was by road. Major routes out of Dammam would be clogged though.

A private charter plane was an option. I had companies on my rolodex that specialised in evacuating large numbers of personnel from conflict zones, but they weren't cheap. Companies with emergency evacuation insurance would be covered of course. But you still needed a convenient and secure airfield you could transport everyone too.

Having said all that, companies with no risk appetite would've left as soon as they thought there was even a chance of the Israelis attacking. The Libyan civil war was a fine example of the impact of varying risk appetites. Most could see the storm clouds gathering as Gaddafi's grip on power was challenged but just about everyone underestimated the speed at which the change occurred. Those with low risk appetites packed their bags and left when there were still commercial airlines running and the borders weren't clogged. Companies that waited for the shooting to begin were stuck. Hundreds of westerners were left in facilities across the country, many in the middle of the desert unable to leave and fearful for their lives. AKE sent a couple of operators across the Egyptian border and deep into Libya to rescue the staff of an Italian company, utilising bicycles and camels at one stage to get the workers out. Sadly I was stuck on the Tunisian/Libyan border at the time with a CNN team and missing out on all of that fun.

Vallourec settled for the road option to Jeddah, on the other side of the country on the Red Sea. It was the least risky of all the options in my opinion. Once they arrived in Jeddah I could arrange for a vessel to take them wherever they wanted to go. By that time, through AKE, I was senior maritime security risk advisor to GAC – Gulf Agency Company – the second largest shipping agent in the world.

The most challenging section of the EEP was listing all of the things that could go wrong and figuring out solutions for them. It took me four days to complete the plan outline that included photos, diagrams, maps and contacts. The average EEP could be around 30 A4 pages long, if the author wasn't verbose. It needed to be concise and easy to read and understand, and readily available in the event it was required. Copies would be sent to the company's headquarters for approval and the job was done. And like all plans, components of it would soon be out of date and therefore needed constant maintenance. Risk Management was a machine that never stopped.

One of my more interesting clients was Lloyd's of London Insurance. AKE had a desk in the London headquarters with a particular syndicate. The downside of the job was working in the city and having to commute and wear a suit and tie everyday. It would usually last a week and mean staying in a hotel.

The task at Lloyd's was to assess terrorist or military conflict related insurance covers. When such a request for insurance cover arrived on the syndicate's desk it was handed to the AKE operator on duty to provide an assessment to help the underwriter decide whether or not to accept it. We might be asked to assess the likelihood of a terrorist attack on an oil platform in the Black Sea for instance. They were generally desktop exercises and we usually had 24 hours to come up with the report. Some were only tangentially related to a military conflict. For instance,

IRAQ, SAUDI ARABIA, YEMEN

I was asked to assess if the Indian national cricket team would turn up to play the Pakistan national cricket team in Pakistan that year. India and Pakistan were close to war once again over Kashmir and Jammu and the Indian cricket association, the BCCI, was looking for insurance in case the team didn't turn up. I can't remember the insurance premium but it was around £1 million for a payout of £20 million.

I began by looking at the history between the two teams, then the current conflict and the potential threats. The Pakistanis had given every assurance the Indian team would be protected. But the cover was specific. It wasn't to insure the Indian team against an incident while in Pakistan. It was insurance against the Indian team not turning up at all.

I finally called a cricket enthusiast I knew who had friends in the Indian team which eventually led to a call to the captain himself. When asked if there were any circumstances in which the Indian team would not turn up to play in Pakistan, the captain roared passionately for anyone to hear that there was no force on earth that would stop him and his team from playing in Pakistan. That sounded good enough for me and I submitted my assessment suggesting it was a safe enough cover. The underwriter chose to ignore my decision and India went on to play Pakistan in Pakistan. He just passed up a million quid. It was one of those occasions where I wondered if I was in the wrong business. But then, living in the city, wearing a suit and tie every day... No thanks.

Not all of the jobs were desktop. Some couldn't be assessed by sitting in the Lloyd's building and surfing the internet. Boots sometimes needed to hit the ground. One such assessment ended up coming to me.

FIRST INTO ACTION AGAIN

The lad on duty at Lloyd's was handed an interesting conundrum concerning a large oil production facility in Yemen, near the town of Riyan on the south coast near the Oman border. It consisted of two large oil drilling and extraction blocks inland, 138km of main oil pipeline interspersed with pumping stations that led from the blocks to a huge oil storage depot on the coast that fed the oil into visiting supertankers through a string of single-point moorings out to sea. The oil company that had the contract was Nexen from Calgary, Canada. The terminal had suffered a terrorist attack a few years back, which was a dismal failure as far as business interruption was concerned, but Nexen wanted insurance in case another attack was successful. The deal was that if an attack halted oil production for 30 days the underwriter would pay out for 36 days of production which was valued at $50mil. This would cover the cost until the oil field could repair the damage and recommence production. The underwriter wanted to know if it was possible for a terrorist attack to shut down production for 30 days. It was clearly impossible to figure out from a desktop computer and therefore someone had to go to Yemen to assess it on site.

I happened to be home when the task was raised and AKE called to see if I wanted to go to Yemen and conduct the assessment. It was right up my street since, being SBS, I knew how to cripple an oil facility, its pipelines and terminal. The question was could the local terrorists have the knowhow and capability of mounting an effective attack and, if so, could the Nexen engineers repair the damage and get the site back up and running within 30 days. The terrorists didn't have cruise missiles for instance or anything nearly so sophisticated. Neither could they muster a huge force of manpower. And the blocks and terminal were protected by the Yemeni army. The last terrorist attack had utilised AK47 rifle fire, an RPG hand-held rocket launcher and a vehicle packed with explosives. They managed to kill half a dozen security guards at the main entrance and make a small hole in a large storage tank that, little did they know was almost empty at the time and therefore failed to even pause oil production for a minute. They would no doubt learn from their mistakes and try again.

I agreed to do the task and left home the following day for Yemen hoping to complete the task within five days. I'd spend a day at the blocks, a day inspecting the pipeline, another two at the terminal, and the rest with the site engineers learning their capabilities with regards to repairing the proposed damage.

Nexen's oil facility security was run by three former SAS operators. I felt the indignation as soon as I arrived. It was no doubt partly due to a former member of the SBS being assigned to assess the security they provided, but there was another somewhat nefarious reason. Several years before, AKE had won the contract to provide security to the terminal and they employed the same former SAS lads to set it up. Once the lads were established they made a behind-the-back deal with Nexen to provide the same security services for less money by cutting out AKE. They would make more money than their salaries by sharing what would've been AKE's portion of the fee. Nexen would lose the support of a major risk management company but they obviously decided it was a good deal. It was pure coincidence that Lloyd's was a client of AKE.

I'd never been to Yemen before. It was a hot, sleepy desert of a place. Small flocks of skinny little goats roamed the countryside watched over by their herders as they searched for what little shrubbery there was. If gravel ever became a valuable commodity, Yemen would be a rich country.

Most of the Yemeni soldiers I saw were flagrantly high on Kat, their cheeks bulging with the leafy product that was comparable to a light hashish. They weren't grinning all of the time and promoting peace with the V sign. More like looking vacant.

The oil extraction blocks would be the most difficult to put out of action simply because of the vast number of oil derricks and pumps. There were hundreds of them over a vast area and would take an army of rampaging terrorists to destroy even half of them. I could cross that off the list.

The pipeline and pumping houses looked like obvious targets but the engineers said they could replace a hundred metres of pipeline in under a week with ease. There was no shortage of spare pipes. As for a pumping station or even two being taken out, the engineers could reroute the pipeline around the damaged stations. The pumping stations in total were powerful enough to skip one or two in the chain that failed to operate. Each pumping station had its own army protection. Once again, the local terrorists didn't have the manpower or organisation to mount a hugely destructive attack on all of the pumping stations. I could cross the pipeline off the list.

The port terminal was a large affair. Its most attractive targets were the oil storage tanks. But the facility was well managed and run within capacity which meant the storage tanks were mostly empty or very low. I could also bring in an empty super tanker to act as a temporary storage tank. So the storage tanks were off the list.

Next was the power grid that ran the facilities. The engineers reckoned there were enough portable generators in the region to provide enough temporary power to run everything until the main grid was repaired. Cross the power grid off.

Apart from some other minor modules, that left one major component that if destroyed could shut down the facility, and it turned out to be a significant one. The main oil pumps that pushed the oil from the fields into the pipelines. There were four pumps, each custom made and, according to the engineers, would take 10 months minimum to replace. It was the Achilles heel of the entire oil transfer system. And they were exposed in the open. I could stand on the road that passed along the block HQ and see them, inside a fragile chain-link fenced area the size of a volleyball court. A handful of determined terrorists could get inside the compound and a few pounds of explosive intelligently placed would destroy them. The former SAS lads had not protected them well enough and I could sense their growls when I brought it up at the engineers and executive meeting. I confess putting the knife in and twisting it a little. It was payback for nicking the task off AKE.

It was not only my job to find the weaknesses but also to mitigate them if I could. Reinforcing the pump compound was not enough. After further discussions with the engineers I was fortunate to find a solution. The four pumps lay side-by-side and when I inspected them I realised only two of them were operating. Redundancy had been built into the equation of pumping the oil. The pumps were designed to pump 100% of the expected capacity of the oilfields but they had been running at 65% capacity for some years. This meant that two of the pumps could be dismantled and placed in a secure storage. If the working pumps were destroyed they could simply be replaced and in a matter of days. It would be a solution until another couple of pumps could be built and stored elsewhere in the event of an emergency.

I completed my report with all of the various attack scenarios and mitigations, advising that the terminal could continue production within 30 days no matter what the local terrorist organisation could achieve based on capability and probability.

The report turned out to be a double-edged sword. Lloyd's could see that the insurance was a good bet. But Nexen could also see the risk was less than they feared and decided to self-insure, saving themselves $20 million in premium fees, which is what they did.

12

ISRAEL & PALESTINE, SRI LANKA, AFGHANISTAN

THE MAJORITY OF MY WORK had been in the background, advising, planning, teaching, below the parapet. But every now and then I found myself thrust into the light. Working for news organisations for many years I gained some recognition as an authority on certain security related subjects and was on occasion invited to give my opinion on TV. It was never something I jumped at. I was always worried about putting my foot in it, being too direct, not politically correct enough and generally inappropriate. I also tended to think of a better way to say something after it was over. That annoyed me the most.

I was passing through Atlanta, Georgia on my way to teach crisis management to the executives of USAID in Washington DC when I popped into CNN's HQ to visit a colleague from AKE who was head of CNN's security. My old comrade Anderson Cooper heard I was in town and invited me to link in to his New York studio to give my opinions about recent Somali pirate activity. It was a long show but I managed to get through it without a noticeable blunder, or so Anderson assured me. At the end of the show he was gracious enough to thank me on air for hanging with him in the Congo. That was a nice moment. It's not often one gets a thank you in my line of work.

Such events were short and sweet. It was the long exposures I wanted to avoid. I managed to dodge the high-profile tasks that occasionally came along that thrust the team, in particular the team leader, into the spotlight. But I was unable to duck them entirely. I should be pleased that I only had one in all my time in the business.

It came a month or so after my return from Yemen. AKE Ops called to ask if I'd like to run a high-profile close protection team. I was wary but I showed interest. CP wasn't my thing, but it was different. It depended on who and where.

The client was Ted Turner and Kofi Annan and the location was Israel and Palestine. My interest peaked. I had fond memories of both places and fancied a return. It turned out to be one of the most stressful tasks I've ever run.

There were so many moving parts, with Ted and Kofi often going in different directions while meeting the most powerful players in Israel and the Palestinian Authority. Kofi was low key and hardly caused a ripple, but Ted was unpredictable and something of a loose cannon. But he was also great fun and quite the pleasure to hang with.

The main problem with high-profile tasks like this was that every man and his dog seemed to become involved. I had endless advice from the UN Chief Security Advisor for Israel, the West Bank and Gaza, the UN Close Protection Team

ISRAEL & PALESTINE, SRI LANKA, AFGHANISTAN

Leader, the External Relations & Projects Officer, and Ted's publicity and communications executive. They all had their jobs to do but the problems usually lay in the overlaps. I liaised with the Israeli president's assistants to discuss meetings and schedules, the Ministry of Foreign Affairs, the Head of Israel NGO and Division for UN, and Shimon Peres's residence to work out various dinner schedules. Then it was over the border into Ramallah and the Muqata to work out hotels, transport and more meetings. The Israeli secret service seemed to be irritated by the extra burden of foreign guests meeting with their main concern which was Prime Minister, Ehud Olmart. The couple of days we had to prepare were non-stop. And then Ted and Kofi arrived, and Kofi's wife too, and the workload really went up a notch.

The days rolled into each other. I don't remember sleeping or eating. The climax in Israel before we moved to Palestine was a speech by Olmart at Ayalon Canada Park. As Ted and I were walking towards it we were diverted into a building where a team had been waiting to give Ted a presentation about a recycling plant. The designers hoped that Ted, a fervent philanthropist, might invest a few dollars. Ted took a seat but became bored of the pitch after three minutes and bluntly interrupted to ask how much money they needed. The speaker was uncomfortable, more a scientist than a salesman, and waffled on about the project being valued at $14million then chuckling nervously as he suggested that if Ted could spare $100,000 they'd be grateful. Ted got to his feet and said he'd finance the entire thing and with that we walked out of the room leaving the Israelis speechless.

We attended Olmart's speech and as it ended Ted told me he

wanted to get to Jerusalem and Shimon Peres's house for dinner with Olmart. Olmart was heading that way in his cavalcade and I asked the Secret Service if we could join it. They said no. I argued my case, how important it was that Ted was there. They finally caved and said we could tag on at the end. As the cavalcade set off Ted decided to take a piss, something he did often. I waited patiently and then it was a mad dash to our car followed by a hair-raising drive to keep up with the cavalcade that was blue-light speeding to the holy city. We made it in time and Ted had his dinner with Peres and other dignitaries.

Ted was an immensely entertaining raconteur. He often regaled us with stories about his experiences, rubbing shoulders with the all powerful. Mikhail Gorbachev was a friend, Fidel Castro was a drinking buddy, and there was even a ditty about Jane Fonda which I will take to my grave.

The task didn't pause for my team at night. There was only six of us and we had to provide a rotational watch on Kofi's and Ted's rooms.

Much as I enjoyed the experience and the uncommon insight into world affairs, sitting at the back of the room listening to the off-the-record chatter, I'm glad I never had to do any more tasks like that. I was fortunate that nothing went wrong. On the final day we dropped Ted off at the airport, Kofi and his wife at the Jordanian border, and I fell into my seat on the first flight home and was asleep before take off.

****

I don't know how a working relationship between AKE and Greenpeace came about. I liked to think we strived to be apolitical, other than avoiding anarchists and extremists. There was a fine line between managing an organisation's security risk and

ISRAEL & PALESTINE, SRI LANKA, AFGHANISTAN

assisting them with operational planning, even if that wasn't the intention. One cannot be achieved without influencing the other. When I began my career as a security risk manager I didn't think twice about planning CNN's operations or those of any other organisation I worked for. I saw no compromise of my morals or principles. I did question my impartiality when I occasionally witnessed the dishonest side of news gathering such as lying by omission, one-sided reports, staged backdrops. Geraldo Rivera's fake 'Hallowed Ground' report for instance, witnessed by his AKE security team, miles from the true location, watching him scatter his own props to the ground – spent casings and a US army helmet he'd brought along, so clearly a planned deception. I do believe the vast majority of journalists want nothing more than to report the absolute whole truth, but not all.

When I was asked to work with Greenpeace I had reservations. I did sympathise, broadly, with many of their objectives, but at the end of the day they were anarchists. They might not directly support eco-terrorism, but many of its members were also affiliated with such groups.

Greenpeace was certainly a successful organisation. Bags of money. Influential at the highest levels and access to the decision-makers of many governments. I reasoned that if the UK government actively engaged with them then I could too, although I would never directly become involved in their operations.

My first task for Greenpeace was in Mexico City where I taught the local team the fundamentals of crisis management that included a table-top exercise. It was a dangerous place to operate and the risks to Greenpeace personnel was high. The task included a trip to Guadalajara to conduct a risk assessment of their offices. I thought that would be my one and only job for them, but by then I was the senior crisis manager in AKE and I tended to take on most CM related tasks. I went on to conduct CM training for the Greenpeace Istanbul team followed a month later by another training session in Jakarta. I also ran a technical surveillance counter-measures eavesdropping inspection on their Paris headquarters.

It was my final task for them that shone an interesting light on the disconnect between Greenpeace staff and its hierarchy. I was sent to Colombo, Sri Lanka to spend a week on board the Greenpeace vessel Esperanza. They were planning a fisheries documentation project that would take the ship and its crew into the Indian Ocean at a time when there was a significant threat from Somali pirates. My task was to advise and assist in preparing the vessel against a pirate boarding that included erecting razor wire defences, cable drags to foul the propellers of pursuing speed boats, and implementing a remote-controlled high-pressure water cannon. I also advised on creating a citadel for the crew to lock themselves inside the boat in the event of a boarding from where they could broadcast a mayday and hopefully delay being captured long enough for a naval vessel to arrive and rescue them.

Part of my training package was to prepare the crew for the worst eventuality which was the vessel being successfully hijacked and the crew taken hostage. I explained the general process of hostage negotiation, the events that would be taking place in the background to secure the crew, and give advice on how to manage captivity.

There were four or five young women amongst the crew and one of them asked about the probability of being raped. In

ISRAEL & PALESTINE, SRI LANKA, AFGHANISTAN

my experience of hostage taking around the world, I would have to summarise that the chances were high. Somali pirates were aggressive but they were not known to deliberately harm their hostages, mainly because they saw them as valuable commodities and therefore had to be kept alive and well. Since few ships crews included women, few had been captured by pirates. However, the year before, a South African woman had been captured by pirates and was repeatedly raped before her release.

At the end of my talk I made it clear that anyone who was having second thoughts about taking part in the adventure was welcome to leave the vessel prior to sailing. The girls were nervous but courageous and none chose to abandon the voyage.

At the conclusion of my training I introduced the crew to the concept of the ISOPREP form – Isolated Persons Report. This was a confidential document to be filled in by each crew member and then sealed, only to be opened in the event of being kidnapped.

The document contained essential personal information for the Greenpeace negotiators and included next of kin details, any private potentially serious medical conditions the employer did not know about, half a dozen Proof Of Life questions that only the kidnap victim would know the answer to such as the colour of your bedroom curtains or your pet's name, and any visual distinguishing marks such as tattoos or scars to assist with identification.

The ISOPREP form came about due to complications we'd experienced in the past. One kidnap victim was suffering from a serious illness that he'd kept from his employers because he feared he would be released from employment if they found out. We had to inform the kidnappers that the victim would soon die in captivity if they didn't receive specific medication. Another victim's wife was contacted to inform her of his kidnapping only for her to reveal he'd left her and children a year before after declaring he was gay and was living with his new partner having kept it a secret from colleagues.

As the forms were being filled in and sealed in their envelopes I explained they would be sent to Greenpeace HQ where they'd be stored in a safe and on completion of the voyage the forms would be destroyed or returned in their sealed envelopes to the individuals. To my surprise, suspicious glances were exchanged between the crew and almost all refused to hand the envelopes over to me. Keeping the forms at the client HQ was standard procedure because in the event the vessel was captured it was where the crisis team would assemble and where the negotiations would be centred. But the crew didn't want their secret details to be kept at Greenpeace HQ. When I asked why, I was told that the Greenpeace hierarchy couldn't be trusted not to open the envelopes even if the crew weren't kidnapped.

In all the years I'd been conducting crisis management preparations for organisations I'd never experienced such a division and suspicion between executives and operational staff. The forms were essential for the well being of the crew in the event of capture and so I took the step of assuring the crew that I would personally hold on to the forms since, in the event of a kidnapping, I or another member of AKE would most likely oversee the crisis management team at Greenpeace HQ. With that assurance every member handed me their completed forms. It was extraordinary that they would hand over their secret information to me, a complete stranger, as opposed to their Greenpeace bosses.

ISRAEL & PALESTINE, SRI LANKA, AFGHANISTAN

The expedition was a success, no pirates were encountered on the voyage and AKE destroyed the ISOPREPS.

****

My first hands-on venture into the kidnap and ransom business took place in Baghdad. The victim was journalist Jill Carroll who worked for the Christian Science Monitor. The CSM wasn't a client of AKE at the time of Jill's kidnapping. Its bureau was in the Al Hamra Hotel where I lived and ran the AKE office. I knew Jill only well enough to say hello in passing. The CSM couldn't afford a risk manager or even an adviser on call. There were many small news outfits and individuals operating on a shoestring budget. We gave the occasional bona-fide advice when we saw them operating in an unsafe manner.

Parts of the story that I have about Jill's kidnapping is not quite the same as has been reported in the various media, that's because I was working with the FBI's Baghdad office at the time and was privy to some of its intelligence.

I ran the Local Management Team (LMT) for Jill's kidnapping, or the latter part of it. The Crisis Management Team (CMT), where the negotiators were based, was in the USA, which meant there was a significant time difference between the two teams. This meant the LMT had to sometimes make time-critical decisions without consulting the bosses and negotiators.

Kidnapping was one of the greatest concerns for westerners in Baghdad at the time. Close to 40 journalists had been abducted by the time Jill was taken, and many more western civilians were missing. The missing persons department in the US Embassy was run by a former Navy SEAL. Ricochet we called him, which sounded like his real name, a cognomen we didn't share with him because it wasn't exactly complimentary, bless him. On the wall of his small office was a list of over 450 missing western contractors or visitors since the end of the conventional war. Some westerners arrived looking for work, got a lift into the city and were never seen again. The city streets were a dangerous place. Gangs roamed in vehicles looking for westerners to pluck. Victims were either financial or political commodities, depending on who the abductors sold them to. The financial ones had a chance of survival. The political victims had little. Once a victim got handed an orange jump suit it usually meant they were going to die.

During that period, which lasted several years, many journalists never left the safety of their hotel rooms throughout their stay in the city other than to travel to and from the airport. The bigger players that could afford to, networks and some of the print news, travelled with armed security, mostly in armoured cars. It reduced the chances of getting kidnapped but still left them exposed to road-side bombs and ambushes.

I had over a dozen small clients in the Al Hamra I regularly trained and advised on operational procedures, keeping them updated with the changing threats. There were various fundamental bits of advice we gave. How to conduct meetings and interviews was an important one. The first rule was to get the interviewee to meet at your hotel to save the risk of travelling. If they wouldn't come to your hotel then find a safe public place to meet such as inside the Green Zone or at one of the big hotels. Members of the Iraqi government or any other political or religious persuasion were not to be trusted, even if meeting at their offices. I would advise against meetings at private addresses and offices. If there was no other option, the advice was to avoid on-the-dot meeting times and not to make them

ISRAEL & PALESTINE, SRI LANKA, AFGHANISTAN

too long. And, most important, if the interviewee wasn't there on your arrival, to immediately leave.

Such restrictions would be anathema to most journalists, even in Baghdad. I gave that same advice to Rory Carroll of the Guardian when he first arrived at the Al Hamra hotel to take over the bureau. Rory wasn't the type to take security related advice or be interested in any kind of security risk management training with AKE. A few months later he was kidnapped in Sadr City while interviewing an Iraqi in his home for three hours. Rory's driver returned to AKE at the Al Hamra in a panic. I was on leave at the time.

The office was being managed by a couple of most capable former SAS lads. They bid the driver take them to where he'd dropped off Rory then contacted the British and US embassies asking for help. The first 24 hours were the most important when it came to kidnappings. The victim was most likely still being processed locally by the kidnappers who were rarely the end users. Both embassies were unable to respond. The AKE lads got a message to mates in the duty SAS team stationed in Baghdad but they were also unable to assist due to commitments.

How Rory was rescued is contrary to what was conveyed in the news reports.

The AKE lads knew of an Iraqi SWAT team in Baghdad that had recently returned from London having spent three months being trained by the Metropolitan Police. They were led by a colourful, energetic and most capable Iraqi named Sunny.

When Sunny learned there was a kidnap victim to be rescued he couldn't have been more enthusiastic about helping. His team arrived at the house a few hours later and after a briefing by the

AKE lads they stormed it, capturing those inside. Unfortunately Rory was no longer there. Sunny promptly 'interviewed' the senior occupants of the house who had set up Rory's abduction using various Iraqi techniques and not what he had learned in London, and soon found out where Rory was being held. The subsequent rescue was swift and had little to do with the British or Irish embassies. That's the short version.

Sunny turned out to be a useful contact for me. The team leader of NBC's security, a large, happy individual and former SAS, knocked on my Al Hamra Hotel room door one afternoon looking for some advice. One of NBC's Iraqi fixers had been kidnapped. We went to the NBC bureau to listen to the finer details of the abduction from the bureau chief which included unusually modest financial demands made by the abductors. The victim's car had been found in the city by a friend. There was something odd about the entire abduction.

Due to the dangers for westerners on the streets of Baghdad, many news organisations sent their drivers and fixers out to gather news. These individuals were encouraged to take photos and video footage. Despite being locals, it was still a risky business for them. Several were caught and beaten and their lives threatened because they worked for infidels. Some were too scared to tell their masters they no longer wanted to take the risks. But work for locals was in short supply in Baghdad and risks had to be taken in order to put food on the table.

We were never asked by any news organisation in Baghdad throughout that period to train their local drivers and fixers in any form of risk management. They were sent onto the streets with scant preparation in the hope they'd return with the goods.

When the NBC bureau chief finished his description of events

ISRAEL & PALESTINE, SRI LANKA, AFGHANISTAN

there were several clues that pointed to a self-kidnapping. The bureau chief dismissed my assessment as ridiculous. I called Sunny, who had much more experience than me, and asked if he'd come to the bureau and listen to the same story. He did, and at the end of it agreed with me that it was a self-kidnapping. Sunny visited the fixer's father and eventually got the truth out of him. The fixer had become too frightened to continue in his new role as NBC news gatherer. The ransom money, which he assessed was small enough for NBC to pay, would be used to fly him to Jordan and a new life. When Sunny explained to the father the game was up but that NBC wouldn't hold any grievances, the fixer gave himself up. The episode was brushed under the carpet and the fixer was released from his employment and, I believe, was given enough funds to move to Jordan.

Two years after Rory of the Guardian was rescued, Jill Carroll made an appointment to interview a Sunni politician, Adnan al-Dulaimi, at his offices in the city. Jill arrived with her driver and fixer to learn al-Dulaimi was not at the office. She waited some 20 minutes and, finally growing uncomfortable, decided to leave. As they climbed into their car to drive away, several gunmen appeared. They'd been waiting for Jill. The driver managed to make a run for it and escaped. Jill and her fixer were captured and driven away. During the journey the fixer was shot dead and dumped in the street. Jill was taken into captivity somewhere in Baghdad.

Al-Dulaimi later gave a press conference demanding the return of Jill. His innocence in the setup was questioned. It's possible that if a version explaining the true purpose of Jill's abduction were true, one that the world's media was unaware of, Al-Dulaimi might well have played a small part in it.

FIRST INTO ACTION AGAIN

I took over the local management of the kidnap for the last month of Jill's three-month captivity. The American FBI had set up an office in the Green Zone not far from the July 14th Bridge and AKE was invited to meet with them and share a few beers in their bar. I attended with Andrew Kain and a handful of others. The FBI was considering employing AKE to assist with some of its field operations. The Bureau had no jurisdiction to operate outside of the Green Zone and needed ears and eyes on the ground beyond their local spies. They needed specialists that could mount urban observation and conduct surveillance. The FBI had clearly done its due diligence on AKE and knew that our capabilities were far beyond ordinary security providers.

The FBI was working on another high profile kidnap case in Baghdad at the time. Four Christian Aid workers had flown into Baghdad from Chicago in order to spread peace and love and criticise the occupation of Iraq by coalition forces. They were promptly kidnapped by Sunni insurgents and threatened with beheading. One of them, an American, was eventually executed, probably because he let slip to his kidnappers that he was a former US Marine. I understand he was also arrogant and rude to them. He was trying to sell peace and love to the wrong people. The FBI hinted that AKE might be given tasks that would assist in the peacekeeper investigation, as well as provide information on Jill. This would certainly go hand in hand with our responsibilities for Jill and we were keen to get involved.

I was having a cup of coffee one morning when I received a call from the Washington Post bureau chief asking if I had news about Jill. I had nothing new. It was an odd call. Short

ISRAEL & PALESTINE, SRI LANKA, AFGHANISTAN

and sweet. Washington Post was a client, its bureau was in the Al Hamra. I visited it regularly. They knew I was running the LMT for Jill's negotiations and that I'd tell them nothing. Yet they called to ask. I was suspicious.

Five minutes later my FBI contact called to tell me Jill had been released and was literally on the streets of Baghdad in Amariyah. That was a total surprise. There had been no warning. Negotiations had been going nowhere. The kidnappers wanted $10 million and the release of various prisoners. The FBI asked if I would pick her up. Amariyah was not a place for westerners to hang around in. She could easily be grabbed by some other gang and taken into a new captivity.

I immediately assembled my team in two armoured cars, armed with rifles and pistols. I called Scott Peterson, Jill's CSM bureau chief. I'd been closely liaising with Scott throughout the abduction and he joined us to collect Jill, who would be highly stressed and in immediate need of a friendly face.

The Washington Post somehow knew something about Jill's release and had called me to find out if I knew. I obviously conveyed I didn't know she was on the street. If they knew they should've told me. As we drove out of the hotel and along the street I called the Post only to learn that the bureau chief was on the road. I had to assume they were driving to pick up Jill. It was a dangerous choice, for them and for Jill. They were going for the story and ignoring the risks to Jill and themselves.

We were halfway across the city when I received a call from my FBI contact telling me the US Embassy was on the case and sending a heavily armed US special forces team to pick up Jill. We immediately pulled over to wait and hear how it played out. The last thing Jill needed was different groups vying to pick her up. I called the Washington Post and urged the desk to message their team not to proceed to pick up Jill if that was their intention. My warnings were ignored. It later transpired that Jill had borrowed a phone to call the Baghdad Washington Post bureau because it was the only local number she could remember and was desperate to get picked up. What could've been a clusterfuck turned out okay in the end and Jill was successfully picked up by the USSF and brought to the US Embassy in the Green Zone.

It remained a mystery why Jill had been released. The kidnappers claimed the US gave concessions, but that was highly unlikely and the FBI mentioned nothing about it.

A few weeks later my FBI contact called to ask if I'd like to meet for a coffee in the Green Zone. He was the tight-lipped type, however, he decided to tell me a little story.

A year or so prior, the Saudis had been monitored trying to contribute money to Iraqi Sunni insurgents and their fight against the occupying forces. American intelligence could monitor the movement of large amounts of money and the Saudis could ill afford the risk of being caught sending money to assist in the killing of US soldiers. And so a cunning plan was hatched.

The Iraqi Sunnis would kidnap an American, someone sympathetic, ideally a woman (the Christian Science Monitor would be perfect), and then after an appropriate amount of time, the Saudis would generously offer to pay the $10 million ransom demand. The Saudis would appear magnanimous and saintly, the Sunni insurgents would get their money and the victim would be released. This would all be done secretly of course and when the Americans discovered the payment, well, it was for a good cause, saving the life of a young Christian lady.

ISRAEL & PALESTINE, SRI LANKA, AFGHANISTAN

A UAE Emirati was given the task of managing the money handover. Apparently he arrived in Baghdad and presented the kidnappers with a suitcase containing $5 million, explaining that it was all he had been given. He was promptly kidnapped and warned that if he did not arrange for the other half of the money to be delivered to Baghdad he would be executed. It was around that time that Jill was released, her part in the pantomime having been played. Two weeks later the Emirati was seen leaving Baghdad International Airport, suggesting that the transaction had been completed.

Perhaps the story was fantasy, but I did like my FBI friend's version of events.

****

A chance to manage my own kidnap for ransom came in Afghanistan. It wasn't a high profile case. I wouldn't have been invited to cut my teeth on anything too complex. But the life and well-being of a human was at stake and therefore it was a most serious matter.

The victim was an Afghan named Gul who was a field coordinator for DACAAR, the Danish Committee for Aid to Afghan Refugees. They were a humanitarian group teaching communities how to manage their development while also providing solutions such as water to isolated villages by digging boreholes. Gul was abducted by armed men while riding in a taxi, a planned, economic kidnapping.

It was decided to run the task and negotiations from the DACAAR offices in Kabul. I arrived a few days after the kidnapping. After meeting the main players and assessing the kidnapping, I set about organising my crisis management team (CMT) which would be made up of DACAAR staff and therefore mostly Afghans. I ran an intensive crisis management course over a couple of days that aimed to teach the team the components of a CMT and how the crisis management system functioned when it came to kidnappings. It was a relatively new training course for AKE that I had developed over several years, which began in Scotland with a company called Serimax near Inverness. Crisis Management training was a fairly new concept in those days. There were no comprehensive courses to be found. Those of us venturing into the business had to write our own. Some years later, when instructors and responders like myself were being pushed to possess degrees on the subject as proof of our capabilities, I wrote to Leicester University who had just begun providing a Crisis Management degree. I wanted to know the course outline and the background of the professors. What I received was disappointing. It was all theory and, in my experience, failed to relate to the practicalities of real world crisis management. The professors had no experience of managing a crisis. I decided not to waste money on a two year course and could better spend the time writing another couple of books, which I did.

DACAAR employees had been kidnapped in the past and ransoms had been paid. This was probably known to the criminals and why they chose to kidnap a DACAAR employee. The repeat DACAAR kidnappings created a particular challenge. My task was to ensure the safe return of Gul, but this had to be achieved in such a way as to discourage further kidnappings of DACAAR employees. There were several thousand of them dotted about the country. Repeated kidnappings would also result in DACAAR being unable to get high-risk insurance in the future.

ISRAEL & PALESTINE, SRI LANKA, AFGHANISTAN

There were a myriad of outcomes and complications to kidnappings, but the three broad, likely results were: the ransom or demands were met and the victim was returned; the victim was rescued; the ransom wasn't paid and the victim was left to their fate. We worked hard to find the kidnappers, but we mostly planned towards paying the ransom, which had come down to $35,000. Paying was usually the safest solution for the victim.

One of the first steps in a kidnap negotiation was to demand proof from the kidnappers that the victim was still alive. Proof of life. But getting our kidnappers to understand that we couldn't proceed without that proof was a struggle. We came to the conclusion that our kidnappers were unsophisticated and inexperienced. Thick, was my personal conclusion. The point of contact between us was the victim's son, who I believe was suspicious of us from the start and often tried to act alone, which was unhelpful. But having him as the main communicator suited the plan I had in mind.

In order to keep the insurers happy and to dissuade future kidnappers from snatching DACAAR personnel, we had to solve this case without the insurance company or DACAAR paying a ransom. To that end, we needed to either capture the kidnappers and rescue Gul intact, or get the family to pay the ransom, or at least appear to.

I won't go into the details of the negotiation because it was a very monotonous affair. There were only a handful of mildly interesting moments followed by long periods of inactivity, setbacks, frustrations and incompetencies. But at the end of several weeks, the case was resolved, the ransom was paid by the family and Gul was returned to us slightly shaken but in otherwise good condition. He'd been held in a hole in the ground, most uncomfortably, his sanitary needs had not been catered to, and his food thrown to him in plastic bags along with water. DACAAR conspired to pay the family the equivalent of the ransom money at a future date once the dust had settled and therefore maintaining the illusion that DACAAR did not pay the ransom.

That was my first and last negotiation. I had no interest in doing another. The Hostage Negotiators circuit was a tough nut to crack for the likes of me. It was made up mostly of former police and government negotiators. Former Special Forces were discouraged from joining the fraternity. It was a very catty, back-stabbing, character-assassinating community that fiercely protected its hold on the business from outsiders. Even if I had been the perfect case officer, which I was not, I wouldn't have gone far. I went to a function in London soon after my Afghan experience and stood in a hall amongst dozens of male and female negotiators, sipping drinks and nibbling canapés. I might as well have been amongst a group of sheep-shearers for all that I had in common with them. I discovered some months later that I'd been stabbed in the back by one of them who complained to the insurance company who provided cover for DACAAR that I wasn't a serious enough negotiator. She was probably right, even though the task had been a success. The insurance company conveyed to AKE that I was not a preferred negotiator. It left me with ill feelings towards her.

A couple of years later I was invited to Denmark to design FALK's crisis management system and she was there as an advisor. It was the first time I'd met her. I was pleased to note that although she was probably a capable negotiator, she was a poor crisis manager. I hated being in a suit and I hated the

ISRAEL & PALESTINE, SRI LANKA, AFGHANISTAN

small-mindedness of many of the corporate types. I yearned to get back into the field where I'd never meet that type. They wouldn't last five minutes in the places I felt most comfortable.

I was, thus, at another crossroads. I was getting too old to be running around dodging bombs and bullets. The madness of those early days, when I was young and reckless, was clear to me. I didn't feel entirely past it, but it was time to look ahead. I fancied taking on crisis management but it had so far been little more than classroom work for me, preparing companies for crisis events. The problem seemed to be that the companies that I had prepared for crises – and was the standby responder to in the event one might occur – didn't get any crises. Serimax, the Scottish/French cable-laying company sent me to a vessel in the middle of Persian Gulf for a few days to assist with a minor crisis in Iranian waters, but it didn't turn into much.

However, my chance of a large-scale crisis management task was to come. It was a classic drama for a major high-profile company in the middle of a conflict zone, the type of crisis that responders dream of, far more exciting and rewarding than a hostage negotiation. It was all on my shoulders, and had I made the wrong decision, hundreds of people could've died.

13

KURDISTAN

THERE WERE OBVIOUS WARNING SIGNS it was time for me to move on from field risk management, one in particular occurred during a brief return to Baghdad after several years' absence. I was conducting an assessment of CNN's bureau with a view to down-sizing when AKE's team leader found me to ask if I'd care to join the crew on a drive through the city with the duty correspondent. One of the lads was unwell. I was obliged to help in such circumstances but I wasn't looking forward to it. It would be hot, dusty, boring and I had things to do.

I donned my body armour, grabbed a rifle, pistol and ammo and climbed into the front passenger seat of an armoured Mercedes saloon. After an uneventful four hours drive I was relieved to return. As the team and client climbed out, I pushed open my half-ton armoured door and paused to enjoy the fresh, cool air before commencing the laborious process of hauling my arse out of my sunken seat, weighed down by my gear. I was keenly aware my spritely youthfulness had diminished somewhat. As I leaned forward to push myself upright, a grenade fell out of my pouch and hit the floor. There was never a chance of it going off. I always had the pins well bent over, but it was most annoying and unprofessional. Worse still it had rolled under the car and I had to get down on my knees and reach underneath for it. The team leader saw me puffing and straining and asked if all was okay.

'Just getting my grenade,' I said. One always had to be honest in my business. No doubt eyes rolled. They didn't invite me to join them again.

I had turned my attention to crisis management which was the next logical step for me. It was a cerebral, academic, civilised, complex form of risk management, and the wardrobe was smart jacket and shirt, and no guns or grenades.

Security risk Crisis Management as a marketable corporate product was in its infancy. The theory was being well documented by various organisations and government bodies but the mechanics of the ground application was still being worked out by a handful of competent security companies. I found the concept most interesting. Having spent many years operating in the field I could see its advantages. But all of those years gaining down and dirty ground truth experience had its disadvantages. You can take the man out of the field but you can't take the field out of the man.

Corporate crisis management involved dealing with senior executives, boardrooms, CEOs and chairmen, and outside advisors were under the scrutiny of generally intelligent, critical corporate types. Corporate management was also usually a nit picky, back-stabbing, bitchy, egotistical environment. Compared to them, I was unsophisticated and rough around the edges. When asked if I had a degree in the business and on receiving my reply that I did not, I was looked down upon. Fortunately, some executives recognised my field experience as the more important qualification for the job.

Our German office called one day to invite me to take part in a selection process run by Siemens of Munich, the largest company in Germany and indeed one of the largest in the world. Siemens was looking to retain an outside crisis responder. Crisis Responders had to be experts in their field. They usually worked for a security risk management provider of renown. Most major companies that operated in hostile environments, or their insurance companies, held one or two on retainer in the event of a crisis. My competitors for the Siemens position were amongst the top security risk management companies in Europe and the USA. Control Risks for instance sent a candidate to Munich to be assessed by Siemens.

The test consisted of a two-hour scenario in Siemens's crisis centre, the assessors, a dozen or so managers and analysts. The scenario was set in Libya during the recent civil war. The plot involved two of Siemens's employees. They had been stranded in the centre of the country surrounded by various warring factions and lethal militias. My task was to demonstrate how we would get them safely out of the country.

The crisis centre was an opulent, glass-walled, high-ceilinged room with multi-screen monitors, pulsating with communications technology. I was familiar with addressing corporate senior management types by then. I had to quickly inspire my audience to have confidence in me. A technique I had cultivated when faced with civilian corporate types of rank and stature was to feel contempt for them. I was a different species and there because they'd had the misfortune of stepping into my

KURDISTAN

world, no doubt due to their own incompetence, ignorance or penny-pinching on security.

All phone conversations between me and my various contacts and facilitators were broadcast to the room over loud speakers and a storyboard of my progress was displayed on the monitors. I stood in front of the group who were seated in a semi-circle and, ignoring introductions, I brusquely got stuck in by asking for Siemens's Libya emergency evacuation plans. They didn't have any to hand. I asked for their security plan, crisis policies and procedures. They didn't have them to hand either. My contempt was justified. I don't know if the missing documents were a part of the test, to see how I managed without them, but I had my doubts only because there were exchanged glances when I asked for them and no one seemed to know who was responsible for them not being present.

I quickly proceeded, asking my Ops room in Hereford to place two AKE operatives on immediate standby to head into Libya. I accessed intelligence reports on the conflict, prepared a medical response option in case the Siemens personnel were injured, checked on the environment and examined road risk and air options into and out of the country. I found a military airfield a few miles from where the two Siemens personnel were in hiding and AKE ops sent satellite imagery that showed the runway was in good condition. I initiated an emergency air response group we had a relationship with based near Gatwick called Air Partners that specialised in high-risk flights into conflict air spaces to fly my two guys onto the airfield. They came back to me within 15 minutes stating they had an aircraft on standby and the Libyan runway was workable for them.

The process up to that point had taken almost two hours. I

announced the small airfield was as far as I was prepared to send my men at that point.

A Siemens executive pointed out the obvious that I had not collected their two men and taken them to the airfield. I explained that it was dangerous enough for my men and the aircraft to hang around the airfield for too long. A recovery of that nature in land would require a fighting force in vehicles of some description such as motorbikes or quad-bikes. If Siemens's two personnel couldn't get themselves to the airfield I could organise such a rescue team, but Siemens would need to pay up front to cover the costs. I didn't have a figure to hand and suggested US$1 million deposit might cover it.

The stroppy intelligence executive scoffed at my proposal and suggested I had not completed my task. I bristled at his naivety and snapped back that I wouldn't risk my operators to move outside the airfield without support. I went a step further, adding that the crisis could've been avoided if Siemens had an effective emergency evacuation plan with built in triggers and security alert levels that would've warned its employees to get out of Libya before it was too late. I offered to write the plans and triggers for him if he wished.

My German partner, who had sat silently throughout, wore an expression that pleaded with me not to go any further.

Siemens's senior security manager intervened to bring the scenario to a close and thanked us for coming. I assumed we had failed to impress. We were invited to lunch before we left and to my surprise the Siemens manager joined me at my table. After some polite chit-chat I asked if I'd ridden the analyst too hard. He said I had, but added that Germans didn't mind getting a roasting regarding such security matters from the English.

KURDISTAN

Three weeks later our German office informed me Siemens had called to let them know that I'd qualified as a Siemens responder. It was quite the feather in my cap. Smart people those Germans.

I went on to complete an examination from Allianz in Frankfurt, winning the responder position there too. I became senior responder for FALCK of Denmark, commencing the design of its global crisis management system, and later for Caterpillar Europe and the Middle East. I also had clients I visited in China and the USA.

It all sounded very exciting, but that was just it. It wasn't. It was all chat, airplanes, hotels, lunches, teaching, assessing, surveys, writing policies and procedures and playing table-top scenarios. It was fun at first but as time went by it became mundane. There was something very obvious missing. I was not getting adventure. What was the point of being a crisis responder if I never actually responded to anything? I wanted a major crisis to manage.

It was to come.

Another of my clients was one of the largest airport services companies in the world, dnata, a subsidiary of Emirates Airlines based in Dubai. I spent my first week with dnata at its HQ teaching executives crisis management theory, creating a CMT (crisis management team) and writing its general security plan, policies and SOPs, etc.

dnata had good reason to want to create a CMT. They ran airport operations all over the world with several of them in high-risk locations such as Afghanistan, Iraq and Pakistan. Anti-western feelings were extreme in these countries and, despite dnata being Arab, like most major UAE companies, it was run by westerners.

Several months after my visit to dnata in Dubai I was at home near Hereford when a call came in from AKE ops. dnata was experiencing a crisis.

ISIS was continuing to expand its reach across Iraq. Having captured the city of Mosul, it had set its next target as the city of Erbil in Kurdistan Iraq, which I was familiar with, and where dnata ran the airport and had almost 200 personnel. The ISIS advanced party had reached the Great Zab River that ran North East, South West and at its closest point was only 30 kilometres from Erbil. ISIS was a formidable force of irregulars that had smashed its way across Iraq and threatened to sack Baghdad itself, which many feared it was capable of doing. Erbil, on its flank and therefore important to control, was expected to fall quickly.

There were only three road bridges over the Great Zab River that ISIS would have to use to attack the city in order to keep its supply lines from Mosul short. The Kurdish military raced to defend the bridges but ISIS were heavily armed and powerful and it didn't look as if the Kurds had any chance of stopping them from crossing once the main force arrived.

Private western companies, some at least, had learned lessons from the Libyan civil war a few years earlier when many were trapped by the conflict after failing to act quickly enough to evacuate. Most companies were already getting their people out of Erbil or preparing to. If ISIS came over the bridges, 30 kilometres wasn't much ground to cover. Mortars would precede them and the destruction of Erbil and the outlying, oil-rich countryside would be at their mercy.

My task was to supervise dnata's CMT in the Dubai HQ. Finally! I was going to be a real responder.

KURDISTAN

I packed a bag and took a taxi to Birmingham airport to catch the first available flight to Dubai. Since dnata was a part of Emirates Airlines they were able to prioritise me onto any Emirates flight. If I had any sense of self-importance, which I confess I did a little, it deflated when I discovered dnata had put me in economy. I had taken for granted that, considering I was on my way to assist dnata in a major crisis, the company might've acknowledged my importance by putting me in business. I did have reading to do and notes to make, and was expected to hit the ground running. I decided that perhaps business class had been full or it had been a mistake on the part of some secretary. But when I arrived in Dubai there was no one to meet me and I received a text telling me to make my way by bus to the Premier Inn where a room had been booked for me. The Premier Inn was probably the cheapest hotel in Dubai, although it was owned by dnata. I sucked up my injured pride with a harumph and pressed onto the hotel to clean up and change.

When I arrived at the dnata offices it was all go amongst the executives. I briefly met with the CEO, Gary Chapman, an Australian with a pleasant, easy-going manner. My main point of contact was Stewart Angus, a member of the CMT and another agreeable lad, who filled me in on the situation.

In summary, ISIS was moving to capture Erbil and dnata had to get its people safely out of the city. The tricky part for dnata was the importance of the airport to everyone else who wanted to evacuate. Without dnata the airport would struggle to operate. It also managed tons of air cargo daily. Many essential services in the city would grind to a halt. But dnata ultimately had a responsibility to its employees. Their lives were without doubt at risk if ISIS invaded.

FIRST INTO ACTION AGAIN

I was asked if I would fly to Erbil and supervise dnata's evacuation. That sounded far better than hanging around the offices in Dubai. Erbil was where the real excitement was to be found. Within a couple of hours I was back at Dubai airport and on a plane to Erbil. They gave me a seat in economy.

The flight was practically empty, but on my arrival it was no surprise to see queues of people lining up to leave the country. I made my way to the dnata offices to find the boss, Oliver Mathwich. He turned out to be yet another easy-going, competent gentleman who was welcoming and eager to assist me with my job.

The list of first things I had to do was comprehensive. Top of it was to get an assessment of how long we had before ISIS swarmed over the bridges. I needed accurate information. I knew the yanks were heavily invested in the city. One of the US military's main operations centres was close to the airport and a large number of American servicemen and women operated it. I called some old friends who put me in contact with someone who had access to US intelligence and who would be of help in assessing the threat. Oliver also had many contacts in various embassies and consulates and worked on digging up as much information as he could.

The next on my list was to muster and evacuate all non-essential personnel. Oliver decided how few people he needed to keep the airport running. The fewer people that remained when it came to the final evacuation the easier it would be.

I had two evacuation options out of the city. One was by air, the other by road to Sulaymaniyah, a city I knew well, a 200km drive east towards the Iranian border. Both had their challenges. dnata didn't have its own aircraft in Erbil standing by.

KURDISTAN

Once ISIS broke over the river no aircraft would land in Erbil. Neither did dnata have enough transport to drive its people to Sulaymaniyah. Flying people out would be safest once they were in the air, but getting everyone onto an aircraft with the pressure of an invading force bearing down on the airfield was too risky. I opted to keep the minimum number of employees in the airport to operate essentials, which meant I had to find the vehicles to drive the remaining personnel to Sulaymaniyah at short notice. Flying out of Sulaymaniyah would then be a much simpler process.

My first piece of military intelligence informed me that the main body of the ISIS force was not yet at the river. That gave me some time at least. I found a bus company in Erbil that had several coaches I could use, but the owner wanted cash only. That was normal in such circumstances. I had already asked Oliver how much cash he could get his hands on. He had around $350,000. We would also need fuel, generators, food, water, medical supplies and sundries, all to be paid for in cash.

My next piece of military intelligence to arrive was illuminating. It was from my American contact. He basically said, if ISIS looked like they were going to cross the river, they wouldn't. To put it another way, he said, 'We ain't going nowhere'.

I didn't know what that meant exactly. It would probably involve US air assets in support of the Kurds. If the yanks said, 'Thou shall not pass,' that was not to be ignored. I couldn't depend on it, but it influenced my planning.

While I was going about my business around the airport and in the terminal building, assessing safe locations and muster points for remaining staff, I overheard a bunch of Brits waiting to depart. They were air traffic controllers from a company that had the contract for Erbil, and they were bugging out while, in their eyes, they still could. There were enough local staff to just about manage the air traffic control, but the Kurdish authorities didn't look kindly upon the British company's desertion of post. The company was informed in no uncertain terms that if they left their posts they need not bother returning. The contract would be lost. They ignored the threat and departed.

I discussed this with Oliver. Erbil was dnata's most profitable hub, worth some $12 million a year. If dnata deserted its post, they would not be allowed back. The desertion would also send a message to all of the other dnata hubs they managed in other countries that dnata would desert its post at the first sign of trouble, leaving the airports in disarray.

At the end-of-day conversation with dnata Dubai I was asked when the evacuation would be complete. I told them I was looking at remaining as much as I was evacuating. The dnata execs were not pleased to hear that. They were focused on duty of care to their personnel, which they were absolutely correct to do so. I put it to them that I was confident I could keep dnata running the airfield and if ISIS did come over the river I would get the remaining personnel to Sulaymaniyah.

The executives were understandably disquieted by my suggestion, but they didn't override me at that point. We were already evacuating non-essential personnel. I would be down to around 60 the following day, enough to cover dnata's main responsibilities. I expected the executives to give me their decision the following day when more information was available.

The dnata personnel who were selected to remain were obviously highly concerned and I needed to reassure them and instil confidence in the plan. They were made up of Indians, Sri

KURDISTAN

Lankans, Filipinos, a few Brits, and Oliver who was German. I conducted a series of briefings to each shift of workers which included detailed instructions in the event of an evacuation with muster points and procedures. I included medical training and weapons awareness, which had to be delicately delivered so as not to cause alarm. Having said that, I was extremely impressed with the dnata personnel who showed great stoicism in the face of such an extreme threat. They were given the opportunity of evacuating if they chose to but none of those selected to remain took advantage of the offer. I spent the rest of my time supervising the storage of emergency food, water and fuel for the generators that were on their way, organising safe operating locations and ensuring the evacuation coaches were on their way to us. We would work and sleep in the terminal. Only essential offices would have a window in case of mortar attack and all other workplaces were internal.

The following day was spent continuing with preparations. No news had come about ISIS. The dnata executives had still not pulled the plug which showed some courage on their part, and confidence in my plan. I suspect they had discussed the repercussions of losing the Erbil contract. It was a tense time.

Day four I received the news we were all hoping for. ISIS had turned back from the bridges over the Great Zab River and had either returned to Mosul or gone south. Apparently Baghdad was still a target for them, but Erbil had been cancelled. I suspect American threats had been taken seriously. The Kurds were also putting up a courageous defensive effort on the three bridges and had successfully repelled several attempts by ISIS to break through.

At that point my job was done. My visit had been short, but

frenetic. I was confident my evacuation plan would've worked if ISIS had broken through, but I'll never know. There was always the chance something could've gone wrong. I had plenty of redundancy if a coach or two had broken down. Our route to Sulaymaniyah would've taken us in the opposite direction to the ISIS advance, but we would still have needed some luck on our side.

Oliver booked me a business class seat back to Dubai. When I arrived there was a limo waiting for me and I was driven to my hotel, not the Premier Inn but a very expensive hotel in downtown Dubai, the Marriott, with all expenses taken care of. The following morning I was invited to join several dnata executives for breakfast. All were in a celebratory mood. We were graced by the arrival of the big boss himself, Gary Chapman, and afterwards he invited me to join him in his vehicle to head back to the offices. A couple of executives assumed they were to accompany us but Gary asked them to make their own way. I was told over breakfast that by not evacuating, dnata's immediate savings had been $21 million. That did not include the annual losses for years had dnata lost the contract. I was pleased with myself.

I left that morning and headed to the airport in a company saloon and enjoyed a business class seat back to Birmingham. I'd completed the task I was hired to do although I had hoped they might have slipped me a few free air tickets for my family and I to enjoy, but as soon as I was out the door it was back to business as usual. I didn't even get the air miles for my flights.

EPILOGUE

THE DNATA TASK IN ERBIL was to be my last action adventure. I had a handful of fun tasks afterwards, such as taking Anthony Bourdain into Gaza to film one of his chef episodes. He was a greatly troubled man, but very entertaining to share a few private hours with.

My last opportunity for the kind of tasks I most enjoyed came during a visit to Dubai when I was asked to attend a secret meeting with two former 14th Intelligence Detachment commanding officers. They asked me to join them in planning an operation to extract a Saudi businessman from Saudi Arabia who feared for his life. As is often the case with these kinds of extractions, it was left to the client to make their own way to a place where we could then take them to safety. Like countless defectors from the Soviet Union during the Cold War who had to make perilous journeys to the nearest point that agents would risk meeting them in order to extract them. In this case the client had to get himself over the Saudi border into the UAE. We offered advice on how he could achieve that but it would be up to him to make it through. Once he was in the UAE we would get him over the border into Oman. My task from there was to drive him to Salala on the Oman coast. We rented a small ocean-going vessel under the guise of filming a documentary on piracy. I put together a manuscript and hired a team of former Royal Marines, acquaintances, who would act as my film crew.

I was the director and producer. I used my writing company as the bonafide film maker to give us legitimacy should we be examined by the Oman authorities. I would wait with the client until dark then make our way to the beach where my lads would pick us up in an inflatable and transfer us to the vessel. From there we'd sail to Sri Lanka then fly to South Africa and then the UK to complete the mission. The green light would happen once the client had transferred a large sum of money to our bank account. My payment would be £250,000 and my lads would receive £50,000 each.

While we waited for the money to drop, Covid struck and everything went into lockdown. I never heard from him again. I developed atrial fibrillation soon after which put the brakes on all of my activities for a while. It was time to find a new road to take.

What does someone with my appetite for the kind of adventures I was used to do when they are too bloody old to do them anymore? The answer is press on and find an adventure you can manage where no one else suffers if you bugger it up because you've become a silly old twat.

I found one. My wife and I bought into a small farm in Africa with one of our kids. Now there was something I hadn't expected. I was aware that being a white farmer in Africa was statistically the most dangerous civilian activity in the world.

Perfect.

EPILOGUE

The dozen or so adventures I have described in this book are only a handful of the many hundred I took part in over the years. I selected them for variety as well as stepping stones through that period of my life.

To echo comments I wrote in the prologue, I don't advise anyone to follow in my life's footsteps. Any one of the various roads I chose could have so easily led to disaster. I certainly don't feel as if I was in complete control even most of the time. Perhaps I had more luck than sound judgement, but with the occasional promethean moment.

My deepest thanks must go to the Royal Marines and how that incredible organisation prepared me to face the paths I ended up taking, and to make the most of them. The training I received, and the camaraderie I experienced was priceless. I suppose, at the end of such a life of adventures, and having the hubris to write a book about them, I should conclude with some words of wisdom. The simplest advice I have is to never give up and to trust in yourself. When times are dark and at their worst, you may be all you have to get you through. Keep your focus, choose your path, and hopefully it will be a good one, and you'll get the chance to do it again.

ACKNOWLEDGEMENTS

RAM, for his early guidance and leadership in Special Forces and civilian security and for providing details on several of his own adventures as a civilian security specialist.

Andrew Kain for his years of support and for providing me with a wealth of knowledge and the opportunities to gain experience in global Security Risk and Crisis Management.

My darling wife for putting up with my unquenchable appetite for adventure, long disappearances into many dodgy and dangerous parts of the world, and making me feel most welcome and much missed on my returns, over and over again.